SIMON & SCHUSTER   New York London Toronto Sydney Tokyo Singapore

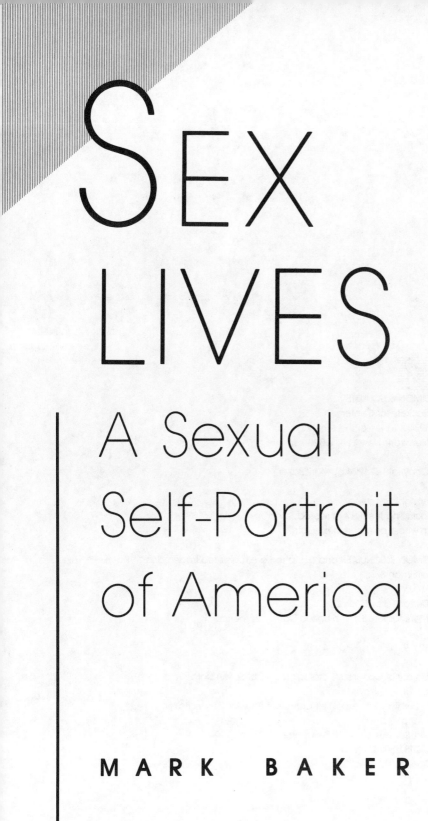

SEX LIVES

A Sexual
Self-Portrait
of America

MARK BAKER

SIMON & SCHUSTER
Rockefeller Center
1230 Avenue of the Americas
New York, New York 10020

Designed by Liney Li
Manufactured in the United States of America

10 9 8 7 6 5 4 3 2 1

Library of Congress Cataloging-in-Publication Data
Baker, Mark, date.
   Sex lives : a sexual self-portrait of America / Mark Baker.
      p. cm.
   1. Sex customs—United States.   I. Title.
HQ18.U5B28   1994
306.7′0973—dc20   93-30575   CIP
ISBN 0-671-70253-X

A C K N O W L E D G M E N T S

The men and women who agreed to be interviewed for this book took a big risk. When people talk honestly about sex, they reveal a part of their lives that is exclusively personal, far beyond the everyday secrets they keep from others and sometimes from themselves. To give a virtual stranger such an intimate glimpse of one's deepest desires and innermost thoughts and feelings takes real courage. Thank you, ladies and gentlemen, for having the courage to be a part of this book.

I extend my thanks to Bob Bender, my editor. The shortcomings of this book are all mine, but much of what is good about this book is there because of Bob and his talent as an editor, his ability to see to the heart of what matters. Production editor Ted Landry and copy editor Andrew Hafitz did a beautiful technical job on the manuscript.

Carolyn Reidy at Simon & Schuster and Bill Grose at Pocket Books have managed between them to keep me afloat long enough to get this book to the readers, and believe me, it wasn't easy for them. Thank you both for keeping your eye on the future.

Esther Newberg achieves the impossible on a daily basis. There is no other literary agent to match her. She's a pretty wonderful human being as well, although she doesn't want that to get around. Thank you, Esther. Her associate Sloan Harris has also worked tirelessly in my behalf.

Johanna Li and Amanda Beesley are reliable, dedicated, and they made my life easier, just as I know they have made life easier for Bob and Esther, respectively.

My sounding board, devil's advocate, confidante, and critic is Frank Fortunato. He's a smart man, clear and compassionate on the subject of the human condition. His contribution to this work was essential.

So many good friends and members of my family have helped and encouraged me in this project, given me a place to stay or their acquaintances to be interviewed, or pressed upon me a little hope when I needed it most that I'm afraid to try and list them all now. I might forget one, and that would be a crime. I'll thank each of you in person when the time comes.

The idea for this book wasn't mine. Veronica, my wife, thought it up. She's much more intelligent than I am in many, many ways. So why didn't I dedicate this book to her, or any of my five books for that matter? The answer is that, rightly or wrongly, I'm saving that. I want the book I dedicate to her to be as singular and extraordinary as she is. I'm not sure what it will be about, I'm not even sure I can write a book that special. Until then, Ronnie, I love you, now and always. Everything I write is for you.

—M.B.

THIS BOOK IS DEDICATED TO BOB AND GLORIA BAKER.

THEIR LOVE MADE ME, THEIR GENEROSITY OF SPIRIT NURTURED ME,

THEIR LOYALTY SUSTAINS ME.

C O N T E N T S

INTRODUCTION

magine that one warm spring night, under a full moon, all your neighbors dragged their beds outside, onto the lawns of their ranch-style homes, the driveways of their condominiums, or the sidewalks in front of their apartment buildings. Then, unself-consciously, they went about their sex lives just as though they were still inside, behind drawn curtains and closed doors. Would the only sounds be the deadly serious drone of Ted Koppel punctuated by the fake laughter of late-night stand-up comics? Would the shrubbery and streetlights ring with the moans of pleasure until the crabgrass began to ripple and the blooms quaked off the hydrangeas?

Now suppose, whatever happened, you were allowed to wander about from bedside to bedside taking a closer look and asking intimate questions:

"What was it like the first time you had sex?"

"Do you masturbate? How often?"

"Did you ever have an affair? Tell me about it."

And very matter-of-factly, the men and women answered, telling you, in detail, about their personal sexual histories, about kissing and gooseflesh, tongues and orgasm, about love and jealousy, ennui and desperate passion.

That is the experience I've tried to approximate in the pages of this book. I talked to a few more than a hundred people, almost equally divided between men and women. They are from all over America, Boston to Little Rock to San Diego, Olympia to Omaha to Orlando. The youngest person I talked to is sixteen, the oldest is sixty-seven. The majority of them are Baby Boomers, between the ages of thirty and forty-five. This generation certainly didn't invent sex, but they were the first generation of Americans to explore and experiment openly with their sexuality.

Among the women are a bond trader and a homemaker, a bartender and a television director, a factory worker and a psychologist. The men include a banker and a piano mover, a waiter and a CEO, a contractor and a mystery writer, an elementary-school teacher and a rock-'n'-roll guitarist.

Although I have attempted to gather a diverse and comprehensive assortment of individuals, I was restricted to those people who were willing to talk to me in depth on this subject. I believe the people who will speak to you in these pages are a fairly representative group of Americans, except that their very willingness to talk frankly about sex may set them apart from the majority. Plenty of prospective interviewees told me flatly, "No! I'm not talking to you about my sex life! What, are you crazy?" and hurried away. I have to admit, I never would have agreed to be interviewed.

But once people made the decision to go ahead with the interview, I believe they told me the truth about themselves, as completely as any of us can tell it from the limited perspective we have inside our own skins. Although that means what you will read here is the subjective truth —not the Absolute Truth—at least there are no ringers here, either. I didn't troll the personal ads in *The Village Voice*, place solicitations in swingers' magazines, or pay professionals to trump up tales of sexual encounters with the rich and famous and dead.

I didn't show up for interviews with a legal pad full of questions like some psychiatric researcher taking inventory of sex acts. In fact, I didn't really ask questions. I'm not much for verbal sparring; I don't even try to pry. But I'm a good listener. I'm more interested in what people will bring up on their own. My experience is that if I just keep my mouth shut and let people talk, eventually they will tell me what is most important to them. A little patience has always rewarded me with anecdotes and insights that I couldn't have imagined, much less elicited with some sly or penetrating line of questioning.

I guaranteed anonymity to all these people who allowed me a glimpse into their lives. That's been my method in all my books, but it seemed particularly appropriate in this case, to put people at ease, so they could tell the truth about themselves without fear of subsequent embarrassment, ridicule, unwanted advances, or, in a few instances, divorce proceedings. In fact, I conducted more interviews than usual over the telephone, even when the two of us were in the same city. We could speak intimately, lips to ear, but the other person could remain concealed, could feel safe even from me. There was a lot of fear involved—fear of discovery by a lover or spouse ("If my girlfriend knew I was here telling you about us, she'd kill me"), fear of not measuring up to some impossible imaginary standard ("I don't know why you want to talk to me—I don't swing from the chandeliers or anything"), fear of being all too typical or, conversely, fear of not fitting the stereotype, fear of speaking aloud an innermost desire, some secret need people hide even from themselves ("There is only one other person in the world who knows this about me . . . ").

It was disconcerting to find that sex is still such a dangerous subject in this country. A quick scan of American popular culture would make it seem that there is nothing of a sexual nature that hasn't been publicly discussed, displayed, exploited, and exhausted. It's standard procedure to use sex to sell everything from chewing gum to chainsaws. Television programming has become one extended sexual innuendo, soap operas have stripped down to their skivvies, the glut of talk shows has become a common folks' *Kama Sutra*, and music videos bump and grind around the clock. Fashion magazines are falling out of their brassieres with erotic images. And movies are reduced to dredging the backwaters of sexually violent kinkiness for a little shock value now and then.

Despite all this commercial sexuality, there's not much information available on Americans' actual sex practices besides a few white-coated clinical investigations, like the Kinsey report, or compilations of lifeless statistics gathered through surveys in college psychology departments or in self-help magazines. There are several hardbound volumes of women's sexual fantasies, companions to the tonnage of glossy, full-color pornography printed monthly for men. Most telling perhaps is the continuing popularity of sexual manuals that teach people how to have sex, to do it better and more often. These are often accompanied by revelations of newly discovered points of physical arousal, charts and maps where G marks the spot. Many writers (of the nonmedical, general-nonfiction type) attempting to explore the American sexual psyche seem to get sidetracked into sexual big-game hunting. They become preoccupied with polygamists or sado-masochists, prostitutes or lifestyle prophets, thinking that if they can just bag this big concept or encapsulate some trendy sexual fad, they can then explain what really drives us all.

Something is missing between the professionals' data and the constant suggestive buzz emitted by American commercialism. There's a big, empty spot where the human beings should be; lots of naked bodies, but no people. Talking about real sex, the simple physical acts, describing the actual sensations of sex, admitting what we like or don't like remains a shameful and treacherous activity to engage in. In the absence of meaningful communication about sex, we have begun to accept the psychobabble and banal perfume ads for reality. As our sexuality is depreciated, our humanity is diminished.

My primary occupation since 1979 has been listening to people talk about their lives. Every time I interview someone new, I am amazed at the complicated twists and turns, the quirks of fate, the depravity or nobility of their experience, the new chapters that spring open just when I thought the story was over, and the surprise endings in ordinary lives. I never pigeonhole people anymore, or put much stock in scientific analysis of the chimera called normal human behavior. I knew there had to be something more sexually real, more individual and idiosyncratic, something more humane, yet exciting, going on in this country than mail-order lingerie catalogues, Madonna in bondage, and a rap singer pulling down his pants in public to sell designer jockey shorts.

I took my tape recorder and went out to talk to real men and women about sex in their lives. No braggadocio, no coquettishness, no Krafft-Ebing props or staging, no censorship or airbrushing. I didn't ask them to give me any numbers. I told them I wasn't too interested in their fantasies. I wanted to know what they felt in their guts, as well as in their genitals. Most people I talked to were very good at using their brains to decipher where their instincts had carried them.

I heard stories full of candor, self-deprecating laughter, sometimes anger and brutality, most importantly love—and all the joy and sorrow only love can bear. Every living thing on Earth reproduces; only human beings fall in love. It is emotion that makes this exploration of American sexuality different—the range and depth of emotion expressed by the men and women I interviewed and the compassion their stories evoke.

I've carefully preserved the context of their words as well as the speakers' voices. The language is like brushing against a lover's body—explicit, glistening with sensuous detail, and bursting with a palpable eroticism that couldn't be invented. But there is no manipulative sexual crescendo here. It won't make good masturbatory fodder for the voyeur. These people didn't tell their stories to turn us on. This is the artless passion of real life.

For organizational reasons I've grouped these interviews in certain categories, but I'm not trying to simplify or to demystify sex in America. On the contrary, I hope the complex and varied strata of individuality laid bare here helps restore the mysteriousness of sex to a society that has mistaken self-indulgence for sophistication and jadedness for boredom with the bombardment of disconnected, mechanical images of body parts.

In the limited, suggestive language of sexual politics, I am a male heterosexual. I am sure this had some effect on exactly what was or was not said to me in these interviews. But I have no political or philosophical ax to grind in presenting this book. I can't change my gender, and I don't hide my sexual orientation. I am personally committed to equality and diversity, but I despise the tyranny of political correctness as much as I deplore intolerance and the censorship of ideas.

I do hope, though, that once you finish this book, you will walk away saying: "I feel like I know these people."

ONE

INITIATION

1. PROTOSEX

"I had a dream when I was just a child about one of the guys in my class at school. In the dream, he was hurt. I was trying to be helpful, because I had a schoolgirl crush on him. I went up to him, looked at his broken arm, and then I got down and bit him. He didn't scream." When I asked a woman in her thirties to try to recall her earliest sexual memory, this faraway dream, suddenly vivid and incisive, was immediately on her lips.

"I was very disturbed by it and woke up thinking, 'Wow! There's something going on out here!' That was the first time I knew there was *something else* to life, that this thing, whatever it is, wasn't just another playground game like tetherball or four-square. That was the first time that a boy looked different to me than my brothers, who were just the guys I fought with constantly trying to get space in the bathroom."

Even as children we are sexual beings, but sexuality is like a distant, troubling dream. Then one day we awake and find the dream is reality and childhood itself has been the dream.

It all begins simply enough with gender. Gender is a big deal in America. Infants all look remarkably the same with their diapers on, so we color code their clothing—pink booties for girls, blue for boys. Mothers attach ribbons and barrettes to what little wisps of hair their daughters have on their heads. Fathers poke baseball caps down over their sons' tiny ears or toss a regulation-size football into the crib. These days, parents who consider themselves more enlightened buy dolls for their boys and encourage the girls to play with trucks. Still, God help the stranger who has the temerity to take the fifty-fifty chance, guess at the sex of a baby, and get it wrong.

"Oh, what a cute little boy."

"She's a *girl!*"

It's important that boys be boys and girls be girls, but Americans don't like to discuss the physical differences. This thirty-nine-year-old advertising executive's childhood experience is typical: "I didn't know what a vagina was. The girl next door called it her bicky, so that's all I knew it was—a bicky. My mother had no reason to call it anything and never did. We didn't have girls in the family, so she didn't have to call hers dink.

"As far as our penises, they were our gigmos—not gizmos. So we had bickies next door for the girls and gigmos for the boys. I remember sitting in the tub and saying, 'Now, Mom, what do you really call this . . . this . . . gigmo?'

"'It's really a penis,' she said, but she didn't like to say that word one bit. She was not happy about it. So I didn't bring it up again. Even at an early age, it was obvious to me that *penis* was a dirty word, while *gigmo* is acceptable, because *nobody* on the planet knows what a gigmo is."

But the curiosity of children is an inexorable force. Is there a man or woman alive today who did not as a child experience some version of this age-old barter of simple sexual information: "I'll show you mine, if you'll show me yours"?

Children begin to share among themselves the scraps of facts, innuendo, and suggestion they have managed to tease out of the world around them. This description from a forty-five-year-old piano mover and part-time artist is a stock example of that childhood exchange: "There was only one guy I ever hung out with. He used to draw what girls looked like with crayons on the slates in the backyard. His father was in the merchant marine and had tattoos. This guy had seen the tattoos, so he knew what girls looked like. They were fish from the waist down, and if his father made muscles, they'd move. Turned out, girls didn't look anything like his pictures. But he told me they did."

When puberty springs its chemical ambush, the trickle of idle speculation, fueled by gushing hormones, becomes a torrent of confusing sexual misinformation composed of improbable myths, misinterpreted euphemisms, and just plain wild invention. Sex seems so improbable, so physically gross, so utterly enigmatic. Yet the urges of the body are undeniably real. As a forty-eight-year-old antiques dealer remembers it, "At fifteen, we were horny as hell. Anything would give you a hard-on. Cindy Fuentes' leg in history class. She'd just sit there with her legs crossed, rolling her knees one over the other. You'd get this hard-on, this boner, this rigid dick that would stay that way for forty minutes. Then at the end of class, because you wore real tight pants back then, and you didn't necessarily want to walk out in the hall with a stand-up in your pants, you would have to concentrate with all your might to will your dick to subside a little bit. That was just a routine thing, rigid hard-ons that men dream about in middle-aged life that went to waste at age fifteen in one of Nature's mistimings. Tragic."

Faced with menarche and budding breasts, breaking voices and tufts of hair sprouting here and there on once smooth bodies, some parents realize the inevitability of sexual maturity in their children, and they give their teenagers "the talk." Presumably, a few adults can overcome their own embarrassment and speak plainly about sex. They manage to be thorough but not clinical, serious but sensitive. One woman in her mid-thirties describes the quintessential sex talk she got from her mother: "It went like this: 'A man puts his penis in a woman's vagina, and he plants a seed, and they should be married when it happens.' "

Most young people get parental giggles or a book, if they get any-thing other than silence. The vast majority of people I talked to were told absolutely nothing. A clothing designer and entrepreneur in her early thirties wondered aloud at how little she was told about her sexuality. "Sex is the one thing we don't get taught how to do. We're taught how to walk, we're taught how to say thank you. We're taught all these things, but then we are not taught anything about sex. Just laid bare, and dropped into a kind of void.

"You should be inspired, as if it were some religious activity. It should be something that you're excited about, but you should also be aware that it's a very special thing. You can create life. It's a very holy act in a way. It's pure."

With little basic information and less guidance, distracted by the rush of their own blood, teenagers—young men and women—do what comes naturally. They begin to experiment with themselves and with each other. If sex was only physical, it would be easier. But it's not. Instead, so many contradictory feelings are involved. The feelings men-tioned most often in these interviews were guilt and shame, not love or even lust. They dive or are thrown into the protosexual stew, bubbling with movie romance, dirty jokes, bra hooks and jockey shorts, sweaty palms and saliva, the electric thrill of skin on skin, hickeys, unbearable anticipation, and total, desperate fear.

For almost everyone, it all starts with a kiss.

Anthropologists suggest that the kiss evolved from the primitive mother transferring chewed bits of dinner from her mouth to the mouth of her child as the infant advanced from nursing to taking solid food. Kissing is about the only physically intimate activity American children are allowed to see their parents engaging in, so at least there are some examples available for them to mimic. As simple and innocent as that first kiss can be, it is a moment most adults still remember:

"My first kiss was okay, but I panicked, so I remember feeling like, 'Oh, I'm going to be sick.' "

"What I remember most is I had a fat lip for two days afterwards. It didn't work out too well. The boy and I were both novice-rank kissers."

"I was real reluctant to get into the kissing thing. That was all frightening to me. Still I remember *Love Boat* fireworks from that first kiss. That was like, Wow! It's amazing that anything so simple can have such an impact on you."

"No one ever told me about tongue kissing. It was a strange thing when the first girl put her tongue in my mouth. I was very surprised—*very surprised*—and not altogether pleasantly surprised at first. But after a few minutes, I began to experience it as a pleasant sensation."

The kiss is the last familiar landmark for youths entering the vast, uncharted world of sexuality. Reluctant or intrepid, terrified or elated, the explorers set out.

The events and emotions recounted in this chapter occurred twenty, thirty or more years ago, but they could have happened yesterday. Despite the radical cultural changes perceived to have taken place in that time, children's early experience of their sexuality has changed hardly at all. Little girls and little boys still want to peek inside one another's clothes, and they still find ways to do that. Young couples explore each other furtively in the backseats of cars, under a blanket on church choir trips, in a corner of the backyard where the porch light is blocked by a tree. Although children today may see many more images of sex than their parents did, and teenagers face even more ferocious peer pressure to be sexual earlier, they are just as physically unprotected, emotionally vulnerable, and technically ignorant as earlier generations were.

o o o

In our family, the biggest event, along with dessert, was Mom and Dad announcing that they were going to have another child. It is so bizarre that in a family that large we never got the technicals down. "We know how you buy a car. We know how new things in general come into our lives, but you never told us about this baby stuff." My parents never, ever discussed sex, *ever*. It was embarrassing.

The first time I had my where-babies-come-from conversation was when we had Father O'Sullivan over for dinner on St. Patrick's Day. The Catholic-school kids had the day off from school, so we were these little vagrant kids hanging around the neighborhood. Right down the street all the public-school kids were in school. At the junior high, they were all hanging by the fence during recess. I was in third grade. I was skateboarding on the sidewalk by their playground. My friend and I skateboarded over to this fence, and we were talking to the big guys over at school.

That's how I found out about men making babies with women. They were very graphic, using their fingers and saying, "This goes in here, and it's like wall sockets or something."

My knowledge to that point was that there really wasn't a sexual act. God (somehow) Gives Man the Seed, and (somehow) Woman Gets the Seed. I thought maybe Woman takes it like an aspirin. I had a vague notion of how this might happen. Then all of a sudden, the Seed Gets Planted.

"How does the seed get planted?"

"Well, you know . . . "

"No, I don't know. How?"

"Then Woman Has the Baby."

I got the whole other side of this theory at the public school, and I was reeling. I was just trying to put it together. I was debating this kid out on the street. "Nah, that isn't how it happens. I'll tell you how it happens."

"Oh, you Catholic school-kids."

"Oh, you public-school kids."

So I was a little disturbed when I got home that day. But things were going on, they were getting ready for dinner. We had this huge dinner table. When we sat down at the table, my parents would say, "What did you do today?" They'd go from the oldest to the youngest, or they'd take drop shots at random.

Boy, did I have something to say. Father O'Sullivan was there, but I didn't care. It was a real shocker for me, and I needed to discuss it. So I figured, "This is the place to do it. This is where we talk about most everything." So I said, "You're not going to believe what I heard today."

I was sitting next to Father O'Sullivan, so I was three places removed from my mother, who was at the top of the table. I was looking the other way and I said, "This kid at the public school told me how babies are made today. But I set him straight."

"We . . . will . . . discuss . . . that . . . *later,*" my mother said.

"But . . ."

"We . . . will . . . discuss . . . that . . . later!"

My older brother Hal, the black sheep of the family, was just howling. He loved it. He's kicking me under the table, mouthing, "Go, go, yeah!" But the conversation was just cut off on me.

"But I want to talk about this."

"We'll discuss that later."

"Promise?"

Then when I had the conversation with my mother, she just embarrassed herself. She never fully explained it to me. She said, "Well, honey, that boy has a point." Trying to be diplomatic, but she would never go into any kind of description. I was made to feel like I was a little messed up, because I needed to have this cleared up. I had to take God's word for it.

We lived in a little house with chickens in the yard. My mother, my father, and I are sitting out on the porch. He points to this rooster attacking a hen. He says, "See that, Buck?"

"Yeah," I said. "What's he doing?"

"If she lets him do it, that's called a fuck. Whenever she won't let him do it, that's rape."

My mother just blew up. She didn't explain it any further, but the graphic evidence was right in front of me. That's the most I ever thought about it.

A couple of years later, I went and spent a few weeks in the summer with my cousin Todd. He hung out with a crowd at the country club and played golf, ran wild, went drinking. He told me about French-kissing. He said, "You stick your tongue in this girl's mouth, and she does the same thing to you." I'm about to throw up. He says, "I know it sounds gross, but it's great."

That turned me off for about a year, literally, to the whole idea. "This is gross. These people are insane. Just weird."

My mother and father were not demonstrative at all toward each other.

I don't remember when I ever saw my father kiss my mother, and certainly not with his tongue. The only thing I knew from romance, man and woman, was in the movies when the cowboy kisses the girl—on the mouth, maybe, but it's just a real innocent sort of thing.

Then about a year later, my mother was pregnant again. My brothers and I really wanted a sister. We never had a sister. She ended up having a miscarriage late in the pregnancy. My father woke me up real early one morning when she was in the throes of agony, got me out of bed. My mother was in too much pain to go anywhere. He couldn't call an ambulance—there wasn't one in this little country town we lived in. So it was quicker to go get the doctor.

He had me climb in bed with her to sort of hold her and help her. She didn't have any clothes on, you know? There was blood. It was awful. I didn't understand what was going on with her. She was kind of out of it. I didn't know how to help her. I tried, but I couldn't.

Later, no one took me aside. My father didn't. No one explained what went on. It was that wall: Sex is something we all love, but it's taboo. Nobody talks about it, particularly if you're an eleven-year-old kid. That turned me off to the idea of women or anything for a couple more years.

My grandfather had a little ranch. He would breed cattle. I grew up watching bulls mount cows, stallions and mares together. I vaguely knew people did the same thing. One time I saw a couple of dogs that were stuck together. My mother had to get cold water and throw it on them to enable them to dislodge from each other.

I thought, "God, this is weird. My father tells me fuck and rape, the dogs get caught, my mother is bleeding to death with a miscarriage, my dad and my mother never talk about it, and neither of my parents were ever demonstrative towards us, not much hugs." I was sort of like tactilely dysfunctional, I would say, which has a lot to do with someone getting off on the wrong foot. I didn't touch people much.

As a result, I grew up with what I saw in the movies: Hayley Mills as Pollyanna. I believed in this idealized version of romantic love, but no early sexual experience, except for stirrings and feelings, the occasional hard-on in the bathtub. No knowledge of function whatsoever. I never had any example of sexual display among adults that was healthy. You at least expect to catch Mama kissing Santa Claus once. But never, never. Maybe it's a Protestant thing; it was downright puritanical. The guy was supposed to be the strong, silent type. The little woman was supposed to bustle around the kitchen and laugh.

My mother was raising my brother and I on a very low secretarial salary, so things were quite a struggle. She was very strict with us. We went to bed early, because she just needed time to herself. When I was about six, we'd moved into an apartment, and things had just started to settle down after her divorce.

We went to bed at seven-thirty. It was just the law. This was the first time I had ever broken the law. I got up out of bed, because I had this overwhelming question that I didn't know the answer to. I went and looked for her in the living room, and she wasn't there. I found her sitting on the stoop outside. It was nice out, breezy and warm. I sat down next to her, and I asked her where babies come from.

She didn't yell at me for being up, and I felt a little like an adult. *"Okay, this is a legitimate question I've asked, and I'm being treated with respect. I like that."*

She told me—very technically—how children are conceived. A man has a penis and a woman has a vagina, and the whole very technical bit. But she also told me that when people love each other, they engage in this activity, and a miraculous thing happens—children may be born. Then she gave me some statistics, like the mother carries the baby inside her for nine months.

I asked questions. "Can a man ejaculate more than once in a row?" I had some pretty good questions for a six-year-old. "How long does he have to wait before he can do that again?"

I remember thinking, "This couldn't be right. They can't do that. It's the strangest thing I ever heard. People wouldn't put a penis inside a vagina. That doesn't sound nice and loving. That just sounds gross." But of course it was intriguing. Since then I've grown to enjoy it. She told me that would happen, but I didn't believe it for a second.

I had a thing or two up my sleeve. When we would visit Dad in the summers, sometimes I would ask him the same questions I would ask Mom, and then measure his answers. Through this sort of testing, I came to trust my mother's advice and opinions. More than anything, I was just curious what my dad would say, just to see where he stood, get a feel for who he was, and get to know him since I only spent a few months out of the year with him. He was a good man, but one of the reasons my mother divorced him was that they really had sexual problems. He was not very loving, and thought sex was dirty.

This ties right into the response he gave me when I asked him where babies came from. He said, "A man has a pole, and the woman has a hole. The man sticks the pole in the hole." He's laughing. I wasn't laughing. Even though I was only six, I thought, "That's what you're going to tell me about this? Really? Really?" I felt bad for him. "That's too bad that you think like that." Anyway, I didn't choose his version and point of view.

My husband had a vasectomy this summer, and we really hadn't thought it through in terms of the kids hearing our conversation. We should have given it some advance thought. My oldest son is eight years old and very precocious. He listens in on every conversation, doesn't forget anything—Big Ears.

He started asking me questions. I did just what the books say, where you give them just a little bit of information and see where they go with it. I thought I could just do the old, "Daddy and I have decided that we don't want to have any more children. We feel like the three of you take up all of our time, and it would be taking away from your time and our time together if we spread that any thinner by bringing another child into the family. Therefore, Daddy's going to have this operation done to his penis." Little boys are so into their penises, so I tried to pawn it off on, "so Daddy won't be able to fertilize the eggs anymore."

That lasted for about thirty seconds.

"I understand that," he said, "but if the egg is coming from you, how does Daddy get the fertilizer to you anyway?"

So we went through the whole shooting match. I said, "Close the door. We might as well have a long talk about this." We must have sat in here and talked for about an hour.

After I was all done trying to explain sex, or at least reproduction, to my eight-year-old, he looked at me and said, "Why is it grown-ups made up that really stupid story about the birds and the bees and the stork?"

"It is pretty ridiculous," I said. "It doesn't give you guys much credit."

We were going to see his grandfather a week later. At this point, my husband had had his vasectomy, but he hadn't been checked to make sure that he was sperm-free. I was packing. I'd thrown in my diaphragm in its case. Of course, my son and I had discussed birth control in this discussion, too. We had done the whole thing. I figured I'll never have to talk about this again his whole life.

"So," he said, "you and Dad think you might make love while we're visiting Gramps, huh?"

Oh, great, now I have to discuss my love life with my eight-year-old. I looked at him, and I said, "William, my sex life isn't really any of your business. Okay?"

"I just noticed that you were packing *that.*"

I got raped when I was six. It was the most scariest thing that ever happened to me in my life. My mother can't believe I remember this. I blame her for it. She was gone to prison, and my brother with the broken leg was the only one at home. This was by a cousin, an older guy in the family.

My cousin, he had brought a sack of oranges and had fooled everybody outside. We was out under a tree, eating, like kids do. I was going into first grade. I was real close with my brother who had got his leg broke. My brother always called me whenever he had to use the bedpan, because they give us a little white pan to stick under him whenever he had to go to the bathroom. Most of the kids didn't like to do it. But I would always do it for him. I wouldn't make a fuss about it. I always felt sorry for him, because he had a cast all the way up to his hip.

I remember him hollering and hollering for me. It was hot, and we didn't have no fans or nothing. He was up against the window, so he could holler, and we could hear him out in the yard. We had a small house that had a screened-in back porch with one of them little white gas heaters and a bathroom.

He had called, and I went on in the house. He wanted his bedpan, which we kept in that back-porch bathroom. I go to get it. When I get to the bathroom, this cousin is behind the door. It didn't scare me, because I'd known the man. He comes around all the time. He's our cousin. He says, "Wait a minute, I want you to play a game with me."

"No, I don't want to play. I don't want to play." About that time, he put something over my mouth and I couldn't say shit. I mean, nothing. I was trying to fight him, but I was so little. I was really trying to get away from him. He caught my hands behind me and took all of my clothes off. I was getting scareder and scareder. I couldn't scream, and my brother was hollering for me, "What's taking you so long? Bring the pan!" He kept hollering for me, and he couldn't get the other kids' attention. They was all having fun eating the oranges.

The only thing I could think of was to kick that heater over, then my brother is going to come and save me. All this was running through my little mind. I kicked, and I kicked, and I kicked it over. He heard that noise and he knew something was wrong. He had an old-fashioned can opener near him in the bedroom, one of them with the small pointy blade. He used that to rip all the cast off, just tore it off. He crawled to the back porch. He got there and tried to get the door open. But my cousin had bolted the door. My brother kept on till he busted the door open.

I was out of it. I was hysterical. I remember the ambulance coming. These guys wrapped me up in lots of sheets and took me to the hospital. I remember my brother crying, and talking to me, "You're going to be okay." He was crying, and I was hysterical. I didn't know nothing. I remember being in the hospital. There were so many people coming in and talking to me in hushed voices. I went into a little setback. I wouldn't talk to nobody. I was scared as fucking shit.

The worst part was then I had to be in court. They brought me to an old red brick building downtown. I was so scared because these people had kept coming to the house and talking to me and asking me if this is the man who did that to me. I told them, "Yes, that's the man." In court, they had a little stool, and they told me to sit up there. This guy, he was real nice. He said, "Ain't nobody going to hurt you. You tell us step by step what happened."

"Okay." They brought my cousin in handcuffs. He had on white clothes. It frightened me to see that man.

The lawyer said, "Ain't nobody going to touch you. See? There's a policeman with him. Now, say everything that you saw and what he did."

"He pulled his pants down and he had two," I said.

"Two?"

"This man is a boy and a girl." They couldn't figure out what I was talking about. I said, "He had a pussy and a dick, too." I thought his pubic hair was a woman's vagina. They give him eighty-nine years.

I did not see him again until I came back here to live again. He's a old man. He got one leg. He knew me. I did not know him. I was in a country store, and I didn't think nothing. I was just having a good time. I was going to see my family. He said, "Linda."

"I know you?"

"I know *you*. I'd know you anywhere. I'm your cousin, Walter Wilson."

"Don't you come near me."

"I paid my dues."

"I just want you to know, I think you're a very sick person." And I left the store. I couldn't believe that after all them years he would remember me. I thought maybe he had died or something.

I was probably five years old and there was a gang of neighborhood boys. It's hard to say how old they were, because I'm five. In my memory, they were huge, like teenagers, and there were twelve of them. Probably they were nine-year-olds, and there were five of them. But they brought me into a garage, took all my clothes off, and I paraded around naked. I had a great time. I wasn't a victim. I was playing. I didn't think anything was wrong until years later, and I thought about it—"Whoa! Wow! I can't believe that happened." I don't know if that's normal, but for a lot of people who have been truly victimized by incest or other sexual crimes it was pretty heavy. If I was a mother and my five-year-old daughter told me that she was with some boys in a garage and took her clothes off, I would be freaked out. That would scare me. It never occurred to me to be scared. There's a certain level of innocence.

I had this idea of boys' penises being something ridiculous. It was more something that gave me cause to laugh than to want it and go after it. Although, that did change.

It had something to do with urination. If you had a penis, you could pee across the room. This is what I wanted to see and know about. I felt inadequate, because I knew I could never do that. I'd heard stories of boys who could. It was always kept from me as much as I tried to get them to show me. I kept asking boys to pee. Heck, I kept asking boys to fuck me, and I can't believe that nothing ever happened, especially when you think of all the horror stories of the things that happen to little girls.

This girl named Valerie Meadows, she was sort of tomboyish. There were a couple of bullies on the street I had to fight when I moved into that area. One of them got punched out by this Valerie, so they were afraid of her, because she would punch them. But she liked me. We were nine or ten. We used to go out in the woods and play at the bottom of our hill. There was this big, undeveloped field down there with all these rabbits and little animals that could survive in suburban clime on the edge of a woods.

I forget how she put it, and I've thought back upon it many times over the years, but one day she said what amounted to, "I'll show you mine, if you'll show me yours."

"Okay," I go. I remember how she did it, too. She pulled down the front of her pants, and showed me this little bald thing with a slit in it. I was sort of interested.

"Okay, now show me yours," she said. And I wouldn't do it. I happened to be modest at nine years old. On a CYO bus changing clothes to go swimming, I was embarrassed about stripping in front of other nine-year-old boys. It's the modesty that's instilled in you in your home. That's sort of natural, but you don't have to be *that* modest. You don't have to be ashamed of being naked around other boys. You really don't get rid of that shit when it's gotten into you while you're real young.

I wasn't trying to trick poor Valerie Meadows. It's just that I was embarrassed to show her my little dick, even though she showed me hers.

At the time, she did not remain my friend. She was not a nice person after that, as I recall. She was disappointed.

It was a mistake on my part. She grew up to be a little piece of ass, you know? Vincent Vittorio was the guy who got to screw her and not me. I could have had an in from the ground floor. I mean, I knew her when she was in the mailroom, before she got to the corporate suite with her tits and her big, ripe pussy ready to be fucked. So it's something I've come to regret.

She always had this resentment towards me. I probably told these jerks —my fellow jerks—"Hey, I saw her cunt. And she didn't see mine." Probably the boasting thing, and it got back to her. It was one of the tragedies of my childhood, actually. I've relived that scene in a masturbatory fantasy. I know you won't be surprised to hear that I changed the ending of that to all kinds of scenarios.

I discovered masturbation when I was about seven. To me, this was the most amazingly wonderful thing in the world, that I could do something to myself and feel really good. That was the age when you had overnights with girlfriends. When I was staying over at my best girlfriend's house, I taught her how to do it, thinking nothing, thinking, "This is just great, and

I want to share it, because we may be the only two on Earth who know." This was information to be shared. This is really cool. I can't believe that I didn't think something was wrong with it.

My mother got a phone call from my girlfriend's mother, that I was teaching little girls how to masturbate. She didn't think that was such a good idea. My mother told me it wasn't a nice thing to do, not to talk about things like that, and not to really do it anymore.

I remember my stomach knotting up prepubescently at being interested in anything sexual. At going into Phil's Candy Store at the age of ten, before I knew what a stand in your pants was, and sneaking in the back where he kept these artists'-models magazines, which are tame by today's standards but which showed shaved pubes. I'd look at these until he chased us out.

Going to the library, looking for anthropological study books and medical books, showing grotesque diseases and deformed people, the females of whom still had snatches.

I remember being in Palisades Amusement Park, where they had those little nickel machines with the risqué flip movies. Yeah, anything that's forbidden, kids go for. I remember Lennie Green and I dropping nickels in. He said, "Press your cock up against the machine. Feels good, doesn't it?" We were still ten then and didn't know what we were doing. But you have an erection, and you press it up against something, and you get a sensation. So I knew there was promise in the dick at age ten. I didn't know what that promise was to be, but I knew there was promise in the dick.

Sex wasn't something that I grew into as many men do. Sex was something *I knew.* I was just waiting for puberty. I was a little libertine under wraps there, waiting to be released—armed, shall we say, like a ballistic missile of hornstick, waiting for someone to flip the switch that sets my warhead off.

He was my partner in crime. If we were ever going to do anything that we weren't supposed to, this was the brother I would do it with. When we were real young we would sneak out of the house when it was raining and pretend we were African explorers. He was a great creative muse. He was my dream buddy when the lights were on. We used to have conversations about, "If the Martians ever came and landed, and they offered to take you away, would you go? You'd never know if you were coming back." We'd play Catholic church in the garage. Take little orange-juice glasses and Wonder bread and make hosts out of it. Play games when no one was looking.

One day, he made what seemed a strange pass at me at the time. And I got scared. He had been given the sex talk by my parents. It wasn't all that strange that he would be the first one to bring up sex, wondering how they do it and what goes on. He was a little bit older than I was, a couple of years. It was Christmas Eve, and I remember him saying, "I wonder what it's like?" It wasn't as though he was proposing that we do it; he was just saying, "What do you think about it?" I was just becoming aware of sex. I was eight or ten, much before the first kiss, and I was scared. I knew him as being more adventuresome than me, and I thought, "I might be in trouble here. I might not be able to control this type of thing." I didn't understand it, and I didn't know where it was coming from, but I knew it was different. We were best friends, but it made me feel weird. For a couple of days I backed off.

He never brought it up again. We both realized, I think, that we'd hit some place where we couldn't go together. "We can't go that way." But that would have been the next step. That was where we were supposed to go next. It was sad. It changed us for a couple of years.

They'd have these raucous parties in this suburban neighborhood and everybody would get quite loaded. I thought that was normal, until at least in my twenties. I'd find neighbors who weren't married to each other kissing on the back steps. Then, on Sunday, you went to church.

After one of these, when I was just a little girl, about eight years old, I got up in the middle of the night, and all the lights in the house were on. We lived in a two-story house, and I went downstairs into the kitchen. There were clothes all over the kitchen floor. In the Midwest, the crime is just unbelievable. All the really ghastly dismemberments happen in the Midwest or at the hands of Midwesterners. I was aware of violent crime, because one of my first memories of reading a newspaper was about the murder and dismemberment of two sisters.

I thought, "Oh, my God, my parents have been murdered." It was late at night, and I start looking around, following this trail of clothes. I come into the TV room. My father is facedown on the couch, naked. I was really scared. I was sure something really bad had happened to him. So I went to touch his shoulder. He kind of stirred in his sleep, and I could smell booze. And I could see my mother underneath him. I suppressed an "Oh!" because I didn't want him to wake up and be embarrassed, and I went running upstairs.

Actually, I was told a lot about sex. My mom was very forthright and open. Before my period she marched me through the whole thing again —"This is what's going to happen."

Not only did she tell me, she told my brothers, which mortified me. A private lecture for me about what was going to happen was okay. But then my brother found a box of Tampax in my room, and they played guns with them, so she took the boys aside and explained to them what's going on.

It scares the hell out of you when you're a kid. You don't know what it is at first, even though you've seen all the films and you're supposed to understand. My first thought was, "Oh, no, I'm bleeding down there. Am I going to die?"

Then you realize what's happening, become calm, go tell your mom, and let her put the Kotexes on. In those days, there were the belts and hinges, not these little Velcro thingies like now. For years I insisted on using Kotex and not tampons, because I was scared to death something would break up in there. Once something is bleeding out of somewhere, you think it's hurt. So I wouldn't use them. I don't know how old I was before I could insert something in my vagina. It was probably four or five years before I was certain there wasn't something wrong with me that was cut and bleeding.

My mother never told me anything about sex. I vaguely remember her saying, "I like hugging, but none of that other stuff." I was never told what the other stuff might be.

In fact, she didn't even explain menstruation, so when it happened to me at a younger age than she expected—about eleven—I thought something was dreadfully wrong with me. I kept hiding my panties wherever I could shove them. "What's happening to me?"

Finally, when she discovered my panties, she said something. She didn't even use the word *normal.* It was, "This *happens* to women. This horrible thing happens to you, and there's nothing you can do about it. We're all stuck with it, and it will happen every month now."

When we were twelve, we'd go to the beach in Atlantic City, New Jersey. My mother would sit and play mah-jongg with her girlfriends. My girlfriend and I would sit on our own blanket, and all we'd talk about, while the tissue paper fell out of our bathing suit tops, was penises.

"Penises? They are disgusting."

"They're so ugly."

"Ee-yew, what do you do with them?"

"Ee-yew! You put it in your mouth?"

"Ugh, that's awful!"

"Don't make me ill!"

No one could be more intellectual than Eddie Clark, but he was my pal. We thought we were two of the brightest guys around in fourth grade. We had some dirty pictures, and the subject of the blow job came up. We couldn't figure out for the life of us why anyone would want to take the thing that you pee out of in their mouth. We just couldn't understand that. Couldn't understand any of that stuff, but were furtively interested in it. Sex seemed to be something you just could not sit down and figure out. It made no sense.

The kid who gave me my first total misinformation about sex also described masturbation to me. We didn't do it together, but later I started investigating. "What is the deal with this?"

I stayed home one day sick from school, watching *The Price Is Right* and all that other junk on TV all day, laying in my mom's bed. I figured the deal out. At that point, it was the little baby dry heaves, nothing was coming out. I thought, "Now, where is this white stuff he told me about?" All I knew was, "My toes are curling! This *works,* too. This is a hobby. This is something a man can put some time into."

So I spent the whole day at it. If a boy could carry that into manhood, he would really be a stud. I couldn't. But I did get a blister that day. I thought I was going to die. The sucker was big, and it got red. I put Vaseline on it. "I'm dead meat. What am I going to do? My mom's going to find out." It was a terrifying thing.

You're doing something that's clandestine, and you're taught to keep it that way. If sex was something where at the age of twelve there was a big ritual, and the men got you out at the football stadium, told you everything, and then took you to Laredo to get laid, maybe we'd be okay. But we don't do that, so there's a real funny feeling that surrounds all of sex.

Me and several of these guys I hung out with discovered the joys of masturbation about the same time. We'd just pull our bikes off the road in any field, it really didn't matter, and beat off. It was like blowing your nose. "Let's whang 'em!"

The funniest thing was, another friend of ours didn't find out until he was in high school how much everybody else was beating off, because he came from a real strict Christian family. He figured you were going straight to hell if you beat off more than once a week. Here he'd passed up some of the best years of his life. We said, "Oh, yeah. You know, Ten, Two, and Four, just like Dr Pepper. Let's whang 'em!" He was really bummed. He's probably been catching up since then.

Me and my friends had *Playboy* stashed away. We must have kept it for about a year. It was hidden in this construction site under some rocks, buried. We'd dig it up, and look at it. We'd have to have someone standing guard to make sure no one was coming when we'd be looking at it.

Once I got to be twelve or thirteen, my father would start telling me, "We have to have a talk soon." He didn't have the talk with me. Finally, I said, "Look, Dad, if this is about sex, let's not worry about it. I know about sex."

"If there's anything you don't know, or you have any questions about it, come and ask me," he said. But he still never laid it out. Then sometime in the eighth grade, they had some priest come and talk to us about sex —the Voice of Experience.

In sixth grade, I read this book *Candy*. I went to a girls' school, and we would pass this book around in each other's schoolbags. When you finished reading it, you would put it in somebody else's schoolbag. We were all waiting for our turn. The part where he comes inside of her, I thought he had peed inside her. "This is incredible! This is what you do?"

For me adolescence was difficult. My body started changing. I had been very tomboyish and very proud of my body. I was really good at what I did. Suddenly, I started feeling weird and awkward. I was noticing that girls were getting dates, and I wasn't. This boy liked me, and I was so ashamed. He kissed me, and I had braces, so I didn't open my mouth, I was so scared. The fear was much greater than any kind of erotic, sexual thing. It was this new, unknown thing.

The funny thing is that when I first started getting "yearnings," it corresponded strangely enough to watching monster movies. Somebody pointed out later that was pretty obvious developmental stuff, but, boy, Wolfman, Mummy, all them, I was really into the transmogrified monsters. Whatever was coming up in my subconscious, I was having some uneasy times with it. I was totally into the Wolfman with his beard coming in, the monster within you.

I really reached puberty while watching *Goldfinger*. I took a whole birthday party of my friends to see it. The year before, we'd gone to see *The Dirty Dozen*, because we were into army and shit like that. This is the first film where there is almost nudity, and we all totally changed during that movie. We were less interested in Bond shooting people than we were in the naked girls. I came out of there going, "Wow, there's a whole thing happening here that's totally new and different. Enough of this action stuff. Where are the girls?" In those days you could get an erection just by snapping your fingers.

When you are fourteen years old, you are oversexed. My roommate and I, while I was in boarding school, discovered the Satanic Church. What we found out was that, when the Satanists had the rituals, the altar was the body of a naked woman. So we thought, "Yeah, man, I bet that's just the start of what they do." Anyway, we wrote away to become members of the Satanic Church. Typically, we weren't old enough to sign this document. For some reason—I don't know how it happened—the church wrote to my parents for permission.

So we're in school, and I get the Saturday-morning call when you talk to Mom and Dad. I could tell things were a little strained, but it was the usual thing, like how's school, fine. Then my mother goes, "I'm going to get off the phone now. *Your father needs to speak with you.*"

"We just received these documents indicating that you were intending to join the Satanic Church."

"Oh, yeah . . . that. Dad, think nothing of it."

"This is not going to happen. Just know that. Okay? Know that it's *not going to happen.*"

My parents had their own personal standards which were the same as Ozzie and Harriet: separate beds. No sex. To this day, that is their idea of the way things ought to be. I'm forty-five years old, and it's pretty damned amazing for me to consider my parents made love. Other people's parents I can see, but not mine. The funny thing is, I'm right.

My father was a man of very few words and fewer actions. He was the kind of guy who would come home from working all week, and for forty-eight hours, he would be seated in his chair with the television set—a Muntz—and three or four radios all playing different ball games simultaneously. His sandwich is on his left. His cigars on the right. There he reposes until it's time to go to work on Monday. He always had a car sitting out on the curb. He didn't use the car. He took the streetcar to work. The car sat at the curb all week and all weekend. I'm sixteen years old. It's Saturday in October. I've got my driver's license. I say, "Dad, can I use the car?"

"I'm not going to sit around the house all day without the car." This is the kind of guy he was.

So his sex talk was really nervous at this point: "Well, ah, if you hear any dirty jokes, ah, I'll tell you what they mean." That's it. I had trouble remembering the jokes, and the last person I would tell is my old man. He'd be too busy with the ball games anyway. And my mother, I think, was born with menopause, so she didn't want to hear anything about sex.

That's why we have dogs. Human beings need to be able to pet and touch warm flesh on a regular basis. I worked in a restaurant kitchen the summer I was sixteen. I got assigned the job of making baked potatoes. I had this huge Flash Gordon machine. I would bake the potatoes, scoop the stuff out, bake the shells in this machine, put in butter, vanilla, and milk, and whip them up. Then I had to pass the finished potatoes through this window that cut the waitresses off at the neck and the knees. All I saw was breasts and vaginas. I never saw their faces. The girls were competing to see who could wear the sexiest outfits they could possibly show up in. I had the wildest summer, because I worked with this warm vegetable flesh, which I handed off to these sex organs. I was out of my mind, just giddy, punchy. I constantly was trying to come on to the girls. I have no idea how I looked to them. I know my apron had these dried teats of starch all over me, reeking of rancid vanilla. "Hey, baby, want to go out?"

Once in a while one of them would duck down, look at me, and go, "Oh, my God, who is this guy?" At some point, some synapses had snapped, because I was molding this warm flesh and watching this parade of bodies.

I was so terrified when I would have these telephone conversations with boys that I'd write everything down, make a list of questions: "What I'm Going to Ask." I'd never call him. My mother said, "Don't ever call them. Let them call you." I was so terrified of them, those boys, that I couldn't be spontaneous. If I tried that, I would go over the top. I'd go too far, say the wrong thing. I'd babble and go on and on and on.

My house was a matriarchal society, it was all women. Women were the ones that I got things from. But I wasn't getting any help from Mom. The more interest I had in boys, the more my mother knew the baby was not coming back, so the more she kept herself away from me.

I didn't get anything from my father. I didn't have a clue as to who he was. He was this very sad, brooding guy, always on the verge of bankruptcy, always fell asleep in a chair with his hand stuck in the top of his pants. Not knowing who he was and never getting a reaction out of him formed my ideas about men and sexuality. Men were these guys that as a female you had to turn yourself inside out and do back flips for them to see you.

I was so afraid of boys, I would throw up before going on dates. I did this from age thirteen, and it lasted until I got to college. It had to do with seeing something on television that I shouldn't have seen. I was baby-sitting for a neighbor. On the old *TV Guide,* it used to say "AO—Adults Only." I thought, "Oh-ho, here I am, and no one can tell me not to watch this." It was a movie that was on at eleven o'clock at night, and it had a rape scene. I was so traumatized by that. I never told anybody I saw it, because it was something I shouldn't have been doing.

I just panicked at the thought of being alone with a boy—I'm talking about being with a fourteen-year-old whose mother is driving you to a dance. But it is so real. I thought in my head, "If I'm alone with this person, that is going to happen to me, or at least there is a good chance it might." It set a fearful stage, just to be afraid all the time. I saw boys as an oddity, a strange sex I knew nothing about. All I knew was that I was afraid of them.

Two dances I made myself so sick, my mother had to call the boy an hour before he was supposed to pick me up and tell him that I was too sick to go. She was furious with me. I still have never told her what it was that I was afraid of and why this was happening to me. I just fantasized so much in my mind that I made every male a monster.

Once I was on the date, I was nervous, but I didn't throw up anymore. I would be like, "Sit on the opposite side of the car, and God forbid, you should try to hold my hand. Don't even touch me."

I was a late bloomer, not sexually mature until I was over fifteen, which is kind of hard on you at the time. You got friends who have pubic hair and five-o'clock shadows. It kept me from going out for basketball until I was in the eleventh grade. I always felt somewhat inferior because of that. I remember making out with a girl and thinking, "Goddamn. I'd be embarrassed to take my clothes off." No danger of me getting into trouble with her. I'd have been too embarrassed to go all the way.

My first kiss was on Mulholland Drive. I lived in the Valley, but I was up there for a party. It was this guy that I'd liked *forever*. After the party, we went as far from the house as we could. It was hidden. It was really a nice night outside, so it was an attempt at romance. We both really just wanted this one thing. It was an initiation. I felt overdue, because my girlfriends had all done it before. Part of my problem was my brothers. They'd kill any guy if he came near me. Any one of four of them could jump out of the bushes at any time and knock them around. They were big jocks, too.

It was summertime. There was this boy I liked a lot who was a year older than me. His friend lived down the street from us, and they had this go-cart that they'd drive around the block. I'd always go out there and pull weeds or something real unobvious—go throw the baseball with my little brother, something really feminine like that—just so I could be out there when they went by.

I don't remember how it got set up exactly, but we made a date for a kiss. It was all planned ahead of time. That is, neither one of us said we were going to have the kiss, but we both understood that there would be a kiss. Days before that I was practicing kissing on the mirror. Girls kiss mirrors and dolls and all sorts of things. I was all ready for this kiss. I got all dressed up, because I knew I was going to have the kiss.

We met in the bedroom of this empty duplex apartment his parents owned. We had the kiss. But I didn't know you were supposed to open your lips. It was one of those childish, puckered-up kinds of kisses. He didn't want to stop. I didn't know what to do. I cracked my eyelids to see what it would look like with him kissing me. I wanted to see his face. I thought, "Oh, well, I'll just close my eyes again." I don't know how long it lasted, maybe thirty seconds. It seemed like it lasted forever, until I finally pulled away.

"This is it? This is awful! This is boring! I'm not going to do this again." I hurried home feeling like I'd committed the worst sin ever.

It was an Episcopalian coed boarding school. That's where I first became attracted to boys. My first boyfriend was younger than me and really cute. We just kissed. He would try and put his hand down my shirt, but I was really a prude. I didn't like that at all. A lot of girls at school were what I considered loose, and I just never felt like I wanted to be identified with them. God, I was amazed at what they'd do, and they weren't doing much.

They had thirty minutes each evening after study hall where couples could get together. They called it Crossroads. You'd see these couples all over the campus, smooching and doing stuff. It was almost like group sex, somehow. I was really embarrassed. I'd sit there and talk with my boyfriend. I didn't want to do anything else.

The administration probably figured it was safer than having people just sneak off into the woods if they didn't give that time to them. Smooch, make out in the corners for half an hour. Then, "Time's up! Go to your dorms and go to bed!"

The first time I was with a guy in the parking lot of Waverly Park—like a lovers' lane—we were making out, he felt me up and came and was wet all over his pants. He was apologizing. I didn't even know what he was apologizing for. I didn't know that men ejaculated. The first time I even knew that existed was when this happened. I was pretty uninformed about sex.

The most I learned about sex was from my next-door neighbors on each side, who were girls. One was older than me and one was younger than me.

The one who was older than me first taught me how to kiss when she was seventeen and I was fifteen. She would come over to my house and say, "I'm going to teach you how to kiss now." So we're sitting there, and she's teaching me how to kiss. As time went on, she taught me how to unbutton her blouse and undo her bra with one hand. "No, no. Do it again." And I had to do it again and again and again. Over and over and over. She taught me everything a piece at a time. This went on for over a year. The whole time she was doing this, she acted like she was teaching me how to do this for when I went out with other girls later on. I never really caught on that she was having a good time, too.

When we got to the great big one, she stopped me and said, "No, no. I can get pregnant, so you can't do this to *anyone*."

That was it. I diddled her for two years, and nothing ever happened. We played around. In a sense, it was great. But in a sense, it was confusing, because it wasn't like this was my girlfriend and we were going out together. She always treated it like she was doing me a favor.

I was a normal kid. I was all turned on, this is wonderful. She'd suddenly say, "Okay, that's it for today. I'll meet you tomorrow. Make sure you don't tell anybody about this." She was a grade or two above me in school, and she didn't want anyone else to know this went on.

On the other side, there was another girl a year younger than me. We started hanging out together a little bit at a time. We ended up spending

Sundays at my house, because my parents weren't home on Sundays. We would spend Sundays in bed naked, just kissing and hugging, because my lessons hadn't progressed enough to know what else to do with her, and she didn't know what to do either. We were kind of learning as we were going along.

I had an orgasm with this girl. As a matter of fact it was the first one I ever had. I didn't know what it was. I snuck and pulled the sheets up. I thought I'd pissed myself.

"What's the matter?" she went.

"Nothing."

She pulled down the sheet and said, "I know what that is."

"What?"

"You had an orgasm."

"What's that?"

"I'm not exactly sure, but my mother has books at home. I'll bring one over and we can read about it."

I never told anybody that before.

I was a big kid. When I was ten, I could pass for fifteen or sixteen, so I got caught up in situations where I was totally unprepared for the things that came about. When I was a young teenager, this girl who was sixteen or seventeen had pursued me hot and heavy. Finally we'd settled that we would go to a drive-in movie. Back home, even if you weren't old enough to have a driver's license supposedly you could drive as long as you didn't get up on a paved road. I could navigate the entire state, and do nothing but cross the paving once in a while. She lived out in the country—I mean, *out* in the country—so I picked her up, and we went.

She was quite experienced. I didn't know that, nor could I have appreciated that. She's sitting over there, and she's just about ripped my clothes off, pulled my hair and everything like that. The girl was a slut. As things proceeded, I got to the point where I was ready to go. She produced a condom.

I'd had one in my wallet for years. I must have carried a condom in my wallet since I was ten years old, because everybody did. But I'd never tried to put one on in a state of passion. *Nobody* even opened the package. It always used to fall out at the worst times. Your mom would give you the money, so you could pay the cashier at the grocery store, make you feel like a big deal. You'd pull out a twenty-dollar bill, and the condom would fall out on that little tray. Whoops! She'd turn her head like she didn't see it, but God A-mighty, you'd be embarrassed.

Anyway, as I go to put the condom on, I lose it. That's all I needed in the primed state I was in. I just totally orgasmed right there. All of a sudden, here's this girl who's sitting over there across the car from me, and I ain't got nothing to give her. I've messed up the steering wheel, and the front of my pants. So now—talk about having to do some soft, quick footsteps—I'm thinking what in the hell am I going to do?

So I proceeded to tell her that I love her, that I know she's a virgin, and she means too much to me for me to go ahead and do this. This is just a kid coming up with this shit.

The girl becomes livid with me, I mean furious. She didn't have a stitch of clothes on, and she starts beating the shit out of me. I grab the steering wheel and drive out of the drive-in theater, of course, forgetting to take the speaker out of the window. I broke the window of my dad's car.

Here we're going home, and she is still beating the shit out of me. Calling me a son of a bitch and everything. I take this abuse all the way to her house, pull up to her front door, and she jumps out of the car. She continues to berate me. By this time, she is halfway dressed. But you could tell that she is still in the process of putting on her clothes. She continues to cuss me to the point that her daddy comes out on the porch. This is the old proverbial redneck, standing up there with his coveralls on, barefoot with a shotgun right behind the damn door. She's using every word in the book on me. I know I'm fixing to get shot to hell. I've already wrecked the door on the car, what else but show up with bullet holes on that son of a bitch. I whipped it around and made a fast exit, managed to get out of that thing.

I thought about leaving town. Here's this girl, and she's bound to be avenged. Trust me, she's going to tell her daddy, and he's going to come get me. I thought about packing my bags and leaving the state, I was so terrified. Nothing ever came of it, but I spent a lot of time looking out my rear window.

I was in seventh heaven dating the most popular guy in school. He was my best friend's brother, two years older than me, a senior, captain of the basketball team, valedictorian of the class, Mr. Popularity. He was so conceited, but this guy made my knees weak. I didn't know quite what to do with this. I could tell that his old libido was on the move there after me. I was almost afraid of him. He was real big, like six-two, and I was little bitty, weighed about a hundred pounds.

We went on a double date to the drive-in, because everybody went to the drive-in then. We were in the front seat kissing, and he started to put his hand down the back of my pants. I thought, "This guy is crazy. He's not touching me." So I kept moving down in the seat. He thought, I found out much later when we were older, that I wanted more. It made him mad, because he thought I was a little slut. The more I scooted down the madder I got at him, because I thought he was trying to take advantage of me. And the more I scooted, the more he thought I wanted it, so it was total miscommunication. He sat up, and wouldn't touch me. He never spoke to me. When he took me home, he walked me about halfway to the door and left.

I was devastated. I came home and was crying and crying. I had gotten all this advice from my friends—"If you want to go out with this popular guy, you're going to have to give him *something*. You have to." But in my soul, I didn't want to. I knew it was wrong. So I was battling with that.

After that I was, oh, so good, because I determined that no boy would ever touch me, if he wanted to live past that evening.

There was this other boy who asked me out. He would just take me out for Cokes after church. He was always real respectful and everything. Then, about a year later, he came over one evening to take me for a drive. We had a really nice time. We went to a park someplace and just talked. I thought, "This is really nice. I can just be friends with somebody who doesn't have their hands all over me."

He brought me home, and in the driveway the first thing he wanted to do was put his hands all over me. I'd move his hands down and they would keep going down. So I'd take his hand and move it up, and it would keep going up. Three or four times of this, and I finally said, "You're a creep." I got out of the car, and I never saw him again.

That was the only bad experience I ever had with a boy. Boys respected me, pretty much, because the boys I went out with knew what kind of girl I was, and wouldn't have ever attempted anything, because they knew they would be dead.

The first time Jane and I kissed, it was the first really good kiss I'd ever had, because I didn't know anything about it. She hit me, and that tongue was down my throat. She had come from Alabama and I wanted to move to Alabama that day. Obviously, things in Alabama were moving a little faster than out here in cow country.

I was doubling with my buddy and Jane's cousin who had come in from Alabama, so I thought, "Shorty's going to get lucky tonight. He's going to get one of them Alabama smooches."

We went to Spring Creek, just to go parking and to walk around out there. The other two walked and I stayed in Shorty's car. Jane and I started making out. She's still wearing this thing from the drill team. The Warriorettes wore these little sawed-off pleated-skirt things made of gold-and-white satin with purple satin underwear and shiny white tops. I started kind of grabbing around, which was real weird. I had never done any of this grabbing around business. I felt a tit, and at that point I was practically blacked out. Then she takes my hand and moves it down there, and puts it between her legs. I'm going, "This is pretty dang cool. This is slippery. Hold everything! This is wet! What's happening?" Then my finger slipped off the bridge of this little Warriorette thing and fell into the trough. The gates of heaven opened up and she was into the program, I was into the program, and it was just a matter of timing. Shorty and his Alabama date came back way too fast. Two years would have been way too fast for me. But that was astounding. I was blinded and I stayed blinded for several days.

We continued that sort of horsing around. The first time we went on a church-choir trip, it was late at night and we had a blanket thrown over us, sitting together on the big bus. This was the first time she ever put her hand in my pants under this blanket. All this stuff was just such a complete revelation. I was out in that white zone where the adrenaline rush just gets everything incredibly overloaded.

The next real step was we were at Oakridge Park, and I'm getting a blow job in the driver's seat of the car. I'm a junior in high school. All of a sudden, Jane's head is illuminated. A flashlight is shining in. It's a policeman with one of those forty-foot flashlights that has all the batteries on the planet in it. It's shining down on this blonde head in my lap. I'm just terrified. I stand up. Hard-on goes away before it has time to hit the horn getting out of the car. I step out, pulling on my pants. The first thing I said was, "Officer, I love her. I just want you to know that."

I'm sure he was thinking, "I bet you do. Believe me, son, you have every reason in the world to love that girl." He took down our names, but he never did anything. He never told our parents.

In high school, I made out with boys and didn't feel anything. They would stick their hands in my shirt or down my pants and sort of furiously rub up against me. I didn't like it. I came home from a date one day and said, "Mom, what's frigid mean?" I was terrified that I didn't like sex, and that I was not responsive.

"No," she told me. "It's tied in with your feelings. If you don't have feelings for these guys, then you're not going to get excited about it. It's okay if you don't like it with somebody. You don't have to do anything with anyone that you don't like or anything you don't want to do."

Pretty much through high school, I wasn't sexual at all, or if I was sexual, kissing, petting—whatever that means—I can't remember it doing anything for me. I never got all that excited or came home with wet underpants. I went through the motions a few times with people. It's more scary and confusing than anything else. I kept wondering, "Why am I doing this? Why doesn't it feel like all the movies and all the books tell me it is? I see pictures of people in ecstasy with their heads back and their mouths open. Love's Crushing Orgasm?" None of that stuff was really true for me.

My mother noticed that I seemed to be rather hot around the collar, and she said, "I think, maybe, you're probably going to want to take these pills. We'll go see a doctor and he'll give them to you." We had to go to the next town over. We couldn't go to a doctor in our town. That was the big rite of passage, a drive to Wilmington to see a gynecologist.

This doctor I'd never seen before said, "Here's what you do. You take one of these little pills every day, and you won't get pregnant." I was taking birth-control pills before I ever had sex. I was just armed and ready to go. But I wasn't ready. I just had all the medicine. Maybe that's the way it is for everyone. I don't think everyone's mother is that way, so on top of things. It was so organized, unemotional, really lonely and scary. My father wasn't there. My mother never talked to me about it.

This is such a weird world. This is so removed from a mother tending to her daughter's budding desires and feelings. As soon as there was any interest in the subject, off to the gynecologist—"Here's birth-control pills. Okay, you're safe." And that was it. That was considered a liberal-minded, modern reaction. Everybody thought she did the right thing. She thought she was doing the right thing. "No one is going to get pregnant in this house."

I'm fifteen years old and I've got three years' worth of birth-control pills, and I'm like, "Okay, now what?" There was no more conversation, no guidance, no sensitivity. It was, "You get home by eleven-thirty, and that's all I care about."

No one said, "Colleen, just because some guy sticks his hand down your blouse and grabs your tits, you don't have to fuck him." No one ever said, "Okay, so you get excited. You don't have to fuck any joe who gets you excited." There was nothing. You just wing it.

There was no talk about the fact that love might be involved in this. That it is natural to have these passions and desires, and that they are about love, too. They're not just physical impulses that you have a lot of and you need to get rid of them.

When I look at my seven-year-old daughter, I feel protective of her. I think of her as someone I would like to guide, not to just send out with her newfound sexuality someday. It's such a powerful thing that you grow into, and you have no sense of it. It's so powerful you don't even know what it is.

It's very easy to explain how one's body works, but everything else is so difficult. It's all unknown. It's such a big thing in your life. You just discover it. What I would want to be able to explain is the importance of being loved, as well as loving, feeling that you are loved. That's the thing that I think about when I think about my past. The opportunities I had, and I didn't know any better. It's just so simple: You have a say in things. It's nice that people find you attractive, but so what? You have choices.

Thinking about sex and my daughter, maybe she could have some sort of protection that follows her into the backseats of cars, some sort of ideas about how one loves someone else and what it can be. Maybe you start thinking about love later on. I don't know. I just hope that I can pad that period of time when sex is so overwhelming and everywhere, and as a young woman you happen to be the topic. It's nice sort of, but you don't know what to think. You believe you're figuring it all out. Then a few years down the road you look back and you say, "That professor didn't really care about me." You're young, and you want to be part of whatever is happening. It's a natural part of figuring out life, but if you're armed with ideas, you make better choices.

2. FIRST SEX

The aggressive, sex-crazed young male, constantly angling for sex until sooner or later he connives—or forces—his way into "getting laid" is the American stereotype. But it's actually women who control sex in this culture, especially the first time. "Control" is probably too strong a word to describe that confusing combination of hormones, peer pressure, and desire, but the girls generally do decide, "Yes, this boy, at this time."

As a writer in his late forties expressed it, "Earliest sex is much more consensual than most men with their bravado would want you to think. It's the girl who has more courage somehow in the situation. They are the ones who make the decisions. They'll just open the way for you, tap you on the shoulder and say, 'Come on, come on, come on.'

"I had a first love affair that lasted for two or three years when I was a teenager. It was real nice. I was very shy then. There were things that she wanted me to do that I just couldn't do. I was too embarrassed. We had sex eventually, but it could have been so much better. It wasn't all that good because of my ineptitude. She loved me, and I loved her, but I was in awe of her, too."

A thirty-five-year-old television director/producer described the standard attitude for many women of her generation in a very matter-of-fact way: "Made love the first time when I was seventeen to my first real boyfriend. He was the guy I fell in love with when I was fourteen. It was something I wanted to happen, so I orchestrated it a little bit. It was time, as far as I was concerned."

Virginity has never been a condition men in America aspired to. In fact, male teenagers are congratulated—always by their peers, and often by their fathers—for becoming sexually active, and their mothers sometimes join in in silent complicity. But as sexually liberated as we consider our society, it is still a very different story for young women. As a sixteen-year-old tells about her own experience in this chapter, "If you do sleep with someone, the word gets around, and you're called a whore. If a guy sleeps with twenty girls, he's a stud."

The choice to have sex—whether it's a whim, a carefully considered step or a half-conscious, passion-induced relinquishing of control—usually rests with the woman. The onus of having made that decision is hers, and the negative consequences that can result weigh most heavily on her. A twenty-eight-year-old woman talks about her teenage pregnancy: "We used to ride around the park. That was the big deal when we were kids, ride around Delano Park two million times on Sunday afternoon. I met a guy there, didn't particularly like him. But I dated him. I think I went to the junior prom with him. But he was just sort of a replacement, since I really liked this other guy, but things weren't working out. So I dated him, and we had sex.

"That year I'd been elected one of the drill-team captains for the drill team. We all went to the big state university during the summer to learn all the drills and everything, like a camp. I got sick while I was out there. I had these dizzy spells and stuff.

"I didn't have my period when I came home and I kind of figured out, 'Uh-oh. I have one every month, something's wrong here.' So I told this guy. We went over to his brother's house and they made an appointment for a doctor. I had a pregnancy test and, yes, I was pregnant. Welcome to the real world. Who, me? Is that what happens? I was really shocked. I didn't know anything about birth control. I was just totally stupid. We didn't have it. No one in the school did.

"My dad worked for the electric company, and he went in at noon and worked late. Since I didn't like my mom, we drove out to the addition I lived in, which was real wooded and not too many houses back then, and we just waited at this certain place for my dad to drive by that night. Then we followed him home, met him at the garage, and told him. His reaction was, 'You have to get married.' After that, he tells Mom and the whole idea makes her totally sick. They are just outraged. They were always mad at me. I grew up with a guilt complex. I couldn't please them. I could never do it good enough.

"Nobody ever sat down and asked me how I felt about it. Nobody ever said, 'What do you want to do? I see we have several options here. You can marry him or not marry him. You can go to an unwed-mothers' home and have it. You can stay here in school and have it.' Nobody ever asked me anything. It was, 'You will get married.'

"His family on the other hand gave him the choice of what he wanted to do. He had an aunt and uncle in Boise, they could ship him off to Boise and pretend I didn't exist. Or he could marry me or whatever he wanted to do.

"So I got married. He wanted to. I guess he's a nice person. It's hard to say at this point."

Even though first sex is an unforgettable milestone emotionally for both men and women, almost no one can remember the physical details. It is over so fast. The emotion almost everyone mentions that first time is not sexual passion or love or wonder, it's fear. That young men and women are frightened by the unknown is unremarkable, but in the case of first sex what they are usually most afraid of is getting caught. People lose their virginity not on their wedding night, but in the backseats of cars parked along deserted roads; on the family-room couch in front of the television, sometimes with the family not far away in another room of the house; half on and half off narrow beds in a dormitory where a roommate might walk in at any moment; in the great outdoors, behind the shrubs in a park, in a cornfield or on the sand under a pier. First sex almost never takes place in a secure, comfortable environment. Fear boosts the surge of adrenaline even higher.

When we consider the circumstances most of us find ourselves in when we first have sex, it's no wonder that the event sticks in memory as a misadventure, an accident, or a shock. In a few cases, sex is a pleasant surprise. A banker in his middle thirties was fortunate enough to have a good experience. "I first had sex when I was fifteen. I had just gotten my driver's license. Sex was more than pretty good, it was some kind of great. More than just the physical aspects—which were terrific—it was a great and wonderful thing to me to be able to share the otherwise secrets of my body with my girlfriend. She did the same with me. She was a virgin, too.

" 'Oh, touch me here,' we'd say. 'Oh, that feels good.'

"She showed me all about how Tampax work, showed me all the little diagrams on the box. All the hidden stuff. Before then, I thought the vagina was in a different location, a little further up toward their stomach. I had no earthly idea where it was or what it was all about or how it felt or smelled or anything.

"Once we got hold of it, we just couldn't stop. I'd say I'm pretty lucky, because in those days, birth control was absolutely unheard of. We did use prophylactics a few times, but for the most part it was coitus interruptus. And accidents can happen. We were pretty durn lucky."

Perhaps the saddest introduction to intercourse is the person who views his or her virginity as a burden to be shed. Here's a thirty-one-year-old secretary with that experience. "When I was nineteen, I thought, 'You know, I'm still a virgin.' I was embarrassed about it. I was the only one that I knew who had not slept with someone. I thought, 'I got to do it.'

"I was sort of seeing this boy, and he was sort of making advances towards me. I thought, 'Okay, I'm just going to do it with him, so that I can say that I've done it. I want this big thing in my life out of the way.'

"So, I did it, and I thought, 'Oh, my God. I didn't like it.' Of course, I didn't know what I was doing. In fact, he told his roommate that I acted like I was dead. I just laid there. It was really awful for both of us. Course, I was in such a rush to get it over with that I didn't even think about using any kind of protection. I don't think I ever even told him it was my first time.

"That was twelve years ago, and it wasn't even important to me. I broke up with him after that. He'd served his purpose, and it was time for him to get out of here. I really didn't like sex, and I still don't know if I do."

The people who managed to survive their first sexual encounter relatively unscathed or perhaps enriched—whether or not the physical sex was successful or memorable—all shared a sense of humor and the feeling of being in love. If there is some affection, even if it is only puppy love, the two people are sharing themselves, not stealing something sacred. If they can laugh at themselves, at least there is fun along with the fumbling and fat lips.

Regardless of the ambivalent public perception of virginity, whether losing one's virginity is a "loss" or just a change, once the line is crossed, life is different, and there is no going back. The personal importance of this singular event remains undiminished. That first partner is indelibly etched in the mind. That face, that name, some blurred detail of that carnal exchange, in joy or in regret, generates each person's most enduring, recurring sexual souvenir.

○ ○ ○

I'm sixteen. I'll be seventeen in a few months. I'm waiting for eighteen to come, and then I'm out of the house. Me and one of my best friends are going to get an apartment. I'm not going to college. I'm in cosmetology in school now, and that means as soon as I get out, I can make some money.

Never had the big talk with my dad, because my dad's never there. My mom and me are more like best friends than we are mother and daughter. We never really sat and talked about sex, though. She always told me little bits and pieces, and said, "Watch what you do."

I had never been with anybody until last year. So I never had to worry about it. All my other friends, they go out and do anything with anybody. I know friends who are my age and have had twenty to thirty people. But not me. I'm one of those people that stick out in the crowd. That's how I've always been.

There's pressure to have sex, but I just never put myself in that situation. They say, "Come on. This is a party. Go upstairs and have fun."

"I ain't going nowhere. I'm not doing it." I'll leave.

Most of the kids in high school do it. It's not just talk. But if you do sleep with someone, the word gets around, and you're called a whore.

Tommy moved into town from out West. I met him through family friends. That night one of my friends died in a car accident. Tommy helped me through that whole thing. Took me up there to the hospital at least three or four times a week to see a girl who was in the wreck. That's how I got to know him and think of him as a real sensitive guy. He swept me off my feet. He was just the nicest person in the world. Not now. He's not now at all. I hate him. I mean, I don't hate him, but it kind of sucks.

We didn't have sex until a year and three months after I met him. It just *happened* when we did have sex. But if I didn't want it to, I'm the type of person who would not *let* it happen. I'm just not the type of person who would go out and sleep with everyone and didn't mean it, like it *just happened*, because anything could *just happen* with anyone.

I was planning on being with Tommy forever, but he fed me a line. We sat down and told his mom and my mom, because they were friends. Told them everything. One day, they came in, both drunk, and we were laying on the couch watching TV. They asked us about it, and we said,

"Yep." His mom didn't, but my mom flipped out. She just couldn't believe it. She had asked me a couple of times if we had slept together, and I said, "Nope." I lied to her about it.

It was kind of hard to lie to her, just because she had told me all my life, "Don't do it until you're married, and until you know that you love him." I feel like I let her down, but she told me that I didn't. My mom didn't act different towards me, just because she knew how I felt. I don't go out with guys that much. I'm picky. And when I do go out with someone it's going to be for a long time or forever.

Tommy races motocross. His bike was always before I was. Always. The last time we broke up, one of my friends had asked him about me, and he didn't say, "I'm not in love with her." He said, "I broke up with her because I like something better that has two wheels." I knew then and there it never would work. It never will now because I hate him. I just wish they'd move back to where they came from. It would make things a lot easier on me. This is a small town, and I see him out every night with his girlfriend. On the weekends, there's only so many places to go.

I don't feel like I'm missing out because I've only been with one person. Everybody talks about how much better it was with this person than that person. Questions come up like who was your best, and it's just so stupid. I have only been with one person and that's the way I'm going to keep it until I *know*. I won't go through it again.

I just sit back and look at everybody else who's dating people; some of my friends are even married, living with people. I hang out with an older crowd, people who are eighteen, nineteen, or twenty. They got a lot more going for them. They know what they're going to do with their lives. They know that they want to be with that girl for the rest of their life. There's just a big difference between a sixteen-year-old and a nineteen-year-old . . . usually. But I had to pick the one that was an asshole.

That August there was some girl that was in from out of town, the cousin of somebody. While we were doing these two-a-day football workouts, she suddenly showed up, and she would just follow me around like a puppy dog. This is sort of a voluptuous little brown-haired girl who didn't talk much, and didn't have much to say. Just a poor little farm girl, you know? She suddenly showed up at practice.

It was beginning to be a time when all the guys would talk about their conquests. If you were fifteen and hadn't gotten laid, it was getting to be time where it was, "Why the hell not?" We were all real big on calling each other faggots.

I borrowed my mother's car. I had a provisional license. My mother had a pretty good car and they were building the new interstate highway. It was not open yet, but everybody would go parking down there. So that's where we went. I sort of talked a little bit. She knew a lot more about it than I did, but she wasn't saying much. She was after it just as much as I was. So we climbed into the backseat. Then we just sort of coupled. This was something that she had done before and it was almost like, "Okay, this is something that guys want."

It was terrible. For me. I thought, "Masturbation is better than this." I really didn't quite know what to do. No one had ever told me. I knew where slot A was and where tab B was, and that was about it. She only said ten words the whole time. Never said no, it was just roll over.

We were at his mother's house. Just the thought of getting caught was so scary. It was close to Christmas, the year I graduated from high school. It was nice and misty and cool. He called me, and I went over to his house to take his Christmas presents to him. We just sat there, all alone. The Christmas tree was lit. The moment was there.

We went into the bedroom. I got undressed or he undressed me, I don't remember. He got undressed and when he came out I was so frightened. I didn't know what to expect. We had already kissed and cuddled.

"I don't think I want to do this," I said. "This is kind of strange."

"Don't worry, baby," he said. "It'll be okay. I'll be nice and gentle. I'll take care of you." He gave me the whole line. I said okay.

We had intercourse. It was so painful, I could not believe it would hurt so bad. I compare that to having my first child. It was really bad. No shit. I said, "I don't believe this." He enjoyed it probably. I'm sure he did. I didn't enjoy it. I was frightened. When we finished, I got up out of this pool of blood. I'm going, "What did you do to me?" It scared me half to death.

I cried for four days. I refused to see that guy. I just refused. It got to the point where I even hated him. No, no, no, this can't be happening to me. It really wasn't that great.

I thought by then, for sure, I was pregnant. I was *sure*. I didn't know what he'd done or if he did. I didn't even care. I just knew I was pregnant.

I didn't tell my mom anything. I was real sentimental then, so it could have been anything, and I would be crying. If anybody did anything to me at the house, I would just start crying just to cry because of what happened.

When I opened my Christmas presents, and everybody was opening theirs, I cried. My mother thought I didn't like the gifts that she had bought me. I couldn't explain, so I said, "It's fine, if she thinks that way. Let her think that." It was weird and a traumatic thing.

I was sixteen and it was just one of those things. You know how you do that thing where you go in a little bit, but not quite a lot. We had done that a couple of times, not really quite doing it, but enough where you are *kind of* doing it. Then one time, he went suddenly all the way in. And I just went, *"Uh . . . oh."* I really felt something break. "Oh, my God."

"Oh, no. I didn't do anything," he said. "Nothing happened."

"Yes, it did."

"No, no, it didn't." He never finished. He scared himself and he scared me.

"Yes, it did," I said. I'm looking at the sheets, and within minutes there's blood. "Yes, you did!"

I didn't feel horrible about it or guilty. I thought it really hurt. What ran through my mind was, "Gosh, why would anyone want to wait until they were married to have this happen. This isn't what I would like to happen on my honeymoon." Even for the first five or six times, it was very painful. I just thought, "What's the big hubbub about this? What's to like? It hurts." I certainly wasn't getting anything enjoyable out of it.

The next day, he brought me flowers, and he bought me a dress. In retrospect, that was an odd thing to do. He came to the house with these presents. My mother just stood there, hesitantly saying, "Felicity, Mike's here. He has flowers . . . and a dress."

"I wonder if my mother knows what just happened to me," I worried.

This girl, she used to tell me, "I like you. I'm going to come over to your house one night."

"What for?"

"You know." She really homed in on me and was relentless in making sure I went to bed with her.

One night she showed up. We were in my basement. My father might have been in the hospital at the time. He was sick through a lot of my late teen years. My mother was home, but she was upstairs. She didn't really pay too much attention to my comings and goings at this time in my life. I made the basement where I lived and that night there were a couple of people hanging out.

Gradually, everybody left except for this girl and my best friend. This girl and I were sitting under a blanket, and she started wiggling around. She said to my friend, "Danny, why don't you go home?"

"Why should I?"

She threw her underwear in his face.

"Oh," he went. He got up and left.

I sat there going, "Oh, gee whiz, looks like I'm going to get laid now. I wish Danny hadn't left. I'm lonely now. I'm going to have to do this with her." This girl really made me nervous.

That's what we did. We had sex. It was the first time I ever had sex, and it was over quick. Just like that. She wouldn't go home. "You have to go home," I said.

"Not unless you come home with me."

"I can send you home in a cab."

"You have to come with me."

"I don't have enough money to send you home in a cab, and then take the cab back home myself."

"I'm not going home." Lucky for me she was a year older than me, and she was going away to college.

The next morning, about six o'clock, there's this banging on the basement door. I said, "Yeah?"

"You down there?" my mother said.

"Yeah."

"Do you have a girl with you?"

"Yeah."

"You better come upstairs and get cleaned up, because this girl's parents are on their way over now." My buddy, who was her cousin, had ratted me out. She had spent the night out and had never called home or nothing like that.

We went upstairs and got cleaned up. It seemed like two minutes and her mother and father got there. They came in the house. I had never met her parents. She and I were smoking cigarettes. I was skinny. Her father was big. I've never seen anyone bigger. Like he was over six feet tall, and he looked a lot bigger that day. Her mother started saying something. This girl was being a wiseguy, and she started giving her mother some shit back. Her mother smacked the cigarette out of her face, grabbed her by the hair and started pulling her hair. My parents were never real hitters. I might have been hit four or five times growing up. I had never seen anyone get hit like that. I tried to get in between them to separate them. Her father came over and side-armed me, knocked me across the room and into a chair. I slid down into the chair, and I thought, "Kill her. I ain't getting out of this chair."

That was it. They dragged her out of the house. Her mother yelled at her, "You're an animal! We're going to lock you up in a cage! You're not going to college, and you're not getting the car we promised you!" It was a real scene.

The worst thing for me was this woman, the girl's mother, was one of my mother's best friends when they were in high school together. They hadn't seen each other in years. The last thing she said as she was going out the door was, "Emily, how could you let that animal be with my daughter? How could you do this?" My mother had no idea what was going on. That wasn't a good start.

My mother didn't say much of anything. My parents hadn't told me much about sex growing up. They didn't prepare me for that, and when it happened, she didn't say anything. She just brushed it over and said, "You shouldn't do things like that. Don't do it again."

That was it. I didn't see her again, and I didn't talk to girls for a long time after that. I was afraid their parents would come over and beat the shit out of me.

I have always been particularly prone to more aggressive women, rather than being the aggressor myself. The first time I had sex it was completely the American classic, in a cornfield, drunk on rye with an older woman. There was a full moon. It was like the Grant Wood of sex. Oh, my God. There was a dance, a mixer, and I was basically dragged into the field and made to perform.

Here I was fourteen or fifteen. She wasn't much older, but much more developed, had to get me through the whole thing, because I was still holding back. I was going to get away with kissing her, and maybe feeling her up. But suddenly, it got a lot more out of control. She was taking her clothes off, and I was completely unprepared for it. To a certain extent that still is the case with me. I can reason and see myself as sophisticated and in control, but when it comes to sexuality, it still comes as a complete surprise attack.

My brother and I are extremely close and close to the same age. We lost our virginity right around the same time. I was afraid to tell my mother. Although we were all so close and could talk about almost anything, she had told me, "Sex really can wait. It's a whole different aspect of your life, and you can't go back once you start. It's special. Why don't you save it?" I was studying ballet very heavily at the time, six to eight hours a day. She would tell me to focus on my career.

Meanwhile, she had found out that my brother had done the same thing. She was so proud of him, bragging to me about it, "Your brother, you'll never guess what happened. He lost his virginity! Blah, blah, blah!" I got really upset. I don't know if I was angry or just frustrated with that. My cheeks got hot, I cried, and said, "Why is it fine for him? You even encourage it. He's even younger than I am." That really made me angry.

"I raised him by myself," she said. "I couldn't talk to him the way a man might, the way I can talk to you. I never knew if I was saying the right thing. So finding out that he's sexually active, and that he enjoyed it, and it works the way it's supposed to is quite a relief for me."

But it was a double standard, one for sons, one for daughters. She told me, "I don't want you to feel badly that you're no longer a virgin. I hope you enjoy sex. I didn't mean to make you feel guilty."

I didn't feel guilty. I just felt it was too bad we had such a close relationship, and this was something I felt I couldn't tell her.

I joined the Navy when I was eighteen. For all intents and purposes, I was a virgin. I had fumbling experience in Tijuana. I went down to get laid, and she ended up talking me into a blow job. I was pretty tequila-ed up. A minute and a half and fifteen bucks later, I was headed back out on the street. They tried to get me on stage pedaling one of these teeny-weeny bicycles with wheels about four inches in diameter. They always get somebody on stage to try and ride the thing. I ended up falling all over the place and breaking the bicycle. In Tijuana, they don't have much of a sense of humor, so they threw me out on the street, and I got rolled.

I ended up with fifteen cents to my name. I had to get from there, back to Point Mugu. That was my first consummated sexual encounter, in Tijuana, what little I can remember.

The way I finally lost my virginity when I was nineteen was that I went to a whorehouse with Wade Remick. Wade was the first one to discover this place, and he came back and told the other guys about it. Then he volunteered to take me. I don't know how he found it originally.

It was the old Robert E. Lee Hotel. Wade took us down there, and sat in the lobby. He said, "Go on and get into the elevator. The elevator boy will take care of you."

I was with my buddy Ralph. We got into the elevator and started going up. The elevator guy was a young black man. He says, "You guys looking for a little fun?"

We nodded our heads. He stopped the elevator and says, "Tell you what. Go down to the last two rooms at the end of this hallway. One of you take one, and one of you take the other. We'll send you a couple of girls in a few minutes. You guys will have a good time."

"Okay."

We went down and got into our rooms. I looked around. I was nervous as shit. Finally, this girl comes in. Only it's a woman who is maybe ten years older than me, but she was totally unappealing as far as I was concerned. To me it was like she was my mom. She had this kind of bouffant hairdo, all done up and sprayed hard as a rock. She comes in and says, "What do you want to do?"

I had been instructed by Wade to ask for an Around the World. "How about an Around the World?" I said. She just laughed and laughed. She knew I didn't know what the hell I was doing. She just thought it was real funny.

"I'll tell you what," she said. "For twenty-five bucks I'll take care of you."

First thing she did was she took me into the bathroom of this hotel room, she had me stand fully clothed at the lavatory, she unzipped my penis, and she washed it—which was actually the best part of the whole deal. That felt pretty darn good. Then she took me back in, told me to take off my clothes and lay down on the bed, which I did. I was just scared senseless. So she pops off her clothes and hops down on the bed next to me, and tells me to get on top of her.

You know how when you're laying on top of a woman what you do is kind of prop yourself up on your elbows so you don't squish them? I didn't understand that concept, so I just laid on top of her like this big deadweight. I must have weighed 175 pounds. I was a big, strapping fellow.

She says, "No, no, no, no." And she pushes me off. "Let me get on top of you." She straddled me and started playing with my dick. I could not get an erection. She worked on me and worked on me and worked on me. Finally, I got a little bit of an erection, and we managed to kind of get it inside before I came, but just barely. That was it. She laughed and got off. "This is your first time, isn't it?"

"Yeah," I said.

"You tell your friends that you did real good." She put her dress on and just headed back out the door.

There was this girl named Phyllis who was this big, obese groupie who followed us around wherever the band went. I wound up with Phyllis, hanging out one night. She was there, and we were all full of beers and stuff. She did it with everybody. Great training ground for me, she does it with everybody already. We're in the back room there. It was amazing. It was like fucking a whale. She had so much flesh. When I got inside her, I didn't even know I was inside.

But it felt good. I remember it feeling better than anything else in the world. I mean it really felt *good.* It was nice and gushy and soft. This is something. It was great. I came, it blew the top of my head off.

It was the most wonderful experience. *Except,* when it was over, and I looked down, and I saw this person that I had just lost my virginity to, I flipped out. I got totally irrational. I went yelling around the house. I threw her out of the house, chased her down the stairs, out the fucking door. I was crazy. I could not believe it. My friend and his girlfriend are in the other room. I told him, "Flip, I did it with Phyllis."

"You what?"

"Yeah, I did it with Phyllis and I feel like shit."

"Are you crazy?" Then he said, "Nah, nah, it's all right."

It just blew me away. It did. Out of all the people to have sex with the first time, I do with Fat Phyllis. So my first initiation to sex wasn't that good really. It was this pig of a woman, who I look back fondly on now, but at the time I was horrified. It was just that I had been saving my virginity, and I thought it was going to be a special moment. But it wasn't. It was just Fat Phyllis.

My first sexual experience was not great. A good aspect of it was that I was with somebody that I was dating, and he went very slowly, a little at a time. In a month or so, he kind of got me introduced to various aspects of sex. Because my dad was never around me, I'd never even seen a naked man before. I was scared. He was scared, too. He may have been a virgin, but I don't think he was.

The first time we had sex, I was visiting his family's home. His mother was in the house, and we were in the basement. There was a fireplace. It was a romantic winter night. It was snowing out.

Neither of us intended to go all the way with this. It happened, but very quickly. I don't think this guy came. He just got scared that he had done this, and he said something to the effect of, "You're not a virgin anymore." And then felt he had to go back to his room, so his mother wouldn't catch us.

I was left feeling really lonely. This major thing had happened, and now I was by myself. I didn't think to myself, "I'm a woman now." What I did feel was a little more independent. I made a choice, and this is what I did. I was a little frightened by it. After that point where you start having sex or become sexually active, you lose a lot of your childhood. That's how I saw it. Climbing trees and stuff like that would be a little less attractive, I thought. I was wrong, but that scared me. I thought, "Now I'm going to have to start paying taxes, wear stuffy clothes and uncomfortable shoes."

I first had sex on my sixteenth birthday. For some reason, I wanted to "hold out" till then, thinking, "I don't want to have to say fifteen all my life when people ask me when I first had sex." I thought sixteen sounded better. So I waited until then.

Not much was happening until then. I was already very tall, five-ten from the time I was twelve years old, and really skinny. So I didn't have boyfriends right at that time. Plus we were moving through the South.

The people who noticed me first were too old for me to be fooling around with at that time. They weren't really old—twenty-two, twenty-three, up to maybe twenty-eight. I met this ring of people. My peers, the guys in my school, they were great friends, but I'd never had any real sexual interest out of them. I was taller than all of them. In fact, I can think of three of my high-school friends now who probably didn't come up to my shoulders. It was a short class that year. I don't know if that was a threat to them or what.

I also was pretty much like I am today—I wasn't very coy. I certainly wasn't the cheerleader type. I was always like I am, not too flirtatious really, not too *slyly* flirtatious.

I worked as a lifeguard in the summers. High-school coaches did that a lot, too, during the summers off from teaching. The one from my high school was lifeguarding. He was really nice and everything, but when he'd have to hire somebody to help us, he'd hire a guy who was a substitute teacher at school that I didn't remember seeing, ever.

Through that guy I ended up meeting this whole circle of this age group. Some of them were married and messing around on their wives. Some of them were single. They must have just been real wild, now that I think about it. The problem with that is I feel that's had a lot of effect on me, because I was sixteen and the first one was twenty-five. There was a girlfriend of mine who was with me every step of the way. Okay? So to them, when I look back on it, they were probably saying, "We got these *young* girls!" I imagine that's what they were doing, because the minute he dropped me and went on with some woman who was more his age, that just hurt me. In quick succession, I just went around and did the whole group, screwed them all, not at the same time, just one by one by one by one, all the way through.

I know I did it, but I don't like to think about it. It's not that I feel guilty. I don't like to think about it, because I can imagine what they were saying about me.

Then high school was over, and it was time to go to college. Somewhere along the line, it dawned on me that this wasn't very good behavior, or it wasn't going to get me anywhere. It wasn't going to do anything but hurt me more. So I went to college with a different attitude. I had a boyfriend. Of course, I slept with him, but he was more my age and I tried to realize for myself how to tell a scoundrel who was just looking to fuck from somebody who really means it.

Definitely, the first time I made love to a girl, it was her doing. I was eighteen and she was sixteen. She'd already had a baby when she was fourteen. It was back in the time before abortion was legal. They sent her off somewhere, she had the baby, gave it up for adoption, and I met her like a year later. She was in a lot of ways a wounded person because of this experience, and because of the local scene where she was thought of as a tramp and talked about.

I met her quite independent of that. Although interestingly enough, after we went out for two weeks, she came to me and said, "I have to tell you something about me." It was very hard for her to tell me, but it was good timing. I already had a pretty good upbringing in terms of, "Look, this shouldn't mean anything to me." While I had to fight against the ways it did mean something to me, I was successful in that. Within two days, I started getting the stories from other people. "Did you know blah-blah-blah?" I could just say, "I know all that stuff, so fuck you." It was one of those things I was glad I knew ahead of time, because when people came to me I could see it for what it really was—cattiness and gossip—as opposed to the caring it was supposed to be.

Because she had tasted of the forbidden fruit, liked the taste of it, and cared about me, she wanted to have sex in ways which I was still uninitiated. On the Fourth of July, her parents were off at a wedding. She orchestrated this wonderful meal and invited me over for dinner. She had gotten some marijuana from her older brother, because she knew I smoked it. Bought a bottle of Cold Duck, because she knew that's what my friends and I drank when we went to rock concerts. And proceeded to get me high. She then led me into her parents' bedroom, where we made love and I lost my virginity. The act probably took all of thirty seconds, once she had made the way clear. I had already given up any desires to fight against it.

That led *literally* to a summer of love. I had a great job in a supermarket that summer. I didn't go to work until five-thirty or six o'clock at night. Our dance every day would be: I had a car, so we'd go to the beach. I would take her home from the beach at maybe a quarter of five. Her mother would get home at five-fifteen, because her mother worked close by, and she got off at five. So at a quarter to five, I'd say good-bye to her out in her driveway, and she'd say, "Oh, just come inside and give me a kiss."

"No, no. I got to go. I know what's going to happen." But of course, I would go inside. She'd put her hand down inside of my pants, and we'd be up in her bedroom at five o'clock.

It would be five-oh-five.

It would be five-ten.

I'd race out of the bedroom, jump in the car, and drive away. Often as not, I'd be driving away as her mom was coming around the corner.

We were playing, and we were kids. We didn't use condoms, so it was a matter of making sure I pulled out of her before I leaked any sperm. Looking back at it, and being a father now who has children who are, in this day and age, much more likely to be sexually active younger, I should have known better, or someone should have told me. I should have had condoms. It would have been much more enjoyable to me, and safer for everybody involved, had I had a supply of condoms and just used them. Of course with all the guilt and everything else, I couldn't even bear the embarrassment of going to the drugstore and asking for condoms.

I was a virgin when I got married. I did it for my own personal values, my relationship with God. I never would have broken that part of the rule. Although my cousins were all pretty wild and ended up getting in trouble. I always thought in the back of my head, "I'm going to be the only one in this family who's going to turn out good."

I would never disappoint my parents. Every now and then, my parents would throw something along those lines towards me indirectly: "Their kids did, and her kids did, but my kids would never do that." That sunk in. I wanted to be the one that turned out perfect. Then when my brother turned up getting that girl pregnant when he was sixteen, I was the only one in the family left out of eight kids that was going to turn out decent. All of them, girls and boys throughout the family, either got pregnant or got somebody pregnant.

Growing up, eleven- and twelve-year-old girls just didn't talk about sex. The only thing we ever talked about in the locker room was our bra size —that was the extent of our sexual conduct. At least, the little girls that I hung around with. I was a cheerleader and real popular. By the time we were in eighth grade, I could see that there was this group of girls who were going the other way. We could always tell the ones who were going to end up in trouble, and they were always the ones that did. In my school, it was the girls who weren't real popular. It wasn't the cheerleaders and the drill team or the honor society. It was the girls who were just a little left out of that. It was the late '60s, so they were the girls who only wore jeans. By high school, they were out in the smoking court and starting marijuana. It was the group of kids that everybody started to stay clear of. They were going and buying kegs, taking them out on the prairie and drinking Friday nights.

When I went to junior college, I got real active at the Baptist Student Union. By that time I had met my husband. He was a year older than me. After our first date, I never dated anybody else. I was engaged at seventeen and married at eighteen.

I met him on a blind date. I thought he was really cute, but I really did not fall in love with him. It was like, "Okay, so he loves me?" He treated me real nice. I liked him a lot. I held my morals very high, and he respected that. That's the way it stayed, because that's the way I wanted it.

After we had been dating several months, he became a Christian. I had never told him I loved him. He knew I wasn't going to say it back. But for some reason, in my strange little odd mind, I decided that because he became a Christian that I would tell him that I loved him back. All of a sudden, like black and white, that was going to change it for me. I was having a real hard time at home and was very, very unhappy. My parents had become real abusive. I was just looking for an out, so he became that escape.

After that, our foreplay became a little more involved, sitting in the car. We came really close a couple of times to almost letting it go, but I wouldn't. I was the one who held back, and I'm so glad I did.

I turned eighteen on August 15, and we were married September 1. My first sexual experience was with him on my honeymoon night, but it wasn't for him. He had been with two other girls, if you can call it that.

I guess my first time was normal. It was okay. We did it seven times the first night. I thought it was pretty neat. I don't remember the first orgasm I had, but it was not that night. Coming home after our honeymoon, I had a hard time sitting down because we had gone at it like two wild animals. But it wasn't really that closeness, that intimacy, the stuff that you get as you grow older together as a couple. It was just the mechanics of it all. It wasn't until after our honeymoon, and we relaxed more—then orgasms came pretty quick after that.

Sex wasn't that big a deal. I could live with it, or live without it. I still kind of feel that way.

I longed for him. I loved him. He was my guitar teacher. I used to stay up all night practicing the guitar to play for him. Then he would come, and I'd just freeze. I'd make everybody I know listen to me, except for him.

He gave me a present, and I was even more freaked out. This was at fourteen.

"Can I ask you a question?" he said.

"Yes."

"Are you a virgin?"

I said yes. He said, "I may marry you someday." Like, I'd better *stay* a virgin.

The next boyfriend I had I was fifteen. He did this number on my head, because he was really a *bad* boy. He had a vested interest in treating me as this pure, wonderful angel, because also I looked really pure and innocent. At the time, I was reading the Bible, and I used to quote the Bible to him. Meanwhile, he was out getting drunk and into fights. He was also a racist who would say the most horrible things.

I remember kind of sidling up to him and wanting more. He'd say, "Oh, you know, you're too good for me."

I'm thinking, "Wait a minute, I want more." I got in bed with him, and he ignored me. There I was asking for something, ready for something, not knowing exactly what it would be, but he turned me away. I was told, "No, you're like this: You're up here on a pedestal next to my mother." That was basically the message that I got. I longed for this guy. He finally just dropped me because of this issue of my being too good for him.

Then, when I was seventeen, out at a dude ranch in the Rockies I went to every summer, I met a cowboy. He had a harelip and all these drugs. He wasn't a real cowboy. He was working for the summer as a cowboy. He was really a student from the Southwest. I met him and smoked a joint with him, which was the kind of thing you did in those days. I was so excited by him. Also, I was the last person I knew who hadn't gone to bed with anyone. So I decided, "Okay, he's the one. This is the one I'm going to go for."

The first time he kissed me, he reached down into my pants, and I thought, "This is terrible! It's awful! He's offended me!" Nevertheless, there was some kind of gumption about him. He was after me and not worried about it. He was going to go for it. This guy had no interest in my being a virgin or in marrying me.

The night I got him in bed, I said, "I'm a little scared. I've never done this before." I thought I had to tell him.

"I love you," he said.

I thought to myself, "That's bullshit. But that's all right." I really don't remember the act per se, but what I do remember is thinking, "Something should happen. I might be traumatized by this." And waiting for that. It was shocking to me that it didn't have some effect.

I had to get an alarm clock—he had to get up early and wrangle the horses—so I left the bed and went into my sister's room. I was laughing hysterically. My sister said, "Is Chuck in there, or what?"

"Nothing, nothing," I chuckled. And I'm laughing and laughing and I couldn't stop.

When he left at four-thirty in the morning, I found this blood in the bed. I freaked out. I'd never kind of put it all together. Then, I was cleaning up the sheets, and in comes the maid. I said, "Oh, I got my period." She said, "I'll do it."

We proceeded to see each other every night after that and we stayed together about five years. It was about being really turned on, but not knowing any technique, just kind of giving myself over to this guy. It wasn't about giving me an orgasm, nor did I even know about them. It was this experience of not being empowered myself, but giving power to him. In terms of my girlfriends, it was all this talk about how I had a boyfriend, and everybody was excited about that.

It was exciting, too, but it wasn't like it was mutual. We weren't going to please each other. We really didn't even talk about it. Then I got really disinterested in sex. Probably a lot of that was because he wasn't a great lover. It wasn't about pleasing me. I remember one night sleeping with him, and on my own having this incredible desire to have him make love to me and not acting on it. It was the first time it felt like my own desire instead of being caught up in something that was happening to me.

After her first separation from my father, my mother started talking to me about sex. It was always in terms of "getting laid"—that was her expression. Then when she knew I was sexually active, she wanted me to get a diaphragm. These were her words of advice to me. She said, "Always go to bed with your diaphragm in. You never know when he might want you."

The question in my mind was, "Am I allowed to want him, too? Isn't it a two-way street? Or is it just whatever the guy wants?"

My mother brought me up where you're supposed to be a tease, but then you can also say to the guy, "Oh, you just took it all wrong." I always had shorter shorts and tighter shirts than anybody else, but that was okay. She encouraged me to buy those clothes. I had the first string bikini on the block, which sent my dad over the edge. I matured faster than anybody else in the neighborhood. Some guy down at the pool took a picture of me in my bathing suit, blew it up and was selling it in the high school. My mother never said anything about the bathing suit. That was okay. You can promise sex, but the point comes where you say, "Oh, you took me all wrong. I wasn't doing anything to make you think that." Wink, wink, wink.

When my mother found out I wasn't a virgin, she wouldn't talk to me. This was the worst thing you could ever do in my mother's book, to not be a virgin.

I was nineteen, and I fell in love with somebody. He was wonderful. When we used to kiss and make out, I'd get so excited that I just thought that the oceans are really going to part. We talked about it, and he said, "I want to have sex with you." He'd never had sex, and I'd never had sex. We were in love, and we sort of planned it. "We'll do it this weekend. You'll come up and we'll do this and that." It was probably the best it could be for the first time you do anything, because we loved each other and a lot of our relationship was based on laughing and our sense of humor.

So when we were at the stage where it's, "Does this go in here? How long does it stay in there? Are you having fun yet? Are we supposed to move, do you think?" I looked up at him and said, "Chris, I think there should be moaning." So he went, "Uh, yuh, uh!"

It was one of those things where you try sex a few times, and you go, "Thank God, it's done. Now we can get on with doing it again, refining it, getting better—or go back to just making out." Making out was in a way more fulfilling. It was so wonderfully frustrating, that delicious frustration.

He was a very romantic character. He was tall and handsome with long hair. He was very eccentric, a poet who made furniture. At first we worked together and then we began to hang out together all the time.

We would go out and get very drunk at night. We'd pick up women and sometimes bring them back to the same bed. We'd watch dirty movies together and jerk off on either ends of the bed. We came up with wild, romantic plans and fulfilled them. We were a real set on the social scene at the time. We had wild parties and would be out into the night. You never knew where somebody was going to end up. It was so much fun.

But I got to a point where I was really jealous, where I wanted to be with him all the time. And when women were with him, if I wasn't included, I absolutely was possessed. I never had the same experience as extremely—it's that first love, but I was all those things.

I couldn't figure it out. What is wrong with me? I honestly I couldn't figure out what was going on. I finally sat him down and said, "I don't know why, but I am obsessed with you. I sometimes think I want you physically."

He went, "Oh, my God! This has happened to me before. I once had a friend, and he turned out to be gay."

I said, "I'm going to go away for the summer to get away from you and see what happens." One of the first things that happened to me while I hitchhiked to a national park was that I got picked up by this couple. The wife was the one that was really pushing this, but she had no idea that the husband would react the way he did, because he reacted big time. He liked it a lot. She thought she was going to be the focal point, but instead she kind of ended up on the couch, and the two of us got it on, which was a very difficult experience for everybody concerned. I was new to this. I don't know if he was new to it or what, but he certainly took to it.

So that summer I had a number of experiences with men and women, and it started to dawn on me what was going on. Then when I got back home, I finally ended up going to a gay bar. It's a huge gay bar. I'll never forget. I was wearing a double-breasted navy blazer and a tie. They had a balcony as you came into the place over a three-story room with a dance floor. Maybe three hundred men were down there. I looked around the room and said, "I'm home." I had no idea I was gay, and then it was so clear at that moment. I felt like a kid in a candy store, because I was twenty-three years old and all of my sexual feelings had been so confused for so long. "This is it. There's no doubt."

As a kid, my masturbatory fantasies first started out with women. But something wasn't right, so suddenly there'd be a man and a woman in the fantasy. I'd find myself dwelling more and more on the man's sexual role versus the woman's sexual role or their sexual activity. You kind of think, "Something's wrong here," but not really mentally dealing with it.

I had a neighbor who would have sex with anything. He was always trying to have sex with me. I found it terrifying. But one day I let him give me a blow job and came in about three seconds. It was pretty obvious that he had rung my bell. The guilt! I felt so guilty that I smacked him. I just walloped him pretty well and never talked to him again and repressed it.

Finally, when I got out of college and moved to a big city, I didn't know anybody, and nobody knew me, so there was a lot more freedom. I was at a concert one night, and I remember seeing a guy across the room. The minute I saw him, my heart went from my chest up into my throat. I could hardly breathe, and it was pounding. I just became obsessed. Then I didn't see the guy for three months.

When I saw him again, the same thing happened. Random, a stranger. Apparently, this guy got a job downtown near where I worked. I'd see him daily. I'd always make sure I'd be in a spot where he could see me. It was like the highlight of my day just to see this guy. I didn't know what to do.

I started saying hello to him on the street. I remember one day I took a long lunch and followed him just to see where he worked. I wasn't wondering about me anymore. It was pretty clear at this point that I'd become obsessed with this man, and it was time to do something. I had also started to read *Everything You Always Wanted to Know About Sex*. I had seen *The Joy of Gay Sex* in the bookstore, but I wouldn't pick it up. I knew I was being drawn to it, which was telling me something. Okay, I have to at least explore this and see what is going on. Here I was, in my early twenties now, and except for one woman I had never really had a sexual experience in my life.

I actually had to go to his office on business one day, and I started talking to him. It was real nice talking. We agreed to meet for lunch the next day. He was into the outdoors, a real macho kind of outdoor guy. In a week, we had lunch or dinner every day together. I was getting real curious.

He came over to my house for dinner and to watch TV. That night I just said, "I'm sorry, I have to kiss you. If you're offended, I'll back off, but I'm real attracted to you and I can't stand it."

"Oh," he said. "I'm so glad to hear you say that." That's how it started, and I'd never felt so comfortable. I was doing the right thing for me. I could say to myself that I was in love for the first time in my life. I never felt anything that wonderful. To hold this guy or to be held by him, there was nothing that equaled that up to that point in my life. I thought, "What have I been denying myself all these years? This is exactly what is right for me."

Freedom was the word. There wasn't herpes, there wasn't AIDS. There was your kind of brown-bag-version VD, even syphilis, but no one I knew ever got it, and sex was constant.

But I felt like this voyeur. Everybody was doing it, and I felt like a foreigner. It was all disconnecting. But the one thing that stayed in place was the sex. I felt that was one thing that no matter how many changes I went through by chance or by design, my virginity hadn't changed. It was constant. Somehow it was like a rudder.

This was all during the time in my life which would have normally been for sexual experimentation. My friends were telling me about sex. But being virginal had been pounded into my head. This was the right way to go about things. I hate to say it, but I kept seeing my mother's face anytime I thought about the natural progression of a relationship to sex. That would just kill it. To figure it out is such a long process. You're taught that it's so negative, to really bring it full circle, you have to go through a massive catharsis. Abstaining and being a good girl was still in play, because I hadn't grown up yet. Some of us don't grow up for a long time.

The first time I had sex was after my mother died. It was the first time I allowed myself. I was twenty-three. It was like growing up all at once. When my mom died everything changed for me. It was like this: "She's really the only one that I promised. You can't keep a promise to a dead person. You don't have to keep promises to people who aren't there anymore." That's when it changed.

I moved to Boston. The first week I was here this man that I had worked with on the West Coast was in town. He is twenty years my senior. I just adored him. He was bright and sweet. But I never thought of him in a sexual way.

We went out one night, and we were drinking champagne. That made it easier being a little more inebriated. I remember thinking, "This is a perfect time."

Although I really cared for him, I didn't want anybody who'd be around constantly. I wanted to get this over with. I knew I had to have this rite of passage. This *had* to occur. I felt that everyone had gone before me, and

I had no intention of getting married. That was the thing, marriage just seemed so out of context in my world, but I'd been told you can only have sex with marriage. I was getting realistic here—"This marriage thing isn't going to come."

When we were walking back to the hotel, he was just being himself, no come-on. I was the one who proposed it. It was a subliminal thing. I didn't consciously set out to do this. It was just the right time. My mom had been gone for six months. I looked at him in the lobby of the hotel and I said, "Your place or mine?"

He looked at me and said, "What?" Then he said, "My place."

He was so great. He was someone I trusted, someone who wasn't in my clique of family, religion, and friends. He was someone I had made friends with on my own.

He was even a little surprised: "You're still a virgin?" That kind of excited him in one sense, but I wasn't some sort of laboratory test. We were friends. So it was good.

Physically, it wasn't great. I was kind of like, ho-hum. But he explained things. We talked about how sex with a great relationship is so wonderful. "You haven't had this experience yet, but it's something you should look for." That's when he said, "When you really, really care for someone, and when the emotions have the ability to go beyond the physical act, sex will be something that you can have through your whole life that will be very positive." He was the first man who really made up for some of the negative advertising I had heard before. He really helped me to see that there is nothing wrong with this.

Although, the next day I felt very strange somehow. I had given something very important away. I really felt something was gone.

M / F

1. SEX WARS

Picture two naked human beings, one man and one woman, standing at ease, silent, like some Renaissance painting of Adam and Eve contemplating the apple in the Garden of Eden before the fall from grace. They are very similar, like the two distinct sides of the same coin.

But if we put clothes on them and have them speak some remarks made during the interviews reported here, this is what happens:

EVE: "Why can't you guys have other things in mind besides a lot of sleaze. Most men today are weaker than well water, and they don't give a damn about nobody. All they want to do is one thing: jump your bones. That's it. He can be with you, but if you don't have him on a leash—hey! —his head is out the window, and you might have a wreck, because if a piece of ass goes across the street, he's *deep* over there. He can have the perfect woman, and you know what he will choose? Excuse the expression, but he would choose a slut."

ADAM: "At one point, I was the only single professional male in this little town, and it was *awesome*. It was a better mousetrap. They beat a path to my door. I was the quarry, and the sexual revolution was at hand. But have you ever heard people talking about having bad pussy? I have had bad pussy. And guys who haven't, just haven't had much pussy, because there is some bad stuff out there."

EVE: "Men will tell you what you want to hear, and then go do whatever they want to do. Men have that attitude—'I don't care about her. I just care about me. What's in it for me?' Their attitude is like the old joke: One guy says, 'What does it take for a woman to have an orgasm?'

"The other guy answers, 'Who the fuck cares?' "

ADAM: "My third wife was a feminist, and a real hardass about it, very emasculating. She claimed women like sex, but I don't believe it. She liked it fine until she'd made my scrotum into a coin purse and stuck it in her pocket. After that I was lucky I ever got any more mud for the turtle."

EVE: "All men are dogs."

ADAM: "Yee-ha! And thank you, ma'am."

Men and women suffer from sexual anger, suspicion, and disorientation. Each sex considers the other intellectually inferior, sexually deviant, and perhaps slightly deranged. This situation is pejoratively called the battle of the sexes. But the friction is very real, the enmity is very real, and the war smolders on.

In the inertial mainstream of American life, age-old cultural role models for male and female sexual behavior are still intact today—the knight in shining armor, the princess on a pedestal, and the sneaking feeling that sex is dirty. A man should be take-charge macho, a sexually dominant predator, insensitive to others' feelings and his own. Women are supposedly made for submission and dependent on love to evoke physical passion. They are aloof, virginal. In direct contradiction to these concepts, the most common male fantasy is still the sexually aggressive woman who initiates the foreplay, the sex kitten who does all those naughty things, unbidden, with abandon. The most common female fantasy is still some version of the bodice-ripper, the ravisher who takes a woman not by force of violence so much as by pure erotic charisma. For some, the fiction of the virgin/whore or the bad boy "who made me do it" provides the only release for erotic impulses.

In the subjective realm men complain that women don't really want to have sex at all. Women's main gripe is that men *only* want to have sex, without any emotional connection. It's no wonder there is so much finger-pointing and frustration when the assumptions the sexes make about each other are based on such incompatible images.

There are strong undercurrents of change in sex roles today. The liberated woman and the new man would seem to provide exactly what their gender opposites claim to be looking for.

For the last twenty-five years, women *have* begun taking control of their lives, including their sex lives. More women than ever before feel free to seek their own sexual pleasure. They are more aggressive and vigorous in their lovemaking. Confident in their own abilities to survive and thrive, they are unwilling to be dependent on men even for their orgasms, much less to be shackled by conventional marriage. Unfortunately, the majority of men, suddenly face-to-face with their fantasy of a frankly sexual woman who is not motivated solely by her desire for a commitment from them, more often than not turn and run away. She scares them.

Some men have become much more sensitive to their own feelings as well as to the emotional needs of the women in their lives. They are also more willing to talk about women, love, and sex in an open, non-accusatory way that men of former generations have found impossible. But the sensitive man, patiently waiting for a positive response from a woman he finds sexually attractive, exposing his emotional vulnerability, runs the risk of being perceived by women as just plain wishy-washy. He bores them. Although women may not want their bodices ripped any-more, they still want men at least to rumple them vigorously.

American society has begun to feint and shuffle toward sexual equal-ity and gender détente, but as the old order unravels, and men and women begin to redefine themselves, the battle lines have hardened. Women feel exploited and angry. Men are confused and vindictive. What little sexual dialogue men and women stuttered through has be-come a shouting match. It will be generations before we finish shaking off the medieval torpor that surrounds our attitudes toward each other and discover new behavioral patterns that satisfy the civilized animal we have become. If males and females traditionally collide with the fatal inevitability of the iceberg and the *Titanic,* then the situation has progressed only to the point where men and women are passing each other like ships in the night.

LIBERATED EVE: "I'm so sick of sensitive men. I had one, and I didn't like it. There's something endearing about cowboys. You know where you stand with them. They're a hell of a lot easier to figure out than young urban professionals. There's no playing around. They're kind of lousy lays, because they get way too drunk, but there's something appealing about that straightforward, very macho kind of man. Don't tell Gloria Steinem I said that. Don't turn me in to the feminist police."

NEW ADAM: "When I was in college, I was an ardent feminist. All this stuff I heard about women and I believed at the time, I have at this point discovered is *not* true. Just in general, like I always grew up thinking women wanted men who were sensitive and caring and so forth. I have discovered this is not true at all. They are not interested in weak men. They want strong men who are tough. Women actually do like to be conquered. They don't like weaselly, wimpy men who mess around. They want a guy who comes in and takes charge, takes control of the situation. That's the kind of men that they're interested in. I wasted all these years trying to be sensitive, soft, easy, and caring, and I want to go on the record as saying this was a big waste of time."

If they can survive the youthful surge of hormones, overcome the disappointments and the resulting animosity of bad intimate relationships, and rise far above the exhausted cultural stereotypes and the sniping of modern sexual politics, a few people manage to withdraw one-on-one from the sex wars and to resolve a separate peace. Although such a reconciliation takes a certain maturity and sexual experience, it doesn't really have much to do with education, social standing, or financial status. It is not an intellectual experience or a political decision. Both combatants simply surrender unconditionally to each other.

Luke and Judy are two Westerners in their thirties. Neither one of them had a very good childhood or parents who talked to them about love or sex. Battered casualties of the sex wars, they had both been married before—twice for Judy—to spouses who used and wounded them sexually and emotionally, not to mention the physical abuse both of them suffered. Each of them brings children to this relationship. Their Eden is a tract house in a treeless suburb. These comments come from separate interviews conducted a few months after their first anniversary.

LUKE: "Last February, I met Judy, and we fell in love, and got married. This time around, it's altogether different than it's ever been before. Sex is more 'normal,' if there is such an animal. When we have sex, I want to do what makes her feel good, and she wants to do what makes me feel good. We care enough about each other that it's just like part of you gets intermingled together. It's really satisfying. That's the thing I never had before. Sex is not a craving anymore where you just want more and more and more and more. It's not one of those deals where it's thirty-five minutes and when it's over with, who cares? Our sex is something that stays with me for the whole next day. I never was so close to somebody with what's inside. All my other relationships had to do with external things—looks and stuff. Maybe it's what I've been looking for all my life."

JUDY: "I don't have a good trust of men. I don't even trust my own judgment. I figured I attract the weird ones. I met Luke, and he was quiet and kind and put up with my kids. He went to church on Sundays and took my kids with him while I worked. Then he got me going to church. Several months later, he asked me to marry him. I thought, 'What are you, crazy? Why would I get married again?' But we did. I could sense that he was a good person, and it might be a right thing to do emotionally. I could grow into it maybe.

"Luke never came on to me sexually, never treated me like all the other guys did. I didn't know how to handle that. If they don't come on sexually, I don't know how to react in a normal way. Is there something wrong with me? We talked about it several times, and he said, 'You need to like yourself the way you are. I don't need sex to like you.' Over this last year and four months, we've grown to where I understand that now. Finally, sex doesn't rule my life. It's great when we have it, very tender and gentle and nice. I don't feel like I'm being used. It's always very special now, and it's the first time I've ever, ever felt that way."

Peace in the war between the sexes may only come two people at a time.

○ ○ ○

Riding in a car about six months ago with another retired libertine—we'd like to say semiretired for pride's sake, but basically it's retirement of which we speak—we see some tomato cross the street. The other libertine says, "Remember how important pussy was in the scheme of things? The raison d'être and what gave you joie de vivre every day? Isn't it a disappointment now that it's over, it's behind us? It was such a part of what it was to be alive, the pursuit of women, fucking women, thinking about women, and the whole works. And now it's over."

It was a whine, one libertine to another, but it's true. It made me feel like I was in some kind of psychological rocker on the front porch of the fucking Libertine Retiree Home. That's how I see myself these days.

However, sex has been one of the main features of my life from the get-go. I am in my late forties now, and I have probably spent a solid ten years of chronological twenty-four-hour days thinking about sex, fantasizing about sex, pursuing women I had no other interest in whatsoever other than sex, riding to and from sex, jerking off, and actually having sex.

In the beginning, it became a game to fuck as many of them as you could. It was the blue-blazer days. Blue blazers were *in* with turtlenecks. We'd go to Spark's Pub and Harlow's. Those were two places on the circuit. I can remember them to this day, we were there so many times.

It would not be unusual for us to spend twenty dollars on fifty-cent tankards of beer in the course of a weekend. Forty fucking beers in three days, Friday, Saturday, and Sunday, looking in the bars for girls to fuck, which was done before us and which is done today, I'm sure, by young hornsticks.

The girls were there, and they'd fuck you, too, sooner or later. They wanted to get laid. They had this brand-new thing they were ready to use. It's always been my opinion that women are the most experimental at the age of nineteen. A lot of them get fucked earlier, but the majority don't. They're at the height of their sexual experimentation at nineteen to twenty. That's when most girls have their sexual awakening.

So under the mentorship of my friend Kramer, who was a few years older than me and considerably more sophisticated, a kind of cynicism came into things. We didn't have much respect for women, at that point. It became an ego thing. I associate it with smoking grass, being cool, too cool to talk to people, looking down your nose at people for no real reason, but thinking that you have a reason, because you're cooler than them.

With the girls I had sex with, I was quite selfish. The thing is not just to get them to fuck you, but to humiliate them sexually in various ways. You humiliate them by making them serve you and not serving them back or giving a shit about that. Girls will—and I am ass-kissing here—but they'll put up with a whole lot of shit, especially young, naive girls do. Women don't, once they get wise to how selfish men can be.

You could get girls, especially with a good line of shit. But there were never enough. You treat them shitty, they don't stay with you anyway. You got to get a new supply. Like screwing some guy in a deal, he never comes back. Well, it's the same thing with girls: They don't come back. There was a big turnover.

And it was really detached, feelingless sex. I always smoked grass. Grass kind of subdues your feelings. For me it was that I couldn't take my feelings. I wasn't strong enough, or whatever it was. Stuff that kind of squelched your feelings was what I wanted to do. So you became a sort of cool guy.

Girls're so fucking stupid, they go for that, too. They see you're cool, they see the way you smoke a cigarette a certain way. I've had them say to me, "I just love the way you held a cigarette in the hall." It was arrogance. Everything was a macho pose, body language that you were cool. A lot of these little saps went for it. They don't go for the decent guy who's going to, like, treat them right and is nice. He's not interesting. He's nerdy. But the pricks like me who look cool, that reflect confidence to women, they go for. Who knows? I don't know. But that's the way it was.

In one college class, I remember fucking three girls in the class. One after the other actually. That was stuff to brag about. It made you feel cool. It was meaningless. But I thought it had plenty of meaning at the time.

You do drown in it, drown in pussy. I spent a number of years inside this meaningless thing, going from girl to girl and being extremely cavalier about sex, about women.

Besides the time that you put into sex, we would blow so much poetry on them. You screw yourself up to your best creative work, to make up your best line, to impress a girl, to get her to drop her drawers for you, rather than put it into something a little more productive than a piece of ass just to add a notch to your belt. That was a big deal for us. "We're blowing all our poetry on pussy. We're smart here, we got senses of humor, but we continue to chase pussy and are obsessed by that."

Back then, another close friend of mine came down with his girlfriend, and we were driving around in my car one Saturday. The girlfriend is in the store, and we're sitting there. Windsor says, "Look at that girl over there! I fucked Wendy twice this morning, and I'm still horny." You'd physically be sated, you come twice in the morning, you go out, and you're still horny. It's a psychic drive.

Sex was everywhere. A twenty-four-hour-a-day occupation is what it was like. You'd have a girl, and you'd be getting plenty of sex, and yet you'd still want more. They had these porn stores all over the place from the late '60s through '75, like pissoirs in Paris. In the middle of the day, an executive could go in here, watch the films and jerk off in this peep show. They still exist, but back then they were all over the fucking place. They were used like pissoirs. You'd go use them in the afternoon, and then go see your girl at night. Does that mean that you're a stud, and you're extra virile? No. The reason you skewered yourself up into this sexual mind-set was you're always trying to escape, you're always a hedonist, you're always looking for your next piece of pleasure. That was a great part of it. It wasn't like sex was a reward. You just lived for the pleasure back then, that was one of the threads that held us together. There was no work ethic involved. Sex was just part of the everyday gratification. Sex was like eating for a real fat guy. He lives to eat, right? I lived for sex, for drugs, for the total hedonistic, lotus-eaters-run-amok kind of mentality.

As I got a little older, I realized that my manhood is tied in with satisfying a woman, not in how much I can get her to do while giving her as little back sexually as possible, making her pay for all those years that I craved for girls and craved for sex and was too shy and too inept, not the captain of the football team or whatever reasons I couldn't get it. Finally, I'm not continually wreaking vengeance on them for having what you want. There is that self-imprisonment that Norman Mailer talks about, *The Prisoner of Sex.* It's not the jailer's fault that you're in jail. Well, it ain't the pussy's fault that you're sex-obsessed.

Looking back, I see it as very much a vengeance angle there, not just with me, but with millions of men. You look at pornography and where it's at today. You see all these scenes where guys jerk off on a woman's face, come all over her face. Now, I've done that. I did that a lot. I consider it disgusting. When I can remove myself from my lewdness and my sexual turn-on from it, when it is purely looked at, it is like spitting in someone's face, only twice as bad.

I've seen thousands of porn films. Why do so many of them end with scenes like that—money shots, the oral come shots, where men are spewing their seed all over another human being's face? Think about that abstractly, and it's a very disgusting thing, but it pleases men. It's humiliating to women, one of the most humiliating things they can do to women. That's the pleasure in it. You talk to whores, you talk to men who are honest about it, and the desire is to humiliate women with sex. With whores that is the thing almost exclusively, except for guys who can't get laid and these love-ga-ga guys who fall in love with them. But they are tangential.

What I'm saying I'm sure is true. You just have this drive. It is this vengeful, malicious drive to humiliate them. It takes the form of getting your vengeance for all the pussy that you couldn't get because you were a lewd, horny guy, and you couldn't snap your fingers and convince a girl to go to bed with you, because they needed more than that. It wasn't that simple. So when you did get them, you wanted to just dominate them.

Part of it is just domination, too. There is a male urge toward sexual domination, just as there is a natural female urge towards sexual submission—when they like you. The more they like you, the more intimate sex acts they perform. That's how a woman shows her love for you. You're special to them. They'll do something that's special. They'll feltch your butt or something. Just something that's especially intimate. Men will force that sort of thing to feel the dominance over women or to humiliate them.

It's not very nice really, vengeance against women for having what you want and being so inscrutable. They're hard to understand. They're even harder to convince, especially if you're single-minded and all you want is pussy from them. They can read that, and they don't want to give you their pussy unless you're one of the charmed souls, and I was never that.

My first sexual experiences had a lot to do with drugs—sex and Quaaludes, sex and pot, sex and wine, sex and whatever it was—so they were "tainted," I guess. The older I got, the more sex had to do with just wanting to get guys to like me. I was very concerned with just wanting to get guys to like me, because I still had that cootie complex, even though I was grown up and had become attractive and wasn't having pimples anymore.

I found that in my twenties I was promiscuous. I guess many people were in the '60s. I would find myself in situations when it would sort of make me sick to think that I was doing these things with this person, not caring really about him, except that I wanted this person to like me. I was performing sexually with these people, and not really getting anything out of it. It wasn't something I particularly enjoyed. Sometimes I did.

Most of the time it was, "Please like me. I hope you like me. I want you to like me."

Then after he left, I would go through a lot of feelings of intense loneliness. I couldn't figure out why that was. With the guys all the time coming and going, my life was supposed to be very full. I thought that was what it was all about. Yet, it didn't particularly fill me up. We were sold a bill of goods on that line. So, yeah, I spent a lot of time in various relationships doing things, not because I wanted to, but because I thought somebody else wanted me to do it.

It was the Quaalude nights and the Rémy Martin until four in the morning, and Quaaludes until ten in the morning, and coke until whenever. I found myself in weird situations with two guys, and another girl and a guy, all these kind of weird circumstances which I never enjoyed. Never had orgasms when I was in these situations, so why bother? What was the thing that was making me continue to do that? Classic insecure girl wants so bad to find something that she just takes anything that she can get. That's the way I was. Maybe something that my mother would always say to me stuck in my mind. It's about them, *their* pleasure, and what they're going to get out of it. My needs are very secondary. Just get what you can get, and be happy that you have something at all. That was the message that stuck with me for a long time.

When I realized what I was doing to myself, it was a guy. He was a messed-up person, and it was after that relationship that I realized what my pattern was and that I should start looking at things realistically and not be so taken in by anybody who said to me, "I want you."

This particular guy, something had happened to him in Vietnam. Sex became this strange power tool to him. He really used it on me. He was very sexual, very kinky and pornographic. He liked to go to weird movies and wanted me to do all these weird things with him. I started to get into it with him. Then he tapped into something that was in me that he knew that I liked. He played this father role with me, and I responded to him in that way. He was really manipulative and really evil. God! He's fucking evil. At one point, I just realized that this person was going to try to destroy me. I was freaked.

He would say, "If you won't do this for me, So-and-so, my old girl-friend, I talked to her a week ago, and she wanted to do it with me. But I wanted you to do it, so I waited to see what you would say."

"I'm not going to pee on you. I won't do that. That's not my idea of sex. Go away from me." It was at that point that I started looking at myself and going, "I got to get a better idea about sex. There's something wrong here. It's not fun. I'm not enjoying it. I need to change my life."

I was lying to myself more than anything else, selling myself a false bill of goods about what it was all supposed to be about. I wasn't having fun. It was no fun. So I stopped that kind of behavior, not overnight, but I pretty much got out of that rut that I was in, and started working on healthy relationships.

I always had this romantic notion of women, that I was going to meet one that was going to be the perfect woman. She was going to be supportive and caring and wonderful, sympathetic to whatever cause I had. In turn, I would be her protector, take care of her forever and pledge that I would lay down my life for her. Of course, once she knew this, we would have a great relationship, never a harsh word spoken, never a word screamed out.

Sick! Where do I get that stuff from? I have no idea.

What happened to me was that erotically I was attracted to a certain type of guy who wouldn't be expected to treat me well, who couldn't come through in a relationship. In a certain way, the sexual life was always kind of aborted, because I wanted more than what the guy could give me.

I felt like bait for guys. I was very uncomfortable if a regular guy would like me. I felt particularly comfortable if a creepy guy would like me. I would feel really safe. I could like let go, be erotic myself with somebody who was sort of more archetypically criminal and bad. In the meantime, I could have regular relationships with nice guys and not worry about a sexual thing. I don't really understand it at all. I still have that tendency.

Right now, I'm involved with someone. We have this incredibly wonderful time in bed, a beautiful time. It's really mutual. There's a lot of sharing and vulnerability, admitting things and trying things. There is this total involvement or attention that I can get from him in bed. However, as soon as we're doing anything else, or trying to have something to do together, we just don't really have anything in common.

There's a lot of abuse, sort of emotional abuse, except when we're in bed again. He can't relate to me at all and what I want to talk about, nor does he want to hear it. I know it's not good for me, but I do know that it seems very much *like* love. There is this sense of having somebody when we're making love, but otherwise I could never have him. Nor does he want to have me. Sometimes, I feel like he misses the best in me in a regular way. Whatever I have to talk about, he's sort of dismissive of it.

Somehow this thing that works so well in bed has to do with the fact that we're so very different. It's this desire for the other's desire. The Other, the one who is really, truly different. This meeting of the impossible, and the impossible happening. This is very charged erotically for me. It's like an adventure. Everything is possible. This attempt to get the unattainable and getting it, erotically—or almost getting it—I don't understand why it had to take place with someone who is so impossible to have a regular relationship with. That's what my obsession is right now to figure out. This is what I'm up against.

I've met this other guy, who in an everyday way makes a lot of sense.

He's a really nice, really normal guy. That's why I went out with him. He's smart, handsome, and he likes me. But I can't get swept off my feet by him. I would like to reach this place where I could be swept off my feet by somebody like him, somebody it makes sense to be with, instead of some sex situation that doesn't make any sense. It's really troublesome for me. I'm back to where I was when I was seventeen, when I was with this guy who had an aura of the criminal, or what is it—the Bad Boy.

With the nice guy, being in bed with him was kind of difficult, because he wasn't all that exciting, because, you know, he was a *nice guy*. But we had a pretty nice thing, because he wanted me to be happy. He did what would make me happy. But there wasn't this talk of *desire* and this "Do I have you? Do I not have you?" Of course, I have him. He's extremely affectionate. For me, that wasn't sexual. I don't think it was sexual for him either. I couldn't let go with him. I couldn't create an illusion or a mystique with him. We just knew each other. That's a big reason why our relationship failed. I was no longer interested in making love to him. It was frustrating to him, so he found somebody else. I can be in a relationship with a guy and like him, and respect him, and admire him, and just figure I'll give up on the making love. Just give up on it. The guy doesn't feel that way. After a very short time I say, "Oh, don't bother me."

I'm in this sad place where I can feel really turned on and erotic and feel like making love to somebody only if there is some kind of risk, a kind of danger, a kind of not knowing, and all this "bad" aura about a person.

There's always been this male thing about the madonna/whore. I don't know what it's called when a woman has that about men. I tell myself, "Grow up. This is ridiculous, stereotypical. Calling some guy a criminal? It's so imaginary." But I don't seem to get beyond it.

Men are not far beyond the idea that acceptable sex is they bend over, you rush up from behind and have sex with them. To a certain degree, I'm totally accepting of that notion. If we could get away with it, men would still be doing that.

Given the dynamics between the civilizing and animalistic elements of being human, when we are with a woman for quite a while, the best sex comes from very spontaneous stuff. It's not so much going into bed, it's pulling the car over because, "I've just got to have you." That's much more erotic than the civilizing thing of you're being sensitive and generous. The real strong stuff comes from, "I'm going to grab you right now, baby." We get a bigger charge out of that return to the spontaneous.

It surprised me how much women like that. They almost wanted to be mounted. I find women like being surprised sexually—just bending over and just having you at them, and it is really ferocious. That flies in the face of this whole notion of foreplay and being vulnerable. Turning animalistic is very attractive to most women, they really get a big kick out of it. It is more powerful and passionate.

I used to buy into the idea that women's idea of sexuality and men's idea of sexuality were two completely different things. If a woman doesn't feel loved, and if a man is not gentle to a woman, caressing and sensitive and all those things, then a woman can't get off on it. I used to be into that. It's a common female idea that I read about in all the magazines. That the act of a woman in taking a man into herself is a much more intimate act, and that the guy goes around with a dick that sticks out and whatever he can put it in—a fireplug or whatever—is fine. But I don't know, sometimes I feel manly if that's the norm of male sexuality. Sometimes I think about sex just in terms of sex. I think about it in a very physical way, and I could care less about what this guy is feeling. I just want to do and be done. I don't have the sensitive "woman feelings" about sexuality. There's sexuality and sensuality. When you have them both together, you've got it made. But either of them exclusively are not bad either.

At any given moment, when talking to a female, fifty percent of the males are thinking about getting in her pants. When talking to a man, maybe ten percent of the women are really considering that as a real thing. But most guys, it just doesn't take much to get us going. It's because our freaking sex organs hang outside our bodies.

When I go into a drugstore to buy condoms, and there, behind the counter, is a pretty young thing, it provides a semiawkward moment. Which is weird.

Besides the guilt—the loincloth stuff—there's also the sexuality of it. Automatically, how attractive she is comes into the equation. Whether she's someone I'd sleep with comes into the equation. This is all really sort of crazy, sick stuff. I saw this comedian do this thing: It's Saturday night and you're driving home. A woman pulls up in a car next to you.

All of a sudden, there you are being at your macho best. It's totally absurd. You and this woman are never going to have a relationship. She's not going home with you. And yet we play this game as if every woman driving down the street in an automobile is a possible sex partner. There I am buying condoms, and part of that equation is not just the guilt and the embarrassment. The kind of things going on in my head are, "I'm buying a dozen. You want to come over and help me break open the box?" Obviously absurd stuff, that I would never say. But I have friends who might.

Testosterone is really a powerful chemical. Hormones are wild. The recognition of hormonal interplay and the dynamics of hormones in human behavior have been really useful to me as a way of understanding things. To realize, I'm a guy, and when my testosterone level rises I am horny. It's just like that. After having lived with a few women, you realize that because of their cycles and the nature of their hormonal flows, there really is very little matching time when they're really horny and you're really horny. Their hormonal cycle is very different. If you get a woman who really loves to roll in the hay, you shouldn't screw that up.

The relationship I had before I met my wife was with this woman who never, ever, ever once told me, "Not now." Never, ever once. She wasn't the prettiest woman in the world, but she was pretty. And there are times to this day when I curse myself and say, "You fool!"

I genuinely like men, and I like the physicalness of sex. I like strong, up-against-the-wall sex. That stuff where you're panting at the end and sweating, where it's an aerobic workout. I like butterfly-kisses tender, too, but I prefer it to be this animal exercise—rutting.

I'm thirty-five now. I became much more aware of my sexuality in those years from twenty-five to thirty. I became freer to meet someone, and like them, and have sex with them, and to be open to doing that a lot more.

In my early twenties, I still wasn't comfortable with knowing that I liked sex sometimes as sport fucking. Sometimes I just wanted to do that with somebody. So instead, I would find someone, and then manufacture feelings around them, because it wasn't okay just to want to have sex with somebody. There had to be some love or some possible love or some sort of *something*. It didn't feel right that I would *just* want to have sex with you. I had to want to have sex with you, because maybe we could be in a relationship, and I thought you were a really neat guy. I would wake up eight months later once the thrill is gone—that sex-appetite stuff that happens at the beginning—and be living with somebody, or in love with someone, and look at him and think, "Never developed a friendship with this guy. Don't really know if I like him. We had some great sex, but that's over now. Who is this guy, and what do I do? How do I get out of here?"

I would get out in ugly ways. I was pretty heartless sometimes, not on purpose, but because I was confused. I had built a cardboard house of feelings around what was essentially lust. Then once the lust would go away, I would look at the cardboard house and not know how it got there and not know what my part was in constructing it. "Do I want to keep it here? Or should I blow it down?"

I would just tiptoe out of the picture, saying earnestly to them, "I don't have feelings for you anymore." I was not clear enough in my own head to know what I was talking about, and which feelings they were in the first place. So I am just able to piece a little of that together in hindsight.

The last two years, I've been sleeping around a ton. Most of the time safely. I don't understand why in this country it's okay to be a guy and to want to go out and get laid, but if you're a woman, and you want to get laid, that means you're a tramp. So I'm on a crusade about that. Most of the guys I've gone out with lately, I've slept with on the first date. I know *something* is definitely tied up in this.

So many of my women friends sleep with somebody, and they think that guy's got to be in love with them then. If he doesn't call, they always get bent out of shape. I say to them, "Did you want him to call? Did you care if he called? I thought you said he was a jerk." There's always so much of their ego tied up with sex whether they liked the jerk or not. I've picked up guys in bars and slept with them. I didn't really want to see them again. If they didn't take my number, that was fine. I don't have a problem with that. That's one thing that annoys me, that most women think the minute someone sleeps with them that means they're going steady, so to speak.

I just got back from Cancún. I went with two friends of mine. One of them slept with some guy down there. We were calling him Tarzan, because this big brute of a guy looked like he slept in the trees. The next day we were supposed to have gone, but we stayed over an extra day or so. He came to the beach with a woman and had a baby with him. My friend got so upset about that, and jumped to all kinds of conclusions.

She was right. It was his wife or his girlfriend and his kid. But my God, at least he's paying attention to the kid, and what the hell did you want out of him anyway? You got laid. That was the objective, so why can't you live with that? I mean, she didn't go on vacation to be married, especially in Cancún, for God's sake.

This thing almost ruined our vacation, because I was so upset with her that she was feeling that way. Once this guy had slept with her, he was hers. What, they had to get married? My other friend said, "Look, were you going to bring him back to New York with you?" It reminded me of all the Tarzan movies, bringing him back to civilization. But I've known more women like that. I've had more arguments with girlfriends over this. But she's far more in the majority than I am.

So that's the way I feel about sex these days. My female friends are jealous. They wish they could think the way I do, and get loose from their own hang-ups. I don't have them and they can see it. It's easier for me to let go of something than it is for them. I can sleep with somebody and walk away from it. Like the guy I went home with from the bar recently, and he didn't have any condoms. I wasn't going to bother giving him my number. When he asked for it, fine, I gave it to him. But of course, he never called. It was fun. We both got what we wanted. Let's just leave it at that. Don't feel obligated to ask for my number. We're both adults, and we knew what we were doing.

Maybe it's tied up with the man being the poker and the woman being the pokee. Maybe it's different being the pokee than the poker, I don't know. Most women agree with me, but they haven't gotten to the point where they can actually put it into practice. It doesn't take very much for women to get involved. I have friends who determine that the point where you call a guy a boyfriend is when you've slept with him. That means that the guy I picked up in the bar is now my boyfriend. There are still women out there who think that.

The whole thing with me is that generally, I get into these relationships, and then I want to get out. To me the whole way you get a woman in bed is you have to fool them into thinking that you actually care about who they are—unless there's some kind of understanding that it's just a sexual thing. Since that kind of arrangement almost never happens, the way you get them to go to bed is that you convince them that you want more from them than just sex. You have to play this little charade. If you do really care about the person, that's fine. It's not a charade. But if you don't, and you still wouldn't mind sleeping with them, then you do. I'm not sure how good all that is.

The girls are not sterling examples of moral perfection either. They play the game, too, to a certain degree. But definitely, there is some kind of deception going on.

I get myself involved in this mess, and then I want to get the hell out. If I get what I'm after, I sleep with them, then I say to myself, "Why did I do this? Was it worth it? I'd rather have stayed home and masturbated." So you break up after a couple of weeks, or a week, or it doesn't even get that far. You don't call them, and they pretty much pick up the message that you don't want to go on with it.

That scenario repeats itself over and over again. I just had a relationship with a woman where this exact thing happened. I courted her. Made her feel like a million dollars. I wasn't sure whether or not I would really like her. I had a feeling that she wasn't the "right one" for me, but I wasn't one-hundred-percent positive. There's your moral defense right there. You can always say, "I didn't know that I didn't like her." It's feasible to say that you weren't sure whether it was right or not, but somehow after you slept with her it was clear that it wasn't really there, and it all comes to fruition.

I don't like it. I don't want to have sex anymore without love. It's good for chanting: No more sex without love. No more sex without love.

When I break up with someone that I've cared about, it always tears me apart. I always have remorse—"Why did I do this? It was a good thing. I screwed it up."

I lose confidence in my decision. It's sort of like buyer's remorse—as soon as you get home with your new, expensive, technologically advanced stereo, you're not sure you did the right thing. Soon as you broke up, you're not sure you did the right thing.

They never expect it when I break up with them, because I'm such a nice guy. I've thought about it a couple of times. I never know what to explain to them. That's the hard thing about sex without love, or just sleeping with someone. When it comes time to break up, there is no diplomatic way to do it. What do you tell the person? "It's because you're a jerk that I don't want to go out with you." You can't tell them the truth, obviously. "I really mostly wanted to have sex with you, and now I'm tired of even that." It's a bunch of moral predicaments waiting to happen, the way I look at it.

So what I end up doing, I just say, "It wasn't working out. I don't feel right about the relationship. I don't think we're right for each other." I don't tell them what their personality faults are. They don't want to hear it. I don't want to hear mine either, and if you open that kind of discussion, the subject is bound to come around to you.

This last girl had wisdom enough not to ask me why. I broke up with her over the phone. She called me up kind of upset that I hadn't called her in a week. She says, "I'm used to being pursued, and this is funny, you haven't called me back. What's wrong? I've been sad the last couple of days."

"I'm really sorry. I know I should have called you." I was just kind of hoping that she would get the message. But we had been too long together to do it that way. "I think it would be best if we didn't see each other anymore."

"Oh. Okay. Wow. I kind of figured that was what was going on, but I wasn't sure, so I wanted to call you just to make sure."

"I'm really sorry things didn't work out, blah, blah, blah." We made some small talk. And that was it.

To me, it's not worth it. She was hurt. I hurt. Although it takes two to tango, in retrospect I shouldn't have pursued her with the knowledge that she really wasn't right for me. But the challenge was there, and I went after it.

Those old attitudes still persist in men. They want someone who's had some experience. Then you come off as someone who's had experience, and they look at you and say, "Where'd you get all this experience?" Virgin/whore! Virgin/whore!

I'm real mystified by you guys. I thought I had it figured out. I can't read the behavior of men anymore. I don't understand it. I feel as if there was a new rule book passed out and I missed it.

So, I've been out with a few men that I have liked a lot. The feedback I have gotten is, "God, you're sexy and you're funny and you're bright and you're open and you're available and I'd love to see you again." Then, they fall into the Bermuda Triangle. That confuses me. I think I'm being clear and direct, and I get some feedback that I'm not. Then I become clearer, and I get the feedback that I'm being aggressive. It's a big conflict, because I've lost weight, I cut my hair and all of a sudden most of the people I know have said, "You look great. This is the best you've looked in years." And yet it's my driest season ever. I look great, I'm well adjusted, and here I am. Hello out there.

I'm not going to settle for less than a real man. I'd rather be alone than just settle for somebody. I think it will make it even better when I find someone, after the wait.

I openly like men. I like them a lot, but I'm not going to put up with whininess and lack of clarity. If you're afraid of me, then I don't want to have anything to do with you, anyway. I'm not going to tone down to make you feel better.

M y impression of women is that while they are more comfortable with their bodies than men are, I'm not as sure if they are as comfortable with their sexuality. The women who I've gone to bed with who I thought were very comfortable with their lovemaking as lovemaking and nothing more, I could count on the fingers of one hand. The women who are not comfortable with sex, sometimes, or most of the time, or all of the time, are legion.

Renée was one of the very few who was very comfortable with sex and liked it. We had a very intense sexual relationship. I'd say we fit together well. She's the woman I fantasize about still. If I was going to pinpoint one moment that distinguishes her from every other woman I went to bed with, I can remember one morning waking up with her. We were sort of spoon fashion in bed. I was facing her back, holding her. I started to move as though I was turning over. But I didn't turn. She turned over facing me, and we started making love. It always seemed as easy as that, whether it was seven in the morning or seven at night or three in the morning. Men usually are angling for sex. This woman was very comfortable with sex and that is very rare. The far greater majority of women are those who, given the right mood, the right moment, etc., are interested in sex, but they do not take to it as comfortably and naturally as men do. As I do.

The bad thing about our relationship was she wanted me to be her savior, and kept putting me in that role. "I need to have sex with you, because it takes my mind off my pain. You're the only one I have." I didn't want to be anybody's savior. It was the worst thing she could have said to me at the time.

I went to her house one time when she called me from playing racquetball. I go to her house, which I didn't want to do, and she comes to the door with no clothes on. It's like the *Playboy* fantasy, only all I could think of was, "Oh, God, I've got to go in here. Getting laid would be fine, but I know there is something else involved." She was needy in some way, although I don't remember what it was that time. I remember dumping her off at the hospital, because she said she was sick, and I just didn't want to be her savior. "Don't tell me I'm the only person in your life."

Even though I felt like I was smothering, I wasn't going to let go of the sex. But our sexual relationship kept getting more and more sadistic for me. Nothing really kinky, just taking out on her my anger at being roped in in some way. We have never talked about that, so I don't know what her perceptions are. I have a feeling that she would laugh. She's not someone who gets abused by people, so I don't think that she would agree that I was in any way really abusive. But that's the way I felt.

She said one day, "You're fucking me like a dog." That rang a bell. I really am just treating her like a dog, and acting like a dog in the sense of not investing any emotion in this.

I don't know if this was true or if she was just saying it, but in some ways she needed sex from me specifically. I want to use the phrase *true love,* but that's not exactly right. In a way that at the time I just took for granted, this woman had this sense of me being really special, me being important. One time after we had more or less stopped making love, she came over. I was on my way to New York with another woman who I never did have sex with, and who was horrible, but who didn't pressure me like Renée. Renée and I started kissing, and she's moaning and groaning.

"Oh, come on," I said, "give me a break."

"No, look at the tears in my eyes," she said. It was the tears of pleasure. She was really turned on and that's a gift.

Sex has evolved for me. It's changed, and fuck it, it pisses me off in a way. But it's because I've changed in what I want. I used to be able to have sex a lot more freely, and have that be okay. Sometimes after I was done, I'd think, "Ah, that wasn't as great as I wanted it to be. What I really want is some closeness and some comfort. I want some intimacy and some affection." You don't get that stuff from fucking a guy right away. You have to build up to that, and building up takes time. I wouldn't take time. I would jump right in.

Good sex usually takes practice, but there are those exceptions. You just hit. Whether it's hormones or chemistry or whatever it is, the sex just works. One of the things I'm working on is I tend to put more emphasis on the exception, where you get physical with somebody, the sparks go off, and it's magic. It's like you've touched each other a thousand times before. That stuff doesn't happen very often, but when it does, I'll give that more importance than the intimacy and the comfort. I'll go, "Oh, the absolute spontaneity of it! Oh, my, this just came out of nowhere!" I regard that more highly than I will building something. I'm still a child of immediate gratification, I guess, kneeling at the altar of happenstance. It just happens, it just falls out of the sky. Crash! Boom! Unexpected. But that's the stuff you usually cannot sustain, that does not last, so there is conflict within. It doesn't guarantee anything except the power of that moment. Doesn't address anything else.

I'm starting to look around for a life partner for the first time in my life. It's a business deal in a lot of ways. I'm looking at men and thinking, "Is this going to be someone I'm going to want to sign up with for a long time? Will this be someone I will want to share a child with? Is this someone who's going to be relatively responsible, able to commit and be a grown-up, who has an overriding, stellar sense of humor, a decent job, and a *great* pair of legs?" That's the stuff I'm looking for, and that's not necessarily compatible with or inclusive of the stuff that I look for with the fireworks. So I'm retraining myself: "Barbara, he looks real cute, and he starts the fire down below, but is this guy lifelong material? No!"

I'm not having much sex. I'm not finding anybody who meets the quality-control levels. The entrance test has changed. I haven't done it consciously. It snuck up on me. I just can't get excited and give myself away and do that stuff with men with the ease that I used to. It's not giving me what I want at all. It's just not worth it to unbutton my blouse, or make the small talk. Ultimately, the law of diminishing returns has set in. So I have some sort of physical need taken care of for ten or fifteen minutes? What I'm left with for the next ten days or two weeks is this feeling of, "What was that? Is that really what you wanted, Barb? Hello? Isn't it truly intimacy and commitment you're looking for and not a little visit in the Dark Tunnel of Love?"

Sex has all shifted for me, and it's highly weird. I don't know how to be. It's like I'm in Africa, and I don't know the customs. Back in the United States, I know how to walk and talk and change money. But I'm in a different place. I'm competent, well oiled, and maneuver well in all the other areas of my life, and all of a sudden it's gone.

I did pretty well. I've been the stuff of dreams. I'm the one that my friends say, "Who are you seeing now? What's going on? Tell us the story about the Greek guy again and the fireman from England, come on." I've been that for my circle of friends, and they tease me about that. Now, I don't have that anymore. I'm the only single one in my circle, too. They're all in relationships or married. So I'm the one out there with stories, because they've all had the same sex partner for years. They changed positions—that's a sex story? So it's, "So Barbara, what's going on with you and who are you *doing it* with?" I'm just not *doing it* as much as I used to. I don't know what that means.

What I find real frustrating, too, was what happened last year. I went back to graduate school, and found a classmate I liked a lot. I saw him every day. We had the same sense of humor, the same take on politics. He just was quirky, charismatic, and charming and had all those things that I'm drawn to.

So we started going to parties and making eyeballs at each other. There were stolen kisses in corners. Finally, one night, I said, "Why don't you come back to my house?" He did, and it was awful. Awful.

I got an indication that it was going to be awful early on. We were on the stairs making out, rubbing up against each other. My shirt was unbuttoned, his shirt was unbuttoned. We're panting, that heated, shallow breathing. We're gnawing on each other's faces. I grab him by the hair and I say, "Let's go upstairs to my room."

We go upstairs to my room. He closes the door, and takes off his shirt. He folds it very neatly and puts it in a pile. Takes off his pants, lines up the creases, and spends ten minutes disrobing. His erection dies. I'm sitting on the bed just going, "Ted! There was a momentum going here! Fuck your clothes! Get over here!"

Sex was very methodical: step A, step B, step C. I don't think he liked it. I don't think he was having any fun, he sort of had his jaw clinched. That was yucky. I just thought, "Oh, God, there are no guarantees." Even if you like somebody, all the other stuff is in place, you spend a lot of time with them and you build up this friendship, then there we are in bed, and it ranked among the worst sexual encounters I've ever had just in terms of awkwardness and bloodlessness.

Sometimes I wish I could just go back to yesteryear when I could sleep with a friend and it would be okay. That's what I'll have to do, because I need some sex. More than sex I need somebody to touch me. I don't need penetration, I need some affection from a male person. I need someone who will make out with me for ten minutes and then go away. That would be okay. I would be happy. I'll just have to come right out and say that to some people.

I tried it with one guy who's sort of a friend. He said, "You know, I'm not really interested in being sexual at this time."

I don't want to ask why. I don't want to hear it. I just said, "Okay, Rick, how about this? Let's just sort of kiss. Can't we kiss, and rub up against each other, and get worked up, feel desired and desirable?" And he just ran away. When he did, I said, "Rick, you're being an idiot. I am offering myself to you without the entrapment or anything else. That's really all I want."

I want what I call an electric friendship. We're still good friends, but we can touch each other and do that stuff. He thought I was interplanetary. I do have a few men friends I can do that with, but they all live in other cities. Five hundred bucks and a six-hour plane ride for ten minutes of your tongue in my throat? Sorry, I just can't swing it these days, the economy being what it is.

I don't know how much AIDS has to do with it. I think AIDS is coincidental to my sexual history. Even without AIDS this would have happened. I'm just older. I'm tired of the dance. Instead of a period of expansion, like in my twenties and early thirties, I'm nearing a period of contraction. I'd like to withdraw, focus my energy on a few projects rather than spread myself out as much as I have. One of those projects is a commitment. You know, I've had plenty of men. I've had wonderful relationships. There are great men out there. I have been really blessed with sharing time and laughs and touches with a lot of them. So it's not like I'm one of those people who say, "Oh, I got to get out there and get all I can before I get married." I've already done that. It was fun. I ate a lot of candy. I sampled the thing. Now I just want slowing, narrowing, refining.

The last eighteen months, I've been treading water, looking around, meeting people, spending time with different men. But I don't have the patience for it. I just want a grown-up. I want someone who's in the same place I am, and not everyone is. I'd like to commit. I'd like to start a life with somebody. Men say they want that, too. Then you go out with them, say that, and they run away. I'm going to start handing out little cards that say, "Be clear about what you want, then call me."

I'm not getting excited for men who don't make me laugh, don't have a brain, and don't have a sense of themselves. It's not working, the juices just aren't flowing the way they used to.

I have a female friend now who is seven years younger than I am, so her experiences are very different from mine, because the culture is very different. She talks about the boyfriends and the lovers. I say, "I just don't want to think about it. I don't want to talk about it." Because to me, it's not like, "Wow, I had these experiences." It's, "Jeez, what did I go through all this shit for? Why the hell did I put myself through all this? What was I thinking? Why didn't I get my head together first, and think about something for a while?"

Because I didn't think about anything for years. I just acted on things, or didn't act on things. But even when I didn't act on things, there was no thought involved. I'd just jump into the fire. Jump into relationships without ever once getting to know a person, never talking to them about what they liked and didn't like, what they wanted or didn't want out of life, what they expected from the person in the relationship and what I expected, what they were willing to give and weren't willing to give. In the '60s and '70s we dropped all these issues that are the whole courting process—wooing and courting, getting to know and taking time. "Now, you're my girlfriend, now I'm engaged to you, and now I'm married to you till death do us part." That all happened like a shot in the dark, "but it's going to be a miraculous thing." That's how I jumped around from fire to fire.

There was never any dialogue. That's what I've learned from all my experience, and that's how I'm being educated by this new friend. You have to build a foundation of trust, openness, and honesty before you get to first base. To get to second base, you have to keep building on that foundation of trust and honesty. You really have to know that you can depend on this person, that you can rely on this person to tell you the truth. It's a very slow and painful process. You really have to deal with your feelings of possession and jealousy. You have to be open and talk about what you want. And not conceal things from one another.

My last boyfriend was a nice guy. A sensitive man, and I just hated it. When I was fooling around on him, I wanted him to leave me. I wanted to give him some reason to get out, because I'm really bad at ditching people. He still wouldn't leave. The guy I was going out with had left three messages on the phone machine about what we were doing that night. My boyfriend came home, and I was sitting on my bed working. He pushed the button on the machine and heard this guy, "Hi, we're going to go do this and this and this. *Beep.* Hi, me again. I changed my mind. We're going to do this instead. *Beep.*" And this guy didn't bat an eyelash. Yuck. I don't like this. Leave me.

I didn't like *Thelma and Louise.* You won't find many women who will tell you that. I didn't like it because men shouldn't treat women that way, and women shouldn't treat men that way. They go to some kicker bar, Louise gets drunk, and goes out in the parking lot with this guy she's been dancing with. He actually tries to rape her—which I am not a proponent of, by any means—so Susan Sarandon shoots him.

I haven't actually gone out with any cowboys that did try to rape me, but this guy that I want to jump when I go back out West is exactly like Harlan in the movie—the short sleeves rolled up, the Wranglers, and the beat-up ropers. The guy owns the Hickory Hut in this little town.

There's something to be said for blue-collar men. They're just a lot easier than ya'll educated people. They usually say what they mean. They're not as willing to sleep with you and forget you.

All my friends in the city have to go out with a broker or a bond trader. This is why you never go out with a bond trader: I was going out with a bond trader that I met at a very good friend's house. Nebbishy guy, he was so caught up in his bond-trading job, he had this little beeper that gave him all the stock quotes from Japan while the stock market was closed. I was giving him a blow job, I look up, and he's watching his beeper, his little stock quotes. I got up and left. To me that was the most unbelievable behavior. He didn't really understand why I was so upset. Couldn't figure it out. I dated him for a while after that, but only because he had money. That was the worst.

I'd much prefer to go and hang out with cowboys. They're a lot less distracted, although they drink too much beer to be effective in bed. Harlan was a big disappointment that way.

The first wife was my pal, and the second one was truly evil. I was divorced from her, but nonetheless, very lonesome. That's when I got into the pornography business for a few years. Edwin got me started, my fellow lonely divorcé in the Lonely Guys Club on the West Side of Manhattan. Edwin's wife left him for the Chinese guy upstairs. Edwin didn't move. He took the apartment and the tropical fish. She took all the furniture and moved upstairs. I don't know how Edwin began writing those silly-ass letters for a men's magazine, but it soon became an overwhelming job, and he had to farm it out to his friends.

In those days there could have been as many as six or eight of us who were desperately, emphatically lonely, all divorced, living in roughly the same neighborhood, providing maybe forty-five percent of this nation's sexual fantasies. If you think about it, that's exactly what happened. We're controlling the fantasy lives of just hundreds of thousands of people out there.

A really funny business. I worked primarily for one editor who was a real true believer. This woman was a dominatrix. She would walk around Columbus Avenue with one of her boys on a leash. She had a little collar made for him, and she would walk this guy around. This she called a sex life.

We manufactured these things out of complete loneliness that people imitated. You think we were pathetic writing this stuff, think of those people who were paying for it and believing it. People will believe anything. "The effusion of my manhood spread up her tawny thighs like a baker's glaze." They believed that these things that we made up about tawny thighs actually happened to somebody.

I'm writing these absurd things which all begin the same way, which is, "Boy, I thought I'd never be writing to a men's magazine, but man, what happened to me last Thursday at the greengrocer . . ." That's the scenario, always. Always the fantasy that is the opposite of the truth. The great bulk of pornographic myth is the aggressive woman, always the women chasing the men. My particular métier in the pornographic realm is the great male fantasy of the women coming after the men. Naturally. That's what I always wanted to have happen, which maybe is why I missed the sexual revolution. At the time I didn't get it. "Oh, I'm supposed to do the hunting? That is the male experience in all of human history?" Which is nothing, just an innocent difference between the sexes. You know, the guy goes out and hunts the woman, for the most part. There are variations.

So, I'm writing in the opposite way to the real world, and everybody believes me. The whole country believes this stuff. Even people who don't read the stuff in the magazine know about it and believe that something real is happening to guys like me and Edwin, sitting in some pathetic little diner, or watching his tropical fish swim back and forth, commiserating about our divorces.

So one day, I see the publisher of the men's magazine on a television talk show, and someone brings up the inevitable question, "Now, really, those letters in your magazine, I mean, are these for real?"

There's the guy who signs my checks for writing this fiction, and he says, "Absolutely! Bona fide, real people write these letters. We check each and every one of these." Great, isn't it?

See, I think sex in America is like professional wrestling: It's a fake. I've traveled just enough to know that the whole world is laughing at us for our sexual culture, among other things. That is a real mother lode of humor to the rest of the world, just watching us.

I had the best sex I had in a long time last Thursday night with a friend who I've known for years. I've seen him dating people, and he's seen me dating people. We've always had a lot in common. We do the same work, we have the same family situation, and we've spent time with each other, but always as pals. There was always a little bit of sexual stuff in there, but it's never been right to act on it. The timing's been off, until last Thursday night. We got together and it just happened.

It was surprisingly wonderful, it was that stuff that was free and unconditional and really powerful. So I was telling my girlfriend, "I haven't been touched like that by anybody I've cared about and who cared about me back, who I've had a history with, who I've already enjoyed outside of the sexual life in a long, long time. I don't know what to do."

I called him up, and I said, "That was tremendous big fun. I like you. You're funny and you're bright. We know each other, and we share good laughs. I'd love to do it again if you would."

"We will," he said. "I'm disentangling from someone right now. So just hang on."

"Okay, we'll see." And we hung up. Meanwhile, I just want to say, "Will you come over and *touch me right now? Please?* Just once?" But I think I'll refrain. Maybe. I may just show up at his office in a raincoat, naked underneath. I'm serious. Why not? The most he can say is no. Then I'll just go away. Maybe.

In some ways, it's like, "Go away! I don't want to do this. Just get away from me, because now I have to pay attention to all this stuff that I had shut down a little bit." Instead, I'm walking around insane and obsessed. All I'm doing for the past week is thinking about sex all the time, all the time, all the time. It feels great. I have a lot of energy. I've got this smile on my face. La-la-*la!* But in other ways it's, "Shit. Everything was so organized and neat before this friend of mine happened to touch me, so now, *grrrrr!*"

And he doesn't want to come over this morning, and he's not being concrete about the next time he's going to touch me, which is driving me insane. Actually, the guy is exercising incredibly poor judgment. But I'll allow him that. Who knows what's going on in his life, and besides, what am I going to do? What am I going to do!

What I'd really like right now is just a period of consuming sex, where you just can't think of anything else. You touch each other, and you go insane. You have sex ninety-five times a day, everywhere. You're raw. When you pee it burns, because you've had so much sex, in the closet, on the desk, and in the shower. I haven't had one of those—I thought about it in the car the other day—in five years. I would like just a little period of that—six weeks, a couple of months. I'm up for that right now. I really am.

Tell the women of America: If we're going to have a new type of marriage where they're treated equally, then I want our part renegotiated as well. I want more sexual freedom. I want less responsibility, and that's the deal. Otherwise, you're going to find that men aren't going to want to get married as much as they used to. They never particularly wanted to in the first place. You don't find men reading *Groom's* magazine. Or growing up playing like they're grooms and fantasizing about the big day when they will finally get married. Reading books about marriage and planning what they'll wear. That's another stereotype: In the movies you always saw the bachelor who was brought kicking and screaming into marriage —it's all true. Guys don't particularly like to be married. They like sexual variety, and they don't like responsibility any more than anyone else. Boy, I sound bitter today.

Marriage to some man doesn't appeal to me. I can't say that I don't think that there's great things to it, but it just seems like the cart before the horse. Marriage, as a cart to put everything into and bring it along with you, has never presented itself to me as something that I would want to mold my life around. So sex has always been separate for me.

Should I get married? It was the safer way of having sex on a regular basis. Marriage was what my parents considered a very adult, a very full life, but to me it just kept ringing hollow. It was like, "How can I possibly go out with the concept of getting married before I've even met someone that I would want to do that with?" In so many aspects of my life I have to be conscious of my plan. I have to project, and then go to the next thing. But with love and sex, it made me feel phony. I couldn't do it. At the time, almost every one of my friends was getting a divorce. Something's wrong here. So I said, "Marriage? I'm not even going to think about it."

But I would like a relationship that was a little more constant. No one has to sign on the dotted line here. I just want to explore life and sexuality with another human being and go onward. Where's the next thing coming from?

Unfortunately, there were a couple of years spent where the only men I was attracted to or that seemed able to get that next thing going were married men. Every time I met someone that I liked that's what happened. They were all married. If I met someone and realized that I liked him, I would go, "There's something odd here." Sure enough, he was married.

The single men seemed scared of me. I have this friend and we are very candid with each other. He pointed this out. "You scare them. You've got all your burners going. You know you've had a tough time with sex, and you're not docile. You're not always conventional. When men are trying to figure out who they are and women are giving them a hard time, you are giving them an extraordinarily hard time."

On the one hand, part of me was told when I was growing up that I was going to have this partnership in life, but at some point I realized that doesn't necessarily mean that it happens. There was a feeling of loss, that I really missed out on having the normal relationship. But I'm a product of where I've been.

What I've ended up with is being just very much my own person. I am sometimes too much a loner. I still have my affairs and sex comes and goes. A lot of guys don't know quite how to deal with you when you don't really care about getting married. Running from marriage gives them structure. Of course, marriage is a social thing, it gives us all structure. If it's not there to rely on, many people are not all that creative about constructing their lives. So that's kind of where the last ten years have been for me.

When I hear my girlfriends talk about sex, it really saddens me. So much of it is tied into body image for women. They are less willing to be uninhibited during sex, because of their bodies, or what they think of their bodies. Women who get undressed in the dark, or won't masturbate in front of their boyfriends, or won't dance around, or won't let go, or won't say in bed, "I'm going to masturbate myself to orgasm." Or just the simple things we do that reflect that we're okay in the body that we're in.

This manifests itself in various ways, but it can be as simple as having the man compliment a woman on her body, and her retort is, "Oh, these breasts? They're kind of saggy, don't you think?" or "They're not big enough," or "Oooo, I hate my hips." Or the woman positions herself in bed so you don't get a view of something. Or she has that in her head where she thinks, "I have an awful ass. I've got to remember to position myself so that he never sees me from behind."

The way that plays into sex is frightening. When I have discussions with my women friends about sex, I hear them talk about their bodies and their shame in their bodies, or their desire to be thinner or bigger or whatever. That's unfortunate.

I like my body. My friends have said that makes me atypical. I like my weight. I like my size. I feel good in this vessel, and that is probably the largest contributor to what I consider my sexual health than anything else. I have maintained an air of confidence in the way I look, and I am secure in knowing that I'm a dynamic, attractive woman, I just think well. Men might be afraid of it. Some men say they want that, but they don't. They want someone who is a little bit more needy. I'm not interested in that.

I have a circle of girlfriends, and we get together once a month and talk about stuff that's important to us. We call it the Rotating Girl Brunch. Some of us are married, one is gay. We got some Hispanics, we got a couple black women, we have a redhead, we have a Scandinavian-looking one. One day we were sitting around, and one woman said, "My God, we ought to be making a commercial for Tampax or something. We've got just the right casting mix."

We all talk about what's going on or who's having what. It's usually not size or details about the act. It's rare that women talk about the size of a penis unless it's so tremendous that they can't get it in, that it's daunting. We'll talk about if there was romance, creativity, or invention involved.

Miranda, a friend who has been married for eight years, her last thing was, she came home from work, and there were candles all over the house. Thomas is lying in bed naked. He had strung lace up over the headboard, and he had romantic music on. So rather than what happened after that, it was that he had put energy into the invention of something. So we'll talk about that.

From the single women, the married women want to know how is it and are you doing anything unusual, is anyone lighting your hair on fire? It's not so much for the sex, as it is, "Is this relationship potential? Is somebody you're going out with going to love and marry and stay with you for a long time? Are you going to get what I have?" I have some good marital role models.

We'll get down to nitty-gritty stuff. We had a girl brunch on Sunday and I asked them about masturbation. I gave them the details of my first sex with the new boyfriend. "Tell us, tell us," they said. When I talked about it, what made it so great was the whole buildup. We went dancing, and we were openly flirting with each other, and rubbing up against each other. We came home, and he pressed me up against the front door. We kissed, sort of touched each other real slowly. It's that stuff rather than, "Then he stuck it in *sixty-five times!*" It's all the stuff around it that made it so great. They know him, and they know me. So they were all going, "Oh, you're kidding. I've tried to get you guys together for years."

I always wonder what makes people happy in their sexual lives. The only thing in my experience that really makes them happy is to finally get to middle age, because then there's nothing urgent about sex anymore. There's absolutely no peer pressure. Also, all the fantasies, whether you get them from pornography or the stories from the guys lying to each other in the locker room, are revealed for what they really are.

Very rarely as a culture do we believe what we see and hear for ourselves. We have to have it objectified by somebody else. That's why television is God in this society. We don't have a national religion, we have TV. Television objectifies everything. Our peers objectify things for us. Pornography objectifies our sex lives, and to a great extent defines it, or invents it, I should say.

But when you get to middle age, the first little stirring of actual wisdom begins occurring. You know that you can now rely on what you can see and hear for yourself. Surprisingly, you can often rely on your first impressions. When they turn out to be right, you recognize what role wisdom plays in that. You can think. You can talk to the opposite sex.

These things didn't happen when you were in your teens. They didn't happen when you were in your twenties. In your thirties, everything was a crisis. So you get into your forties a ways, and things become more or less as they should be.

No peer pressure. I cannot remember the last time I was hanging out with my buddies, and we talked about "girls." It just doesn't happen, except for one pathetic guy who is so terrible. He's fifty, and the poor guy is continually telling us about his female conquests. When he starts, I'm right back there at Mumford High in Detroit, Michigan, listening to guys lie in the locker room. It's the same goddamn thing. We tolerate him, poor fellow. You make a decision at middle age whether you move into little baby-step wisdom, or if you just disgrace yourself and ignore everything and become really rather awkward.

But most men at forty can think for themselves. We can talk to women more or less as human beings, and we recognize that they have thoughts and important things to say. A good sex life comes out of that. It becomes a natural part of a life of relying on your own instincts and observations, your own senses.

Sex is a very intimate thing. Now that sounds quite obvious, but we don't have intimacy in this country. Our only intimacies are in reading literature, which about ninety percent of this culture doesn't do. Our only intimacies are in written correspondence, which almost nobody does anymore in this country, because that would be the tangible exercise of thought, and you don't want any of that stuff. The last intimacy was in sex. We have vulgarized sex. Sex is no longer intimate. It's public, and it shouldn't be. Sex is not a public thing. They keep trying to tell us it is. When I say a good sex life is intimate, it sounds stupidly simple, but that's what it should be and what it's not. *Until* you get into your early poot-hood, like me—you know, as in, "You old poot." I'm in my early poot-hood, and finally after all this time, and all this searching for the women who knew stuff that I didn't know, finally after all this action and nothing happening, I finally figured out that I could think for myself, and that I could just ask people things, not of a sexual nature necessarily, but that, too. I didn't rely on TV chuckleheads or journalists to tell me things. I now read the newspaper like Russians read newspapers under the old regimes. "They're telling us this, what is it they want us to think?" That's the way you have to be, and you only start doing that when you're about my age.

Then naturally, your sex life improves. My sex life is pretty good, because the life is good, and the thinking is good, therefore the sex life is naturally good and naturally intimate, and that's it. I've learned all that.

I don't think women are conscious of how much control they have over actually having sex. Flirtation can be a fifty-fifty kind of thing, but it's really up to the woman to proceed or give the green light. Guys know that much more consciously than women do. To a certain extent, women like to buy into the open-endedness of things—I know I do. I don't like to be in a preordained circumstance. Maybe something totally unexpected might happen. I don't like to be in control, I guess. You don't want it to be reduced to, "Oops, time to have sex now."

Love and sex take experience. I remember thinking how sad for my mother, who has only slept with one person her whole life, and probably not very often at that. To this day, even though I have a daughter, I think experience is a big, important part of it. I'm not going to care if she feels like living with someone. It's a lot scarier to be married to somebody and find out that you have not done the right thing, than going ahead and taking a chance. You have to find out what you like sexually, and how your body works, what's good for you, what's best for you. You can only do that with time. It's not all sexual technicalities. It's definitely the person and what they bring to it emotionally, and how involved they are with you. But you can't find out about these things until you've tried them.

At almost forty, I'm just beginning to see the diminution, the ending of the sexual life for the first time. It's just beginning to dawn on me that I may not always be able to couple for my whole life. I find that horrifying. It's absolutely terrible. I'd rather choose death than not be sexually active. It just seems such a wretched idea. It must be really wild to be beyond sex and see those girls in the spring. This city always has that one day when their tits come out. Suddenly, they're down to one layer, and this is spring! There is one day every year when your dick gets hard, and, God, they're out there. I feel great. I feel real again. I like the seasons, but that spring morning when lust is out of hibernation, I feel more vibrant as a human being. How could I be alive and not participate in that communal surge of hormones and sexual sap rising?

2. HIGH PERFORMANCE

W hen I asked a person to be interviewed for this book, almost invariably the first response was, "I don't know why you'd want to interview me. I'm not out there swinging from chandeliers or anything."

The most enduring legacy of the sexual revolution is not a greater freedom to talk openly about sex or more comfort with the vagina and penis and how they function. Perhaps assuaging their old-fashioned Puritan guilt over having sex by flexing the old-fashioned Puritan work ethic, Americans instead embrace the concept of sexual performance —the importance of being "good in bed." Under the bad influence of exaggerated sex scenes in everything from pornographic films to daytime soap operas, expectations can become impossibly inflated. Every man and woman should be an aficionado of the *Kama Sutra*. Men should be remarkably endowed and capable of holding off orgasm for hours. Women must be multiorgasmic contortionists with a wardrobe of lingerie to accessorize every fetish.

As one thirty-year-old woman expressed it, "There's too much pressure on people's sex lives. They feel like they *have* to be swinging from chandeliers. When it comes right down to it, the basic act is the basic act, no matter what position you're in or what tools you bring. Then we look at movies like *Basic Instinct,* and people think they have to take an ice pick to bed to be really cool. Everybody needs to come out of the closet about sex in this country. But performance anxiety is driving us all back in."

When I asked ordinary individuals just what their most exotic sexual techniques—beyond the "basic act"—might be, it usually came down to one not-so-astounding answer: oral sex. Fellatio and cunnilingus,

America's "secret" sex kink. In real life, most of us are lucky just to cast off a standard inhibition or two. Virtually no one is swinging from light fixtures. But imaginary as the ideal sexual athlete may be, the negative effects of performance pressure are all too real. Anxiety about sex is at the root of the most common sexual dysfunctions in America, impotence and inorgasmia.

"The allocation of energy, the economics of sex can be very frustrating. What will you do for me? What do I have to do for you? When and how and how long?" A thirty-five-year-old psychologist was musing aloud about the pressures of sexual performance. Because of her background as a personal therapist, she was good at getting right to the crux of the matter. "Usually, there's this thing about me having an orgasm. If I have an orgasm, I feel like the guy has to wait for me. Then there's this demand to hurry up, because there's the messy Penis Issue. Sometimes there's a lot of pressure. Sometimes, you just want to give it up, but you don't really. If I do give it up, and we kind of complete things, it's, 'Oh, shit, I lost out on that one.'

"It seems so easy for the guy, and it's so hard for the woman in a certain way. I remember this guy saying, 'Okay, come on. Concentrate!' It can be this ordeal.

"Sometimes I look at it really as economics. This for me, that for you. Then sex gets too technical—the trade-off. What I find sexist is, when a man is inside me, a lot of times there is this total concern with the penis, and what the penis is doing and how it's doing, especially as you get older. 'Oh, it's erect now! Let me do something with it.' If there is no concern for me, I want to tap him on the shoulder and say, 'Hey, buddy.' But I don't usually."

Marriage would appear to provide a safe, loving atmosphere, where two people can escape from the sexual circus and relax together. But that's not necessarily so. A forty-year-old financial analyst, married for fifteen years, says, "Hopefully, everybody has had those experiences, where the timing is just right, and things click, and the atmosphere is charged, and you're lucky enough to have an electrical storm. Where you just go into another state of mind, almost like you're seeing a universe of stars, where you forget where you are. Certainly, a wonderful thing. Certainly not the kind of thing my pop would have told me about.

"My wife would like to have that feeling all the time. Every time we have sex, she is always searching for the ultimate, sex as a spiritual experience. My feeling is that I'm inadequate in that. Everybody knows what the potential feeling of inadequacy in a sexual experience can do to you. For me, it's extremely denigrating being in search of the perfect orgasm all the time."

Some people are having better sex than others. There is no denying the advantages of experience and practice when it comes to sexual pleasure. But what are more important than spectacular technique and a cultivated sexual repertoire are a willingness to risk making a fool of yourself and the ability to talk about desire in plain language with your partner. Fear is the enemy of good sex. But fear can't exist where there is laughter and sincere communication.

Performance anxiety will ruin thousands of otherwise perfectly ordinary sexual encounters tonight. Afraid of their own simple impulses, worried about everything from their looks to being liked, terrified to tell another person what they feel between their legs, much less what they feel in their hearts, too many people will suffer through lousy sex, whether it's performed in the most basic missionary position or in costume with appliances and gravity-defying acrobatics. Thousands of women will fake an orgasm just to protect a fragile male ego, or just to get sex over with. Thousands of men won't even be able to get an erection. All of them will needlessly suffer frustration, embarrassment, guilt, and anger, most of which could be avoided if they would only relax and talk honestly about what they want sexually, and perhaps laugh a little at themselves and say, "That feels good. Do that some more, but a little to the left."

o o o

Most men are desperately afraid of women in the first place. It's something men should really address themselves to, their fear of women's anger, of women's withholding sex. I've often found myself very jealous and paranoid. In relationships, I became very possessive, the fear of losing this person that I fell in love with would overwhelm me.

The fear of women starts with Mommy first. Mommy is such a powerful image. Mommies don't need to be tyrants, but Mommies are very tyrannical in their own way. They've been given the role, so they become the autonomy and power in the household. They can make or break anything —when meals are served, when you get sex, what the kids wear. I'm not saying Mommy consciously abuses this power. It's just that adults inspire so much awe from children. Then when men get in relationships with women, that's what they see, not an equal—a Mommy. We see someone we have to please and bear gifts to. We have to walk up to her on our hands and knees and ask for forgiveness—a lot of these very religious elements, the Goddess kind of thing. We put women on a pedestal.

We really have to be equals. But it's harder for men to see themselves as equals on an emotional, feeling level with women. To say, "My feelings and my emotions are as important as yours in this situation. Let's put them on the table and talk about them. Let's share these things."

There's a certain amount of power—and I don't mean to use that word in a consciously controlling way—but there is a great amount of power that goes along with the part of the human species that is able to talk freely about emotions and feelings. For men that seems so magical.

To sit and listen to your mother, aunts, and sisters, your grandmother, sitting, talking about their feelings. Then you go into the other room, where the men are talking about the stock market and the teams doing this and that, and it's so artificial, it's so external and limited. It becomes all fact and figure, very cold and in order. To get into all that maleness, you have to give up a lot about who you are. You become the team and the corporation.

The woman is who she is. There she is, talking about the difficulty she is having with her husband, with *your* father or your uncle or your grandfather. You hear this stuff, and if you're open to it, you're not running to the other room saying, "Hey, Dad, they're talking about you again. And I'm one of the guys. I'm spying." You start listening to this stuff in the men's room and in the women's room, and you start to find out that you want to listen to what the *women* are saying. What they're talking about is more real, it's touching your heart. They're talking about what they're *feeling*.

But then who do you talk to about this stuff? Then you have to go and find other men to talk to. Then you're considered a wimp or a nerd or a dweeb or whatever they're calling us this week. Or you're an "artist." A dilettante. So there is a certain element of subjugation, because you want to be part of those emotions. Open that door for me. Let *me* into that world. The women control that door. There's a certain amount of mystical and spiritual fear. That's what I'm talking about: the Unknown.

Men spend their lives going to women for sex. I tell my girlfriend all the time, "You're a real control freak, aren't you? When you want to kiss, we kiss. When you want to go out, we go out. When you want to make love, when you're ready to have sex, we'll finally have sex. Do you have a date in mind? Should I write it on my calendar? It's fine with me. I don't want to be controlled. I don't mind the waiting. Just give me a date and a time, so I can pump iron, the new Chinese thing where I tie a barbell to my penis and lift weights."

That's nothing that women have to change about themselves. It's something men have to change about ourselves. As we become more aware of our own emotions and can express them, we will become equals. Then we can also say, "When *I'm* ready."

That's a real difficult thing for a man to say. "I don't want sex right now. I just want to take a bath. I've got a headache. It's my time of the month. I'm not in the mood." How many men say that? How many men don't just salivate when the wife says, "I'm ready."

"Okay! All right! Yes!"

One young man I go to lunch with—we're just good friends—I'm always fixing him up with young gals I work with at the bank, because he's not married. He was saying, "I think all men reach that point where they can't really have sex anymore."

"I want to tell you something," I said. "That's not true. Not all men have this problem. I don't want you to think that it's going to happen to you. It isn't inevitable. Believe me."

I do know there are women whose husbands this must happen to. There are women who are married to men who have real serious physical problems, and they nurture them and stay with them to the end. I guess you just have to shut off this part of your life, but I can't imagine doing that. That's where I think I'm different than a lot of people. If you go without sex for a long time, you do tend to put it way back in your mind, and you rarely think about it. But if you have some opportunities, and sexuality is reawakened in you, you think, "There's no way I'm going to live without this."

A lot of women sell themselves short, because they've never really experienced a good sexual partner. They don't think it's any big deal to give it up. I can understand why. But when you have a dynamite sexual relationship, who in the world would want to give that up till they bury you? God, it just blows my mind when you read all these articles in Ann Landers's column that say, "If they just cuddle, that's all I care about. It's no big deal. I wish they'd give it up."

Where have they been? And how sad that they must have such a shallow sex life that they don't care whether it continues or not.

We're not past that. How many women have faked orgasms? They're still doing it. That means they're still not experiencing it. The fact is that men are still not knowledgeable, men and women are not open enough, and women are afraid to be honest. They're afraid it will hurt the fragile male ego if the guy hasn't been just wonderful, and the star-spangled banner isn't waving up there over the bed.

It's a real tricky subject to talk about with someone that you're sleeping with as to what the quality of the sex is. It's like the story about the old lady who reaches over from her rocker on the front porch of the old folks' home and smacks the old man. He says, "What in the world was that for?"

"That's for being such a lousy lover all these years," she says.

He sits there quietly for a few minutes, and then he reaches over and smacks her.

"What in the world was that for?" she says.

"That's for knowing the difference."

In this day and age, people should *know* the difference.

I didn't even consider anything but the missionary position. I was so freaked out about sex that it was probably a year before my first girlfriend and I got more experimental. I found that I have great difficulty talking about my needs in sex. That's because of a total absence of any information. Nobody ever got me comfortable with the language of sex, "If you'll do this, then I'll do that." A couple of affairs I had were based on women who were really communicative about what they wanted, and that opened up a whole new experience for me. We could talk very graphically. Part of talking dirty is to get over the barriers of how tense the terms are, and be able to use them with some fluidity. That opens you up to address what you'd like to have happen.

It's an amazingly awkward and difficult period when you're learning about your own sexuality. There's got to be some other way to do it. So much of what I was about, unfortunately, was really trying to get the approval of my male friends to the exclusion of the women that I was with, and almost hiding my real needs from this woman for fear that it would jeopardize me with this group where callousness was what you talked about—who you used or what your score was. The whole deal was to try and get two women in one night at the same party. That really prevented a lot of open communication. It was not as brutal and callous as it could be made out to seem, but the orientation of where you were putting your interest and support was so misguided. What you were trying to do was to have sex, while keeping up as much armor as you possibly could. That doesn't make for great sex.

I was definitely a premature ejaculator for years, when I was first becoming sexual. I was a real mess, and I didn't know how to deal with the situation. I came in with a performance technique and a certain brutal ruthlessness which meant that I would participate, but not let myself go. Invariably, I would set up a self-failing mechanism. I would blow it. It was horrible, because you really are performing and under tremendous pressure. It was not until I lived in the moment that I realized that I could control the situation and make it better.

There was this enormous gulf. I just didn't get what women were after. All my guy friends and I didn't want to let go of our childhoods and admit that there were actually other people that we could care about. We "band of brothers" never could find our way out of it. In the group there was a couple of homosexual experiences from friends of mine which were totally shocking at the time, which now in hindsight aren't at all. In this insulated group, we thought we were the smartest guys in the world. We were doing a Peter Pan number to ourselves. Consequently, some of the more aggressive ones would really try to destroy your relationship with the woman you were with. It was very threatening to them. Try to humiliate you, watch you, bust in on you while you were having sex, pick up the other end of the phone when you were talking with her. It was really hostile stuff.

The point where I gained any maturity at all was when I realized just how insecure I am and became comfortable with that. My big take on the difficulty men and women have is that women really underestimate how insecure men are. There is that humorous dancing that goes on with both of you pretending that you're something you're not. When you fall in love, there is that great period you go through where you're basing your relationship on the illusions you have about each other. It's fantastic, it's all cloudless skies and fields of daffodils. Then that gets cracked. There is a point of disappointment. You have to try to accept the other person, and then you have a chance at a real relationship. The fun part is when you're fooling each other and yourself. Fantastic illusions about how clever, sophisticated, and in control you are. It was only when I realized that I have problems that I began to be easier, not only sexually but socially with women, and to do better with women.

Most of the women I talk to about their relationships with their boyfriends, invariably at some point, I have to say, "But what you don't understand is that the guy's insecure. He's afraid. You're attributing all these qualities and faults to him. The one attribute you're not considering is the one I think guides his behavior. That is, he's kind of freaked out, scared, and he doesn't want you to know."

I do this with my girlfriend all the time. I don't want to talk about the fact that I'm broke. I'm embarrassed by that, so I get really pissed off when a bill comes, and she has to tell me. All I want to do is tell her that I'm not doing as well in the business as I should be. I'm supposed to be the fucking provider and hold the whole deal up, so instead I say, "Don't worry about it. I'll take care of it." It amazes me. Even though I can be conscious of that, I go through that reflex every time. We're having a hard time of it, but if we weren't having a hard time of it we wouldn't be growing as a couple and as individuals. That's the whole deal.

When I was nineteen, I remember talking with a couple of girls and saying, "Do you know what an orgasm is?"

"Oh, yeah," this one girl goes.

"You mean, you really feel something specific?"

"Yes!" she said.

Another girl said, "Oh, yeah, there's something that really happens."

"Shit!" I said, "I don't know how to do it. I can't. I've never felt something specific. I can be all taken along in the emotion, but I've never felt anything real," or anything that was what I thought they were talking about. They couldn't really describe it, but I knew it was some muscle-releasing going on. It wasn't happening for me, because something that was indescribable was not happening to me. I didn't know how to get it. "What do I need to do to have that happen?" I had no idea and neither did my boyfriend. Kind of like the blind leading the blind. Although sex was fine for him, it was nothing special for me. I grew to not like it very much over those four years, just because I felt it was so predictable, and it wasn't very much fun. Sex was just kind of okay. No invention, no fun, no passion.

Until I met somebody that I worked with who I ended up having what

I would call an affair with, even though I wasn't married to my college boyfriend. I had a very strong physical attraction to this other guy. I really didn't want him as a boyfriend. It wasn't like I was crazy in love with him. We just liked having sex with each other.

I still never had an orgasm with this guy who I was physically crazy about. I was kind of going, "Maybe I can't do this." I didn't know what I was looking for. "Maybe I *am* having an orgasm and that's it. Maybe this is all there is, and everybody else thinks it's just great, and I don't experience it that way." That's kind of difficult to admit. "Oh, okay, uh, this only ruins the rest of my life." I remember thinking, "I'm frigid, and it's all my mother's fault, because she never has liked sex. Oh, my God! Sex is nothing! And I'm going to have to do this forever."

The sex with this guy was great, and part of that was that it was very secret. We'd only see each other at certain times, and that was the fun of it—making arrangements and sneaking around. There's something very intimate about holding that secret, just the two of you. But even with this guy I had the hots for, I didn't have orgasms. Nothing.

So then I met Richard, who is now my husband. As I got to know him I got more and more deeply involved with him, but I didn't really know how to break off that four-year relationship or wouldn't do it. It was a tough breakup. Richard was so cool through the whole thing. He didn't fly off the handle or try to force me to make a decision like, "You better choose him or me." He took me out to dinner, he was romantic, and it was a whole new thing. And I had an *orgasm* with him.

I remember vividly when that happened. I don't really know what he did to bring it on. Maybe it was just because I was into it as much as he was. When that happened, there was just that really strong muscle sensation. It shocked me. I thought, "Oh, my God! This is *it!*" I couldn't believe it. I was so excited, because here I was twenty-two, and I'd been having sex for six years and this had never happened to me. I was pretty thrilled.

"Okay, now, I've got to figure out how to do this again. Can this be duplicated?" Because I didn't know *how* it happened. Nothing seemed different particularly. There was no extended foreplay. I didn't know what had happened to bring it on the first time.

Later, I figured it out. I started to be able to feel something coming on, and I started really being able to tell how I could do this—"Here's a whole new world for me." It is something that you learn. Even with your girlfriends, you don't really talk about that so much. I haven't really.

Maybe some people do. You don't say, "Do you always have an orgasm? Is there any certain way you can have an orgasm?"

For me it is definitely a certain way. I can bring that on in a minute or I can make it keep longer. I'm in total control of when I want that to happen, to this day.

My partner—my husband—has to be completely still, and I have to be the one that moves. That brings it on. If he's moving, that does nothing for me, and I will not climax just from that. He has to stop totally, and then I have to move. Then, it's just the easiest thing. I can't believe how easily it happens to me. I don't masturbate or anything. I never have. I don't know why, it just never has interested me, never been something I wanted to do by myself. I just learned as I went along that this is what did that for me. Different positions, even if I'm on top, whatever it is, I can't do it any other way or it doesn't happen for me. Nothing else is involved except that specific movement. Foreplay or anything like that doesn't come into it or have much of an effect. I can just choose to do that whenever I want. It's nice to have that much control.

W hile I was in boot camp, I met all these guys from all over the place, and one thing that everybody was talking about was eating pussy. It was bullshit, and you know how bullshit is. I mean, I knew nobody would do anything like that. I couldn't imagine that. It was one of those things you talk about. I knew they had to be pulling my leg.

Then I transferred from boot camp to my assignment, and everybody up there is talking about eating pussy. I'm thinking, "These guys can't possibly be in on the bullshit from boot camp. What is this? Whew, that's got to be the most disgusting thing I've ever heard of."

I went home for the summer of 1961, so I was just about nineteen. Someone got me a blind date with a girl approximately the same age I was. The girl I had the date with, she was good enough to write home about. Beautiful complexion. Coming back from the movies, she just pushes me down in the backseat, hikes her skirt up, and proceeds to get astride me and just ride away. We weren't screwing—I had my clothes on —but nevertheless it was probably the most exciting thing to happen to me up to that point. Just aggressive sex, and I couldn't believe it. I imme-diately made a date for the next day.

That was a Friday night, so the next day was Saturday. I've got to have a car. *Got* to have it. We had a '59 Plymouth station wagon. But my dad had to work. He was the supervisor at a factory. I said, "I'll get up and go to work with you, and I'll come back and get you."

I had made this date for ten o'clock in the morning. I was ready, but no more so than she. I took him to work, I drive all the way across town, met this girl, and we proceeded to a rock quarry.

Jump in the back of that old Plymouth station wagon, and in a heartbeat our clothes are off. She really had this great complexion, this olive skin. I start kissing her breasts, which is not totally strange, but not well known to me. And she is going nuts. Her nipples are popping up there, and she's grabbing my hair and moaning and groaning.

I started thinking about all this bullshit I'd been hearing about eating pussy. All of these guys and forty million Frenchmen can't be wrong. My throat was getting kind of tight, and my mouth is getting dry, and my eyes are getting sweat in them. I start down her stomach. She is by now beside herself. There is nothing but the back of her head and her heels touching that car. She is making wonderful noises as I proceed down with little kisses.

I pass her navel. I've been to this girl's house, and it's a very nice, very well-to-do family. The people who introduced me to her are nice folks. I look at that navel, and there's lint in it. But I'm going to press on. I get down and I'm kissing all around her lower stomach, and she is in fucking agony. If I had made a ninety-degree turn, my nose would have been in her vagina. That's how close I was. I decided to go back and check that navel out again. So smooch, smooch, smooch, smooch. I look in, and by now the lint looks like a Dempster Dumpster to me. I think, "I hardly know this girl. If she has lint in her belly button, what in God's name does she have down in *that* place?"

So I went back up, sweating bullets. I chickened out. I get to her neck, and she just sags. I then try to screw her. She wasn't having any of that. I had taken her too high, and been too abrupt with her. She put her clothes on. My nuts are aching like they are in a vise. I take her home. My nuts were so bad, I couldn't walk upright. And I have to go and get my dad.

He was in a neighborhood tavern near the factory where he'd gone when he got off sometime before that, drinking with his foreman. He says, "What's wrong, son?" And I told him the story. He looked very serious. He really looked upset. He said, "Son, I really don't know what to tell you. Why don't you tell Jack here? Maybe he's got some advice."

So I ended up telling the whole story to this foreman with my dad looking very concerned. I finished the story, and this guy tried to look serious. Then he started to twitching. Then he started laughing. My dad started laughing. They were guffawing. They damn near fell into the floor laughing. You ever watch a dog that can't get laid, how he kind of walks just edging along? I'm doing that. Anyway, that was my first attempt at erotic gymnastics such as they were.

I'm an orgasm faker. I learned to do it even though I'd never had one, because you can see it in the movies. I started going out with my present boyfriend two years ago. We had a lot of sex when we were first dating. Then, in the regular-couples thing, it's pretty much tapered off. We don't have sex that often anymore. I still don't have an orgasm with him. But I haven't told him either. I feel bad about that. I've been faking it and lying to him for so long, I feel like he would die if I told him the truth. I'm really embarrassed.

I'm afraid it would hurt his feelings. He's really nice, and he's very concerned about me having one first and all this stuff. If I don't have an orgasm, he gets his ego hurt and feels bad. He really does.

Sometimes, I just fake one, because I want to get it over with. Isn't that terrible? Is it normal? I don't know what to do. I'm kind of stuck now. I don't want to keep on lying to him, but I don't want to hurt him. So I just keep doing it. I'm stuck in this terrible routine. Luckily, we only have sex like maybe twice a month, which is okay—really okay—with me.

I have never had an orgasm with a man or in intercourse. Only with the vibrator. I don't know what it is, really. People say that it's all psychological. What is the barrier? What is the big deal with me that's going on that I can't have an orgasm? I personally think that it's partially my fault with these men, because I don't say I need more time. If I were given more time, I would have an orgasm. But it's like people get tired. I get tired of it and want to get it over with. I'm not terribly excited.

Also this relationship doesn't excite me too much. I'm losing interest in this person. I'm not as attracted to him, that has a lot to do with it, I think—I hope. At first I was attracted to him though, so I don't know. I guess early on in the relationship it doesn't happen because I'm scared and nervous.

We've tried different things to spice up our sex. We have. We have. But that hasn't really helped. They've helped him, but they haven't helped me. We've done it in different positions, on different pieces of furniture, in different rooms. We've done the garter belt and the stockings thing. He's aware that I have the vibrator and everything, and he wants me to use it in front of him. I can't do that. It embarrasses me. I don't do that. We really haven't done any of the spicy stuff at all lately. It's pretty normal and routine now.

That's the one thing I really don't like about it. It gets to be such a routine that it's really not very much fun anymore. Just because I don't have an orgasm doesn't mean that I don't enjoy it when it's good. We just do the same thing every time, the same position. We do it this way, and then we turn over and do it that way. I would rather just kiss, lay on the couch, and roll around and kiss. But we get to the sex part, and it's not really intimate to me. It's not a lot of kissing and hugging and caressing. It's, "Get down to business and *do it*."

Making out was fun. I miss making out. It used to be fun when you were a teenager to sit in a car somewhere and make out. Maybe I'll have to suggest that.

But like I said, I've kind of lost interest in him and I'm not really attracted to this person anymore. I kind of don't even want to make out with him. I don't know what to do about this sex thing.

The first time we slept together, I was impotent. It's really odd. I haven't had this problem much in my life, but it's hard for me to actually perform well with her. We've been together four or five times. I don't really know what it is. I know she's had her doubts about us—maybe she doesn't turn me on, maybe we were meant for a nonsexual friendship. But I kind of assuaged her doubts and mine lately. Things got a little bit better. Still, I never had it so rough.

We talked about it at length the other night. Maybe it's because she's the first person I've really cared about in a long time. It may be easier to sleep with and perform well with someone you don't really care about, so you can't really make a serious mistake.

I was telling my friend Joel I was having these problems with impotence. He said, "Girls like that. It turns them on. You're a challenge for them. They have to make you get it up. You're not this mad, hungry sex fiend that every time she turns around you've got an erection." I think that he was right. I can see in this girl that she likes the challenge. It turns her on that I can't service her the way I wanted to. But you can't let it go on too long. They'll think you don't really dig them.

I had my first real sexual relationship when I was twenty-two. I really didn't care for sex nearly as much as he did. I thought he was oversexed, because he wanted to have sex all the time. He really did, and I didn't enjoy it. I never had an orgasm or anything. This is really embarrassing, I could kick myself that I didn't know then that this was really insensitive of him, but if he wanted to have sex, and I didn't, he would say, "Let's just have a quickie, since you're not going to enjoy it anyway."

"Okay." I always felt kind of used, but that went on for several years. I stayed with him.

The sex was just not as important to me as it always seemed to be to the men. They say that women just want to be held and all that stuff. I really think that's true. Sex is something that always comes up. I always go along with it though, pretend that I enjoy it even if I don't.

That was pretty much the way it went. My next relationship was two years later. Sex again just wasn't that big an issue with me, but it was for him. He knew I wasn't having orgasms. We *tried* different stuff, but it didn't work. I had never masturbated at this point, and never would have. I just thought that it was terribly gross. I wouldn't dream of doing that. He would say, "If you would, then maybe sex wouldn't be a problem. You could have an orgasm and you would enjoy it." I wouldn't hear of it. He would always suggest it, and I would always say, "No. I'm not doing that. That's gross." So that's the way it was.

Now I'm in a relationship, and it's still kind of the same thing, but I do masturbate. You know, one day about three years ago, I said, "I just don't think it's normal to believe this is something I shouldn't do." I wanted to do it. I wanted to have an orgasm, because I never had one before. I had thought maybe something was wrong with me. I was real worried about myself. Maybe I'm having them and they just don't do it for me like they do it for other people. Maybe I don't have a clitoris, maybe I just don't have one. I thought everything. I figured masturbating was going to be the only way.

I mustered up my courage and went to this big sex store right in the heart of gay territory. I was really embarrassed, but I went in anyway to buy a vibrator. I gave myself a pep talk before I went in there. "This person is never going to see you again. This is a huge urban area. This is what they sell for their living. They take this in stride. It's not like they haven't sold one to a woman before. This terrible experience is only going to last for five minutes. Just do it."

Turns out I wasn't embarrassed at all until the man said, "We have to test it to make sure that it works before you take it out." He plugged it in and turned it on. There were other people in the store and that was embarrassing to me. The funny thing is I've had a couple of girlfriends who have gone and bought them. They said that the man hasn't tested theirs. Maybe he wanted to have some fun with me.

I brought that vibrator home and used it. Right away, I had an orgasm, like *right away*. It was great.

"Okay!" I thought. "I'm normal!" So I was very happy when I had one. I still haven't had an orgasm any other way. But at least I have them.

I was a senior in college. I am by temperament a perfectionist. I come from an alcoholic family in which I was the fixer, the star, the one who was going to redeem everything and make everybody better. So here I am going out with some girl that I'm falling in love with, and, of course, I want to play that role with her.

The first night that we went to bed together, I thought, "I want to be really good." I didn't have an erection. It was devastating. That's one of the things men don't ever talk about. You don't find out that everybody has that problem at one time or another. I didn't have an erection, and I remember sitting on the couch afterward and just moping around. I went to the college infirmary and got this older nurse who just laughed and said, "Don't worry about it. You're fine." What I needed was, number one, a man who could say, "Hey, this has happened to me. I know how you're feeling. It's a bitch. And I've seen forty-five thousand other men just like you. Your worst enemy is trying to be perfect here. Relax, it will go away."

The girlfriend's reaction at the time was that she didn't want to deal with it. She was embarrassed. I was embarrassed. What I have to say truthfully is, I don't know *what* her reaction was, because I was so embarrassed I wouldn't say anything about it. We tried another time, and I did have an erection that night or another night, but it still bothered me, because it wasn't an on-and-off switch like I thought it was. And I was nervous about not being perfect.

That relationship didn't go anywhere. That was kind of the end of it.

I'm sure from her point of view that wasn't the problem, but for me it was, "Oh, I didn't perform so that was that."

That issue and that incident has shadowed my sexual life from that time on. I wound up going out with a woman I'd been seeing off and on since high school. She came over, and we started to make out. She said, "What's wrong?" I don't even know that she was saying that because I didn't have an erection, but because I was being so freaky about stuff. I was nervous, uptight, pulling away. There's nothing worse than trying to be intimate and you're supposed to be thinking about kissing this girl, and instead I'm worried about whether my cock is erect or not. It's hard to be passionate when you're keeping tabs on what's happening down below. Eventually, when I did have an erection, and I came, she said something like, "Happy birthday!"

Basically, that first incident scarred me. I never really got over it. Since then, any time I get involved with somebody, I'm always wondering, "what's going to happen this time?" I haven't had a whole lot of one-night stands where I just pick up some girl in a bar. This is not only because I am too sensitive and nice and interested in deep things, but I also have to say, "Do I want to share with this woman my failure?"

On the positive side, I've told myself, "That helps me be much more understanding about women's nervousness about going to bed." But in retrospect, this has robbed me of a certain joie de vivre that other men have, and a certain kind of mercenary attitude about scoring that I never shared. I'm not certain that I would have shared it anyway, but getting laid is not something unproblematic for me. Sex is not carefree for me. Instead of, "Oh, boy, pretty soon we'll be exploring each other's bodies," it's like the dread of, "Oh, no, we're getting close to going to bed. What's going to happen? Am I going to be okay this time?"

A lot of women don't even recognize, when I'm in this funk with them, that this is going on. They don't even give a shit. They don't care whether I've got an erection or not. A lot of women really like that they're not going to have to make love right away with somebody. I've had women say to me, "Look, let's sleep together, but I don't really know you that well, and I just want to get to know you better." I feel more empowered now to say that myself. "Hey, I'd like to sleep with you, and I think I want to make love to you, but let's just see what happens. I'm not sure that that's what I want to do right now, or if that's the best thing for us at this moment."

As you can tell, I've thought a lot about this, and I feel like I'm a little bit more free of it. What I realized is that I'm much more of a head person than a body person. So jumping into bed with somebody is not something that comes naturally to me. I'm somebody who wants to deal with people in my head before I deal with them physically. Part of it is that I need to be comfortable with a woman before I go to bed with her, and that's not the message I got in my upbringing. It was, "The sooner you get your clothes off, the better."

One of the realizations that I have is that I am a very sexual being. For a while I had this rap of, "I guess I'm just not all that sexual." When I was in one of these impotence funks, I could go for a year and not have sex. In fact, in the year after my first impotence bout, I didn't have *any* sex, I didn't have any *desire* to have sex. I didn't even masturbate. I was like dead, because I was so petrified that there was something wrong with me.

I really envy women their comfort with and acceptance of their bodies. Perhaps it's because they have periods every month. They know their body at this moment is not the same as it might be in the next moment. For me, if I'm not having an erection now, it's then very easy to extrapolate to, "Then this is the way it's always going to be. What if this is the end for me?" That really made me deny my own sexuality. It's scary.

So I feel like I've come through this in a way. I've spent a lot of years between the ages of twenty and forty alone and not getting laid. Part of that has been that fear about being impotent. I was looking at my dick, but it was the effect rather than the cause. This all came about from the isolation I felt from other men, from the women I was going to bed with, from my own psyche. For me to be able to talk about my experience like this is sort of a graduation exercise for me. To be able to admit this and to see it as a major characteristic—if not *the* major characteristic—of my sexual life is important to me. This is who I am. I don't really regret that it happened, and that this has been a shadow in my life.

I first knew what masturbation was when I was in my early twenties. I don't remember how I discovered it. My mother didn't tell me, and my friends didn't tell me. When I was a kid sometimes riding my bicycle felt good, and there were times where something would rub up against me like tight shorts. I knew something was going on down there. I knew technically that was how a woman orgasms, but I didn't know I could masturbate and bring myself to orgasm.

I was in college. My calculus professor was a grad student. We had sex a few times. Once we were having sex, and he said, "I really like it when women masturbate, and I get to watch them."

"Really," I said. I'd only masturbated once or twice at that time.

"Yeah. Would you mind?"

"Uh, okay." And I did. I liked it. He liked it. That sort of started it. I never felt that it was bad, or that it was shameful. It was just a piece of information I never had. I never knew about that kind of sex. I didn't know it was something that could be shared with a partner until Evan. I never had integrated it into my personal sex life, to masturbate on my own. But I learned about it, I did it, and I included it in my repertoire.

I really like it during sex when I masturbate or the man masturbates. I've gotten some resistance from men on that front, which I don't really understand. In some ways, I guess they feel like they're the ones who are really supposed to satisfy me. I'm not supposed to bring myself to orgasm. They'd rather be the ones to do it. But the men who like it, really like it. It signals a real comfort level with your body and with me and my body and with me taking control of my sexuality.

I do know that with these long periods in between a regular sex partner I've experienced the last few years, I started masturbating more. I'm sort of trained that's the way I come. My last regular sexual partner was last fall for about six weeks, but I had a more difficult time having orgasms with him when I didn't masturbate than I have in the past. It was just because of these long spells in between and me being trained to respond to that touch.

I was talking to girlfriends about this the other day, and I asked them, "Do you find you masturbate more when you're with somebody or when you're without?" I find mine goes in spurts. When I'm just becoming interested in someone, I'll masturbate a lot—that means once a day, twice a day sometimes. When it becomes more regular, my masturbation drops off alone, not including my masturbation with somebody else.

Then when I'm not having sex for a while, masturbation will just go away sometimes. I just become asexual. "Oh, yeah, okay, it's there. I can do it if I want." I'll masturbate maybe once a week. It's almost like I don't want to masturbate, because I don't want to be reminded. I'd rather have somebody else touching me, so I'll shut down and ignore my sexual self rather than be reminded that I'm the only one here bringing myself off.

But during those dry spells, there would be times where—Oh, God—

I would just go crazy for a couple of days. I'd watch a movie and see two characters going at it or something would remind me, and I'd go home and masturbate furiously for a weekend. Then it would go away again.

The first woman I had oral sex with also grew up Catholic. We were nineteen years old, and we were camping with a bunch of other people. She had come off to my tent with me. I had a crush on her for a while, and we pretty much established that we were going to spend the weekend together—without words, of course. There we were, yet we were both really reticent about having sex without birth control. We didn't have any forms of birth control given to us. So we had oral sex.

Even though at that point, I had given up intellectually that this was a wrong thing to do, I wound up eliciting guilt feelings by doing this, that there was something dirty and wrong about it as we did it. I could feel the pulls of that old guilt, even though I didn't believe that anymore. So I ended up having oral sex as much as possible until I got over that.

In my first marriage, my wife after once or twice or three times sucking my dick, she sort of gave it up. I find women will do that pleasurably until they think they've nailed you, and then it's cut back. I've found that to be statistically true. But she loved having oral sex performed to her, and literally of all the women I have known I could make her come like for half an hour straight. I could keep making her do it until she collapsed, but usually I'd settle for four or five times before I'd cut her off. But she could handle it ten or twelve times before she started saying, "Stop." Women, once they've really learned to have that really do get greater enjoyment out of sex than men. I also think it is a learning thing. As far as sex goes for a man, there's a difference between just coming and having a good orgasm. That's also learnable. You can learn how to extend the pleasure of sex.

Also there are blow jobs and then there are blow jobs. I had a girlfriend one time who said to me, "Can you teach me how to be really good at this?"

"Hey, sure." So for maybe five or six days in a row, I gave her instructions. She got to be just great at it. She had been okay at it, but with some feedback she just took off.

When I look back on my relationships, the girls that I remember most were good at giving blow jobs. That's probably the most erotic form of orgasm for a man.

My mother was divorced when I was sixteen in 1944. We became sort of like buddies. We would talk about things. At that particular juncture, most mothers and daughters didn't really have close enough relationships to have mentioned sexual things. But she was going out with men again, and faced with this, she talked to me.

One thing really struck me—and, of course, I always believed this for many, many years. She was dating this prominent dentist. He had a wife, but his wife was in a mental institution and had been for many years. She said that she really cared about Fred, but that he wanted her to do things that were "not natural." Of course, being sixteen years old, I was quite curious as to what was "not natural." It turned out to be that he wanted her to perform oral sex. She truly believed that his wife was in the mental institution because he had requested that of her, had forced his wife to do this.

How bizarre, in this day and age that is what they thought. Oral sex would drive you crazy. That's what my mother had been told; she believed it and passed it along to me. I thought it was really wrong. It was really bad. So I was all hung up on that sort of philosophy for years and years and years.

The only time my husband, after many years of marriage, would even think about performing oral sex on me was occasioned by lots of drinking and wild parties. He did perform oral sex a time or two, but only when he was drunk.

Let me tell you something—I couldn't perform oral sex either. It was so ingrained in me that I could not do that. We had been told it was wrong and bad from the time we were kids. You can't turn that off.

When he was drinking and would want to have oral sex, he didn't know how to go about it, and he refused to read about it like most people of his generation. He and I couldn't talk about things, because we still reverted back to our childhood where we couldn't talk about things. So I couldn't tell him what felt good and what I liked; therefore he would just kind of like push me to take his penis into my mouth. Now, nobody likes that kind of treatment. It's not rape, but it's unpleasant. You don't want to be pushed into something.

The only way that I finally experienced oral sex was with a lover I had an affair with. He was so gentle, so sexy, and so tender. He talked to me and explained to me that this is how it is, and we do this and do that. Let's try this and let's try that. Not everybody can be that kind of person and not everybody can be that kind of lover. I feel very fortunate that I found somebody like that to introduce me to other aspects of sexual behavior. I certainly never would have found out about them at home.

It's so sad that you can't experience that with your mate and grow and change. I don't know what it's going to take in this world for us to get beyond all of our hang-ups and be able to talk about it, tell one another what we want and need.

3. MAKING BABIES

Egg and sperm unite to conceive a new being. Most people idealize the creation of life as serene, natural sexuality. The reproduction of the species is the purest, most basic biological function of human sexuality. As a thirty-year-old mother of two expressed it, "I'm not saying that one is solely involved in creating life when they make love, but that sex is very special, special enough to produce life in itself. We can do that, we can be natural and make life."

In modern America, the proliferation of natural-childbirth techniques and the peer pressure propelling more men than ever to be present for the birth of their children have made most people knowledgeable about pregnancy and childbirth. But for all the emphasis on the words *simplicity* and *natural,* the entire process of making babies has taken on a confusing complexity in modern American society.

There are two terms that immediately enter almost every discussion of conception and childbirth these days: birth control and planned pregnancy. The technology of birth control allows Americans to plan pregnancy. The media image of the thoroughly modern couple is a clean-cut man and woman with two small children exactly three years apart. But the reality that comes across from talking to men and women all over the country is that although the majority of pregnancies do occur from unprotected sex, they're not exactly planned. A musician and composer in his mid-forties put it most clearly when he said. "The general rule of thumb is the more responsible you are, the risk of pregnancy is correspondingly higher from whatever form of birth control you're using. And sex without birth control definitely has more *frisson* than when using it. The less birth control you use, the more exciting the sex can be, and that's all there is to it. That's something human beings are never going to get around.

"Most people instantly know that they've made a baby. That's why I always find it interesting that people say, 'Oh, no! I'm pregnant!' Wait a minute. Of course, she's pregnant. You mean this is a surprise to you? You don't know how you got pregnant? People know what they're doing, but somehow acting like they don't know releases them from the consequences of their actions. They want to have the thrill without owning up to the consequences. Part of the thrill for me was that sex without birth control *had more consequences,* and I was willing to accept them. In that way our babies were planned, because once we started having sex without birth control there was no way I was stupid enough to be surprised someday when the litmus turns blue."

The genuinely planned pregnancy isn't necessarily a carnal picnic, as an advertising executive in her late thirties, pregnant with her second child, recalls, "It only took us five months, which in the scheme of things is not a long time, but for us it was nerve-wracking. Jimmy would come home from work, and I'd go, "Well, today's the day." Forget about enjoying yourself. Forget about foreplay. Let's just get this thing in there, and hope it works. After four months we were dreading the fourteenth day of the month. After a while I decided it was better not to tell Jimmy. I'd just put on all the sexy lingerie I had and not say anything. At least one of us should enjoy this."

Childbirth itself has taken on a special significance which may be unique to our age. Conception and giving birth are no longer considered just the normal, albeit rewarding, biological functions of reproducing human beings; making babies has become a sort of personal triumph. As a new mother of twenty-nine years old expressed it, "I sit around with these women at playgroup for our kids, and they talk about 'birthing experiences' like they were competitors in some professional sporting event.

" 'I had my baby in a birthing room without an epidural.'

" 'Well, when Jake was born, I didn't have an epidural or even Demerol at the end.'

" 'I had Maggie totally without the use of drugs, and we used a midwife.'

" 'I didn't even need an episiotomy with the twins.'

"It's incredible. Ninety-five percent of the women in this country *shouldn't* have any trouble getting pregnant or having the baby once they get pregnant, but the way people talk you'd think they invented live birth while everybody else was still laying eggs."

Incongruous as it may seem, along with the back-to-basics childbirth movement, there have been staggering innovations and advancements in reproductive technology in less than a generation: in vitro fertilization, artificial insemination, amniocentesis, fetal sonograms, microsurgery in the womb, surrogate motherhood, hormone fertility therapy, legalized abortion, the morning-after pill. Combine the inevitable ethical ambiguity of this high-tech wizardry with the present adversarial state of the relationship between the sexes, and the results are downright crazy. A vice president of the United States can incite a national brouhaha by criticizing the portrayal of single motherhood in a television situation comedy. Men are approached by female acquaintances with the suggestion of "recreational procreation." Women in their forties fly off to Central America to go baby shopping, while middle-aged bachelors find themselves spraining their backs keeping up with women half their age to make a baby they won't live to see grow up.

The source of all this controversy, ingenuity, and desire is that, for some ineluctable reason, making babies just *feels* so good and so right. Whether it's a modern psychological quirk or some primeval carnal conditioning, procreation is even more pleasurable than sex for sex's sake.

"I found making a baby on purpose very, very erotic," said a man in his early forties who waited to have children until he'd been married ten years. "After more than twenty years of being so careful not to get my girlfriends and then my wife pregnant, wrestling with condoms and diaphragms, sweating out missed periods—one week, two weeks—in an absolute panic, it was fantastic sex when we made love with every intention of getting my sperm and her egg together and to make a child out of them. Hell, if I could afford it and it was legal—and I could convince Katy to go along with it—I'd have five or six wives, and make all the babies I could."

A woman, fast approaching thirty and poised on the brink of a high-flying career, said, "Every time I make love with my boyfriend, I feel this sense of wanting to become pregnant when I have sex. At this point in my life, this is a strange thing. I don't want to have children yet. I have so many things I want to create. I'm just beginning to move forward with my career. But what makes sex so sexy is the life-force aspect of it. Creation, not of things, but of life."

o o o

The doctor had taken me off the pill, because I had real bad migraines from them. I had a diaphragm. At twenty-two years old, sometimes I used the diaphragm, and sometimes I didn't. So it was no surprise when I got pregnant. I'd been married three years at this point, and when I found out I was pregnant with her, I was embarrassed to tell anybody. Everybody would know what I'd been doing.

Six weeks or so after I had Leslie, the doctor measured me for a new diaphragm. I used it religiously. Boy! I had such a hard time having that baby that I wasn't going to go through that again any time soon. After about four months, I knew I could feel that damn thing inside. But I'd been so vigilant with the diaphragm that when I got pregnant with Heather, I thought she was an ulcer.

"Uh-oh," the doctor said, "the diaphragm was too big." My body had continued to change after he measured me. The diaphragm was then too large, and it had gaps in it, with predictable results. My first two children are fifteen months apart. People had the nerve to ask me if those two were planned, which used to irk the shit out of me. Who would *plan* to have two children in two years? But I did get the second one at a discount. The doctor felt sorry for me and only charged me half his usual fee.

Now, fifteen years later, I am married for the second time for only four months. We had been using foam, but I got allergic to all the spermicidal stuff. It makes me swell up—not all over, just in a particular place. Makes it real bad. So we quit using that and were just using plain old condoms, but just when we felt like we had to. This evening, I thought we were way in the clear. It was just after my period was over, so there should have been plenty of time until I ovulated. Ovulation must have happened on about day ten of my period. As soon as I quit bleeding, Bang!

This time I thought I was going through menopause. My grandmother went through menopause when she was thirty-five. I was thirty-seven, so I went in to be checked for menopausal symptoms. I also had a slight infection, so they were going to give me some kind of medicine for that.

The doctor said, "Just in case, by some weird chance you are pregnant, we'll check that, too." I thought, Yeah, right. Ha!

They dropped that little drop of urine on there, and it didn't take that thing two seconds to turn pink. She said, "Wow! Are you pregnant!" I could not believe it.

I never got a chance to "plan a baby." Never got a chance to *practice* to plan a baby. I always wondered what it felt like. I've heard people say, "We had sex every night for eight months, and still no baby." I would have sex, and it would be the only time that month, and the next thing I knew it would be, "Oh, no, I can't believe this."

We live high up in an apartment building. There's a window in the bathroom by the shower. It's always open a couple of inches. Whenever my wife would take a shower the morning after we had sex, she'd put her diaphragm on the windowsill. I was always telling her it wasn't a good idea. "It's going to fall out the window, Slim," I'd tell her.

This one morning, I came out of the bathroom and repeated that line, and she said, "Okay, okay." She walks into the bathroom, and then comes right back out. "That's not funny!"

"What're you talking about?"

"It's gone. You pushed my diaphragm out on the ledge."

"I swear, I didn't do it." Go look, and there's her diaphragm outside on the ledge below the window. "Don't worry, Slim. I'll get it." I went to the closet, got some tape balled up on the end of a straightened-out coat hanger to snag the diaphragm. I get back to the window, and the diaphragm is gone.

"What do you think happened to it?" she says.

"It blew off. Landed on somebady's head like a little rubber yarmulke. Probably fell in some businessman's coat pocket without him knowing it. His wife will get ready to send the suit to the cleaners, find it, and that'll be the end of their marriage. I don't know what happened to it. It's just gone."

She didn't go to the doctor and have it replaced. And she didn't go, and she didn't go. We didn't discuss having another child at all. But the night she got pregnant, we were playing around a little bit. And then it gets a little more interesting, and a little more interesting, and finally it's the old thing of, "What are you doing?!"

"What do you think I'm doing?!"

I tell everybody we had our second child because my wife's diaphragm flew out the window.

I never had morning sickness in the morning. It always started at three or four in the afternoon and lasted until I was finally able to go to sleep at night. I didn't feel like touching anybody. I wasn't interested in sex at all. Then one morning, I was laying in bed, and my husband opened his closet and I threw up. I said, "Close the closet, close the closet!"

"What's wrong with you?" he said. It was all that leather and shoe polish and his smells. He didn't like that real well.

At three or four months into the pregnancy, when I was feeling fairly decent again and began thinking we could resume our sex life possibly, I went in for the amnio and sonogram. They found out the placenta was low. The first thing the doctor said was, "No intercourse. Zip. Don't touch. You could punch the placenta, and this pregnancy is over."

This went on for a couple of months. By then I'm huge, so my husband did without for quite a while.

At the end of the pregnancy, I was just gigantic and at least a week or more late delivering. They say, "Have sex, have sex! That might stimulate the cervix and make the baby come."

"Oh, yeah! That sounds like a *great* idea. But, okay, I'll try. I felt sorry for him anyway. The closeness was nice. It was great to feel wanted and pretty and like a woman again after being just a big vessel for nine months. But it was uncomfortable, and there was no way I could have an orgasm. No way. And it didn't work anyway. I still carried that baby another week.

The best part about conception is working on it. The worst part is succeeding. It's good to succeed, because you get the kid out of it. However, all these books talk about sex during pregnancy, and that's pretty bogus.

The first trimester, when there's no physical reason to even justify cutting off sex, is when they feel like they're going to throw up on you all the time. Then they start to get big. Some women I am told get super horny at this point. I'm sure this is a great thing, but I can't testify to that. With my wife, not being able to see her feet did not make her feel sexy.

But their tits do get bigger, and that's a good thing, because you can still play with them until they say, "Stop that!"

Even after all this trying to make a baby, I was still shocked when I got pregnant. I sent Fred out for one of those home pregnancy tests. You add a drop of urine, and it was supposed to turn a certain shade of pink.

"Looks pretty pink to me," Fred says.

"I don't know if it's the right shade or not." So that same day I sent him back three times to the drug store for pregnancy tests. We went to the same store every time. I guess they see a lot of this—the women sit out in the car, and the guys run in to get another test.

Nobody talks about how great sex is with a pregnant woman. That's the greatest thrill of all to me. Making the baby only takes one shot, but then there's all this other stuff that goes on. The sensuality of the developing fetus. My wife growing this baby inside. Man, it's just a great feeling. Pride of ownership, I guess. You feel that way about the '56 Chevy parked out in the parking lot, but I like it a little better because you can go to bed with her. The bigger the better. Walk down the street with them, "See this woman? I did this . . . I think. At least, that's what she says."

That's the thing, once they get in that mood to have a baby, they're hard to stop, so you really never know. Then you get the old Big Bull in the Herd Syndrome, start saying nasty things to guys who've been your friends for life. "What you looking at my woman for? You know she's not wearing anything under there. I know you do!" You're walking around with a loaded pistol.

With my third child, I figured I had this birth thing down pretty well. After my last checkup, the doctor told me I was a few centimeters dilated, but it could be another two weeks before the baby was born. I went home and thought about that. The next day, I called him and said, "I'm in labor. Meet me at the hospital."

When he got there, I told the poor guy, "I lied. But this baby's been in there long enough. Snag my bag or something, and let's get on with this." He agreed to induce labor. I sat up there for an hour or two timing contractions and laughing and talking with the nurses. About the third time I pushed, he said, "I see the head. Here, you deliver it yourself."

During the next contraction, he guided my hands down. I just sort of hooked a finger under each of the baby's arms and lifted him out. I loved it. I'm ready to try for a girl with number four.

Sally was in labor a long, long time when they finally admitted what I'd known for two months. Just looking at her belly and then looking at her hips, I knew that baby was going to be too big. And he was. She needed to have a cesarean.

When they got to that point, they went on automatic pilot, just going through procedure. They gown you up and glove you. They take her off and shave her pubes.

There's a section in the birthing class that is about cesarean, but it's not enough. I don't know if they could give you enough. In the film strip, the father is sitting by the mother's head, and he has a partition between him and the action downstairs. No partition for me. You're there about two and a half feet away, and it's right at eye level.

The basketball tournament was on that night. These doctors are standing over my wife doing their thing, just chatting about the game.

"Jesus Christ! These sons-of-bitches!" was my first reaction. Then I realized, "This is the best thing I could possibly hear. It's like me and my friend working on a car, and we talk about the game. We know exactly what we are doing. It's just another carburetor overhaul."

Then I prayed they'd keep talking about the game, because I knew if they started talking about the operation, the thing was going off automatic. I want this to be easy for the doctors.

It's a pretty small incision. The bikini cut, they call it. It's maybe the size of a zipper on a pair of trousers, and they're going to pull a baby out of there. They get the head out. It's just this bloody pulp of a melon thing. Then they start trying to haul the rest of it out. They are literally wrenching the baby out of there. My wife is jerking, but she was doped up, thank God.

"It's a boy," and they hand him off to team number two who have been waiting in the corner. It seems the fluid in the womb was infected, and the baby can't be allowed to breathe in any of that stuff. They get around him, and all I see are *tubes* flying. Squeech, squizzle, suck, suck, suck. My wife is mumbling, "Is the baby okay? Oh, God, the baby's not good."

And I don't know. I really don't know.

What seemed to last at least a half hour probably lasted forty-five seconds. But during that time there is no crying, no breathing. They're not letting the kid breathe because of the danger. But I didn't know that until afterward.

Finally, when he was sufficiently sucked out, they incite breathing by making him cry. Your heart trips over like it never will again. They clean him up a little and bring him over. My wife had just gotten her innards ripped out and was really doped up, so they wouldn't let her hold him. She couldn't hold anything at that point. So I brought him close to her, so she could touch him.

Being a white, Protestant male, you have no real rite of manhood. They stopped putting blood on our faces a long time ago to signify that we had arrived. You get pubic hair when you're thirteen, but you have no idea what's going on. I will tell you this: Watching your wife bear a child by cesarean section will erase any doubt in you mind that you have achieved full manhood, particularly if you handle it well. You find things within yourself that you didn't know were there.

You always hear people say, "That was the best moment of my life." That was true for me. Giving birth is the most incredible act, having a life force that's right there. You meet your child at that moment. Here is something that you made. It's out, and you have it in your arms. That's the most amazing thing that one can do. You can make incredible artwork, you can write stories, carve sculpture, and do all these things, but *I can make a baby!* To this day, I think it's overwhelming. You look at that baby, and you see the skin and hands. It's an individual that is at that second who they are forever. You are just a part of it, and then it goes on.

Childbirth is really unlike anything. It's the only thing you can do really. It's so natural. I mean, so what we're really about, just that moment of creation and giving of life. It was so perfect and great.

Both births were easy. I didn't have any problems, I felt so lucky and blessed. I recommend it.

The other day, I saw this bumper sticker that was an antiabortion bumper sticker, but it made an impression on me, because it was very true. I have strong feelings about abortion. Not about whether abortion should be illegal or legal or anything else. It's just a big thing to do with one's life. But the bumper sticker said, "It's a child, not a choice." That's really the way I feel, that if you're granted this gift, you're responsible to have received that chance at making life. It's a big deal. It's the only thing that you can do in your life to make something that's so amazing.

Those kind of ideas are lost now. Sex is really everywhere in everything. Somewhere along the line, sex became a commodity. The spirituality of sex was lost. Instead of something you shared, instead of communication, sex became something you enjoyed, something you took. Everybody is responsible for their own orgasm. That is the really sad thing in our society.

My first real girlfriend I met in the summer of my eleventh-grade year. My parents didn't like her. She had a lot of problems, but she also had huge breasts, which is what I liked. That lasted about a year. I got her pregnant and took her down for an abortion.

At that age, you're really not that conscious of the pain. Now it would hurt me more than it did back then. Back then I didn't have the concern that I do now for human life, although I'm not antiabortion. Then I just knew the relationship was going sour, and I knew that I didn't want to end up with her. So there was never any doubt in my mind what the correct action, the right course should be. She was willing, too. She knew it wasn't right for us. She went and got tested, and when she was positive, she was pissed off.

I took her there. It was a cool place. I was hanging out with all the other guys. Just sitting there chewing the fat, talking shit. It was fun. We obviously have at least one thing in common, so it was communal. I took her home afterwards, and we had lunch. She felt sick for a few days.

It was an easy decision to make, because I wasn't fully cognizant of the moral implications of what we were doing. We both knew that we didn't want to have a baby together. She would have had the baby had I wanted to have one. But she had a lot of problems, and she didn't really want to deal with a kid. So we did it.

Basically, it finished off our relationship, too. It wasn't much longer after that we broke up.

I've been pregnant four times. I've had three abortions and one miscarriage. The first abortion and the miscarriage that I had, I didn't even tell the fathers, because I didn't like them enough to want them involved.

The third time I was pregnant was when I was with a man who I was with for several years. That was relatively early in our relationship. He really tried to be there for me, but didn't have the slightest clue how to support me through that situation.

This is not necessarily a trait of all men, but lots of men have a tendency not to talk about things. He would try to avoid it. I saw when his mother died that he just refused to discuss the fact that it hurt. That's how he tried to approach the abortion. Eventually, I found myself so frustrated with that I was just screaming and yelling and doing anything to get a reaction out of him. Which I finally did get. He broke down into tears, some sort of tantrum like little kids do. He finally just fell apart—for an hour—but then he was okay.

I wanted him to totally take care of every aspect of setting up an appointment, getting me there, and all that shit. I felt really sick, and I was already having to deal with it enough that I didn't want to have to call up clinics and doctors, research which ones were the place I should go. It just meant having to think about this thing more. I didn't want to think about it any more than I was already stuck having to think about it. I was sick all the time. My hormones were going crazy. It wasn't the first time I'd been pregnant, and the guilt was just incredible. He couldn't even take care of the minor details.

I certainly let him pay for it. I feel like I'm paying physically and emotionally, and I didn't get this way alone. Women shouldn't feel one-hundred percent responsible. I sure as hell know none of the guys I was with asked me before we had sex, "Did you take your pill today?"

Are we protected? is not a bad question. It's interesting how much of a responsibility sex is, how expensive it is trying to get protection, and the consequences, now especially because of AIDS. I used to wonder why would people do drugs when they could have sex instead. I find it's not all that dissimilar in terms of the bad outcomes you can have.

When I was younger, I had a lot of trouble getting birth control pills. I slid through the cracks in the system. My dad made enough money that I couldn't get help in a clinic with a sliding scale. I was still under eighteen, he was my legal guardian, yet I was getting no money from him. This was so ignorant, but I just didn't *know* at the time. I would try to spread out my pills by taking them right in the middle of my cycle, thinking that I would be covered. That's how I got pregnant the first time. I had a diaphragm that I must have worn wrong. I had a condom break. So you see I wasn't just indulging in unprotected sex.

The last abortion I had was just this last fall. I was tripping. I love my boyfriend and I wanted to feel open and free. But I can't believe that I did that. I had to have been tripping or I would never let my guard down like that.

One of my greatest fears is getting pregnant. I'm on the pill. I take it every day, but I'm worried even now, I'm such a paranoiac, that I'm pregnant. My breasts ache a little. "Oh, no, what did I do? Maybe the pills didn't kick in. Maybe I took antibiotics instead of hormones." I'm totally paranoid. It's a big fear. I don't ever want to get pregnant without being willing to go through with it ever again.

I wonder how those little souls think of me. I have lots of spiritual potential, but because of that I'm not really sure I'll ever be acceptable in some sense. I don't have a traditional view of God, but I really believe in some sense of God. The life cycle and Nature are special. I don't feel good about having had abortions. It also hurt a lot physically.

I've never known a man to feel shame about it. Maybe I'm wrong. The men that I've been involved with in this situation have not discussed their feelings about it. I've tried. Like this last time, I really tried to let him know what I was going through. "I'm really nauseous. That's why I'm just laying around a lot." Or, "This is such a terrible thing for me emotionally, that I need a lot of support." The male partner where somebody is having an abortion should be involved. He's needed. This man didn't feel connected. He didn't know how to relate to what was happening, and I couldn't seem to relate it to him or for him.

Here we are happily married, in and out of communication depending on what the circumstances of the year are—if there is money, is there not money? We're basically just shooting the puck there, and saying things like, "If we get pregnant, we're pregnant." No precautions. If it happens, it happens.

Me, I'm okay with that. I have that attitude that babies are fine. The more the merrier. I should be a lot more responsible about it. Is there money to pay for this kid? No. But I just like them. I don't have a clue as to why I like them. I just think kids are great. I'd like to have a whole flock of them around. Can't afford them, but I like the company, you know? I like my son a lot, like having him around, and another one would be fine. I know they're going to be different. Everybody's different. Still it's fine.

So here's Joyce, now she finds out that she's pregnant. She says, "What are we going to do?"

"What do you mean, 'What are we going to do?' "

"We don't have any *money,* we don't have any *coverage,* we don't have *anything!*"

My basic attitude was, you can't let money get involved with the picture here. It can't be a money kind of choice, because we'll always have the money. Somehow. I don't know how, but we'll have it. Maybe magic. You never have enough money anyway. It's not there forever, and it goes places.

Anyway, we've been talking about it for the last couple weeks. It boils down to we made an appointment to have an abortion. It was supposed to happen next week, but Joyce actually moved it back a month. She said, "Maybe I'd better take a month and think about this for a little while."

Deep down, there's this little twinge that gets me in my gut. It goes, "We made it, I want it, it should stay here." That's like the bottom-line kind of thing for me. "Hey, if we can't make this and keep it, then what the fuck are we doing together?"

At the same time, I actually sat down one night by myself outside and had a beer, had a smoke, and just reflected on everything that's gone on. I can kind of come to terms with the fact that she carries the child for nine months, and the responsibility is on her for that time. It's got to be a mutual decision. Not just mine. It's easy for me just to say, "Yeah! More babies!" Because I'm not squeezing them out there. But I like the idea of more family at this point.

That very needy girl I was seeing before I was married got pregnant twice and had abortions twice. I knew when it happened both times. I knew when Joyce got pregnant this time, too, even though she refused to admit that she was pregnant. I said, "You're pregnant. Last week, it happened. I just knew it!"

Anyway, those first two abortions, they didn't rattle me. I was concerned about her, but not concerned about it so much that I lost sleep over it. There was just no connection between us, no love connection. I didn't really feel like I wanted to bring a child into the world with this woman.

This time it's entirely different. This time, all of a sudden, I'm with someone I love. I have a family already. Things aren't going great, but they're not going bad either, so I'm sure we can manage in some way. It's put a whole different spin on the situation. There's a lot more to consider and reconsider and talk about. It's good we had this little consolation time to see what it is that we want to do. Hopefully, I'm going to be okay at the end of that time, whatever the decision is.

I certainly don't want our lives to be harder. I don't see it making our lives hard. It's not an obstacle to me either. It's more like a gift to me. "Here's another good thing in your life. You're going to have to work a little bit harder, maybe, and put things together a little bit better, but it's a fucking gift."

Modern technology is making life more complicated. My baby sister and her husband have been trying to get pregnant. She has to stay on her medication, because the epileptic seizures that she has would be worse for the child than the medication that she's on. Yet, she has miscarriages, and there is this huge incidence of spina bifida and all kinds of other abnormalities with her medication. The doctor said something like three in ten. That's a big risk.

Then this wonderful OB said, "There's nothing wrong with your eggs. There's nothing wrong with your husband John's sperm. Would one of your sisters consider being a surrogate to this child?"

So she hit me up with it this weekend. It really had never crossed my mind. We as a family had all discussed how badly we felt for Loretta. But this was like, "Uh, I'll have to give this some serious thought." She wasn't demanding an immediate answer. Would we consider it? So we're considering it.

My husband immediately said, "You wouldn't be able to give her the baby." Physiologically, I'm assuming that the surrogate mother's hormones are going to be raging and doing all the things like if it's your own natural child. You'd just have to know that there was going to be a real painful time when after giving birth to this baby, you gave it up. You would have to know from the beginning that it wasn't your child and wasn't going to be your child.

It gets very complicated. What do you tell your children? Mom's pregnant, but she's not really pregnant, and it's really not going to be your sibling. It's just going to be a *really* close cousin.

I'd have to go around with a T-shirt on that says, "No, I am not crazy enough to have four children. This is my sister's and brother-in-law's child." You'd have to offer everybody an explanation about something that shouldn't be anybody's business. You can't hide a pregnancy for nine months. That would be a little unrealistic in my life. You'd just have to tell everyone what you were doing, and you'd have to be secure enough in what you were doing to not really care what anybody's remarks were.

You get into our neck of the woods, and it's so conservative. Fundamentalism is running rampant. There would be that whole side of my friends who would say, "Morally this is wrong. It wasn't meant for your sister to have children. If God meant for her to have children, she would. And if He means for her to have a child with spina bifida, she should be proud and thrilled to raise this special child without concern."

My husband was real open about having a vasectomy last year, so we're going to have to send out a mass mailing or something. "When you see me at the grocery store pregnant, do not be afraid to ask me about it. Don't chuckle behind my husband's back."

The surrogate doesn't have to be a family member. Most people who do this hire somebody to carry the child. To me that seems morally more wrong. At least, I'd be his or her aunt. Paying someone, you get into all those ambiguities. Are women going to pay someone just because pregnancy interferes with their job and they don't really want to take a year off to be pregnant or to feel bad? I think it's wonderful, the things that technology has allowed us to do, but I also think that Americans have a tendency to be lazy and find the easy way out. If it's easy and money is no object and you pay someone forty thousand dollars to have your child, just because it's kind of an inconvenience, then to me that's a totally different moral issue. For my sister to pay someone to have it, even though it's just because she's physically not able to, those dollars exchanging hands seem to complicate the issue for me.

You'd like to think that between sisters you wouldn't have to have any sort of legal documents, but I think you would. You'd have to draw it up real unemotionally at some point. If her husband divorced her or one of them died, then it could become an issue somewhere down the road. What if I flipped out after the baby was born? I don't even know if it's legally their baby from the very beginning or if they have to go through adoption procedures. You'd have to resolve all that.

So life is getting complicated, just when I thought it would settle down. I was teasing her that this was just real typical of her to get someone else to do all the work, and she gets all the credit. We need to make sure her husband really doesn't have a problem with this, that it wasn't just something that she talked him into.

I picture the whole family in the labor and delivery room. Rick, you stand here next to me. Bob, you're the father, you stand over there. My sister would be at my side. Mom and Dad, come on in! We might as well have the grandparents in here, too. Maybe my husband could skip it. He's kind of the odd guy out. That's why he said, "Do I have to seriously consider this?"

"Yes, you do."

"I was afraid of that."

"You've got to give this one some serious thought." He certainly needs to give his opinion, and it would affect his life, without a doubt. But he's kind of a swing vote, the way I look at it. I don't think his opinion should weigh in as much as mine. In other words, if I was ninety-nine percent convinced that it was the right thing to do, and he was pretty shaky about it, it would be hard for me not to try to convince him. It would be hard for me to dismiss it, just because he felt uncomfortable with it. Women are weird when they're pregnant, there's no doubt about that. He'd have to live with me afterwards, too, if I flipped out. But at the same time, I'm not sure that he should get an equal vote. We have to put a percentage on his vote. "You come in at thirty to thirty-five percent. If this is close, we might take your vote into consideration."

One of the things that's been disturbing me lately is that I have had in the last couple of years women approach me to father their children outside of my relationship with my girlfriend, which is very long-term. They tell me that it's going to be anonymous. I've had proposals from women who are really flipping out. They want to have a child really badly and can't seem to figure it out.

Wow! Is that a temptation! Recreational procreation. The idea of sex for procreation. I think the best sex is done with procreation in mind. I think there's a real difference if there's the possibility of making a baby as opposed to recreational sex where you know we're going to get off and that's all that happens.

I find it really wild that this has been happening to me. I'm sure that I must be signaling them on some level that this is an acceptable thing to say to me. Maybe I have been more intimate with them than necessary.

It's also really indicative of how kind of fucked up things are that these really attractive women can have this happen to them. It's a condemnation of the age that beautiful, intelligent women are unable or unwilling to make a relationship work and make babies. I don't know why they're not hooking up with the right guys, and it really freaks me out.

It's sort of flattering to be approached in this way, on the one hand. But on the other hand, it's not flattering at all. It's degrading. The degrading part is that it is assumed that it would be easy for me to do this for them anonymously, that I wouldn't want to see this kid, that it wouldn't be a part of me, that I wouldn't be wanting to hold the child and send money every month. In equal measure, I don't believe them when they say that I would be anonymous. For one thing, they're going to go through this hormonal thing, so as far as discretion I don't believe them for a second. And how would I live my whole life as a lie with the woman I'm with? What do I tell my girlfriend? If it was a test tube that would be one thing, but that's not the offer I was getting. This *Murphy Brown* thing is just bullshit to me. I'm really surprised that stuff goes on. The whole thing is sad.

I want to have a kid by the time I'm thirty-five: that's because I don't want to have a sixteen-year-old when I'm sixty. I don't want to go through adolescence with them then. I want to enjoy my golden years. No biological clock really, just a logical projection.

Right now, the job I'm taking, switching careers, that would probably be the most important factor, whether or not I could afford to have a child by myself. That's the way it's going to work. I'll never find someone to marry me with three cats, that's for damn sure. I don't feel any pressure from anybody. My mother's always been after me *not* to get married, and I don't particularly want to get married at this point in time all that much. Ideally, I'd meet some Rockefeller guy who needed a marriage of convenience and marry him. He could go off and do his thing. I'd go off and do my thing. I could spend the money. That would be perfect for me.

Can you imagine being with a woman who decided, "I'm going to have a Nobel Prize baby by going to the sperm bank." Am I supposed to feel insecure about it? What if that was happening more frequently, where artificial insemination became something like DNA manipulation of tomatoes. We men are going to have a hard time, because basically we thought that the attraction of us was the rough, blunt way of penetration.

Women may get more critical about that and say, "You did a great job on my body, but really what I'm looking for is something a little more intelligent. You're too low on the food chain for me, pal. I'm looking for some really good father material." That's another thing that would absolutely split the atom as far as men are concerned. I don't know how men would cope with that on a widespread scale.

My only regret about being gay is that I want to have a baby. I love children so much. I still may. I don't know how I'll do it. I don't know if I'm equipped to do it. I have had men who agree to have a baby together with me. One guy who's gay but clean. Of course, we'd check him out before we did anything. But I don't know if I could actually go through with the sex part. I've never had sex with a man. There's artificial insemination, but for some reason that reminds me of Frankenstein. It's like science scares me. I'd rather have a baby in the natural sense. Then, there's adoption. If I can adopt, maybe I will when I'm financially able. Even adopt an AIDS baby or a black child or any child, just so I can raise someone who can carry on *me* some way.

I hate that feeling. I don't want to be an old lady without anyone. I want roots, and I don't have roots. That bothers me. That's the worst thing about it, that I can't carry on me. If I die, there'll be nothing to carry on. Not my family thing—*my* thing.

There are a lot of children in my family that I love and take care of. But I can't depend on them to always be there as my children, because they're not.

It's not some biological-clock thing that has only recently started nagging me. I've always loved kids and love being with children in the pure sense of it, because when I'm with children, I'm free. No one is judging me, no one is asking about my sex life, or my this or my that. I love children for that.

"No." My first answer was, "No, I don't want a vasectomy. You get your tubes tied. Get out of here! I'm not getting a vasectomy. Suppose something happens to you, I meet a younger woman, and she wants babies? I want to be ready to go." I still kind of feel that way.

She went, "Harrumph!" But you know, everything I say I get the har-rumph. And likewise, she doesn't say too many things that don't get a harrumph from me. We're kind of witty like that.

But getting a vasectomy, man, seemed like it ended that sower-of-seeds imagery that I have. This is my mission on Earth—Seed Sower. The Baby Maker. Here he comes, baby! Spread your legs. It's the Baby Maker, the Baby Man. The Baby Man Can. God, what would I do? What would my function in life be if not to bring joy and make babies? I don't know. What would I possibly do?

There is no intelligence behind this. In fact, it's complete ignorance, but I actually think, "If I get a vasectomy, I'll be an old guy, and I won't be able to do things or think the way I think now, because part of my body will be changed *forever*. I won't be able to make more babies." Isn't that weird? This is stuff I read articles about years ago in my late twenties, about how some of the people felt that after they had a vasectomy they weren't as much of a man anymore. I said, "That's ridiculous. You want a vasectomy, you get a vasectomy." Here I am now, thinking those very same thoughts about how it's going to change me and my image of my masculinity. Suddenly, I'm going to get a very high voice and hang around with the boys' choir.

There's a problem. He's older and has three grown children. The last one was a big problem kid. He loves this life that we've created for ourselves where we can pick up and take off at a moment's notice, and go to whatever country we want, so he's resisting it. I said to him recently, "What would your life be like if you didn't have children? How do you think that you would be? What kind of person do you think you'd be if you didn't have children to enrich your life?"

"You're absolutely right," he said.

"Then how could you ask of me not to have what you have. I want to have that experience, too." You can never really quite say the reasons why you want to have them. The reasons that you shouldn't have them far outweigh the reasons that you should have them. It's hard to put into words, but I really want to have children. I'm wearing him down on that. I think he's going to come around. It's very hard.

I'm the type of person that plans things. I'll fantasize about the way it's going to work out. I create these situations in my mind, and I set out to get them. The way that this one will work is that he will be there in the background, but it would be my kid. It would be me doing most of the work, me doing the three-A.M. feedings, this and that. I would really take the driver's seat with the baby. I don't want to have expectations of him that he can't fulfill. If he seems like a father who's there, but not really there, not a totally participating parent, I think that I could accept that, too. I understand that I'll have to put out a lot more energy with a child than he will. I feel okay about that.

He says, "It could never be like that. I could never take a backseat. I would have to be active—I *would* be active." But that remains to be seen.

I have this idea that we conceive our child in a hot-air balloon. We're renting a house for the summer, and as we're driving back last night, we saw this exquisite hot-air balloon in the air. So as a wedding present to Robert, I'll take him up in that hot-air balloon with a bottle of champagne. And if there's nobody else in the balloon, maybe we can make a baby right then. We'll see.

There is one thing I get sort of wistful about when I see it. I go to the park and see roughly-the-same-age parents together with their child, enjoying the child. I'm envious of them that they're going to do this together. The guy or the woman could drop dead or get hit by a car tomorrow, but for the most part those people are going to have a relationship, and they're going to have this child together. They're the same age range so they'll go through life together. I wish that could happen to me. But, it's not going to happen, so what am I going to do? And that bond that you have when you have a child, I hope that I'll be able to have with Robert, but I have a feeling that it's going to be different for me.

So you miss certain things that a normal relationship might have. *Normal,* whatever that means. Maybe *conventional* is the right word. Who knows? Maybe those people I envy go home and fight about bills and whack each other on the head. It's just some sort of fantasy idea that I have, that fairy-godmother thing about the prince in shining armor and the princess, the happily-ever-after syndrome. But, you got to eat your ice cream while it's on the plate. You've got to get what you can get from life before it isn't there anymore. That's what I feel like I'm doing with this guy. Fuck it if he's dead in twenty years. He's great right now and twenty years is a long time.

THREE

Sex drive

1. FREAKS LIKE US

When acquaintances find out that I worked for sexually oriented magazines in the late 1970s in New York, they often ask me to tell them what was the kinkiest thing I saw during the fading years of the heyday of the sexual revolution. Three tableaux I personally witnessed always come to mind. All three have to do with some variation of sadomasochism, since that was the sexual fad of the hour.

There must have been twenty S&M after-hours clubs all over New York. Two colleagues and I were invited to review the opening of a new club —Mistress Pain's Dungeon Deluxe. The club, in the middle of a long crosstown block in a warehouse district, looked more like a boarded-up storefront than a nightclub. The most sadistic thing about the place may have been the booths and tables, banged together out of plywood by some journeyman carpenter and painted flat black. It was impossible to sit comfortably. At irregular intervals tufts and patches of shockingly red fake fur were pasted to the benches and walls.

A shy, middle-aged man, wearing glasses with those plain gray plastic frames clerks everywhere seem to prefer, offered us a drink from the bar, then explained that really he only had a few bottles of beer. The lights came up on a small stage with a set that reminded me of the backdrop of the *The Honeymooners* on television in the '50s.

Mistress Pain herself, a dead ringer for the overweight witch in the Bugs Bunny Halloween cartoons with the same lilting cackle, presented a brief but erudite college-level lecture on the long history, correct materials for construction, and proper use of the cat-o'-nine-tails.

Next came the sex show. The lights came up on a young blond waif dressed in a cross between her underwear and a high-school majorette uniform. She looked like a flat-chested Julie Andrews in *The Sound of Music,* especially her haircut and her smile. She danced like a hippie at an outdoor rock concert—eyes half-closed, feet rarely leaving the ground. Suddenly, beside her on the stage was a pale, paunchy fellow dressed only in his jockey shorts and wingtips. He looked strangely familiar. It was the bartender without his glasses and missing most of his clothes. He threatened the waif in broad pantomime, but in the end he was tied to a chair and slapped playfully with the cat-o'-nine-tails. Obviously, the waif hadn't learned a thing from Mistress Pain's lecture series. The record began to skip, playing the same four notes over and over.

The second scene took place in a much more upscale S&M club with spiffy dungeon decor, a full bar, and the S&M cultural elite in attendance. The occasion was a bondage demonstration presented by a husband-and-wife team from somewhere in New Jersey. He owned an auto-body shop and restored classic cars. She was dressed in a merry-widow corselet, garters, and stockings, but the piled-up perm and over-size designer sunglasses said suburban real-estate agent or insurance-office receptionist.

The spotlight in the pit threw a ring of light on a ten-foot-high stepladder. The mechanic positioned the receptionist against the ladder, and then went about the job of choosing just the right leather straps from his attaché case to secure her wrists and ankles to the rungs. Head down, with a craftsman's concentration, he took a long time to find just the right tools for the job. Meanwhile, she carried on an animated conversation with the club owner who stood nearby—as animated as one can be with one's wrists tied to a ladder. For the finale, the mechanic, with a practiced flourish, bared the receptionist's breasts and began to drip wax from a fat red candle onto her chest, while she explained in a chatty insider's whisper to the owner that the first few drops were a little warm, but all subsequent hot wax only fell on the layer of drippings that was already in place. Her bosom shook with laughter, which cracked the wax and sent bits cascading all around her high heels. The owner swept up around her feet with a push broom so none of the patrons would slip and fall. With a sigh, her husband began again to get the wax finish even.

The last memory is a young man I recall as Pony Boy, after the children's song. I saw him late one night in a small disco. He was dressed in jeans, cowboy boots, and spurs, but instead of a shirt he was wearing a wool horse blanket and a child's pony saddle on his back. His eyes were hidden behind mirrored sunglasses. He held the bit and reins in his teeth.

Bending at the waist with his hands on his knees, he went silently from woman to woman on the dance floor, offering them a ride, a masochist in search of a mistress to ride him hard and put him away wet. From time to time, a woman would take a chance, put her foot in the stirrup and climb aboard. At first, she would be a haughty equestrian, kicking her steed's flanks and pulling on the reins, laughing and waving to an admiring crowd. Pony Boy would buck and grind, dance and gallop to the pounding music.

As the ride wore on and on, song after song, her face would change, and soon she was holding on to the pommel for dear life, unable to climb down until he stopped, unable to make him stop. It was hard to tell who was taking whom for a ride.

Rather odd kinky stories. All three took place in public, none of the characters took off all of their clothes, none of them actually had sex. Each story begins with the stock conventions of S&M erotica with the all-too-familiar props, but then the standard plot is totally undermined by the fact that real people are playing the parts. Their humanity interferes with the story line. Their fallibility, their unpredictability, their fears overcome the banality of their fetishes and make the stories more intriguing.

This chapter contains the confidential stories of people who have been obsessed by sex and their personal sexuality, for as little as a few hours or for their entire lives. A few of the people who tell their stories here are truly seekers, some merely wanderers through life bushwhacked by circumstances, a few more or less willing victims of someone else's compulsion. With two possible exceptions, any of these men and women might actually live next door to you, and you'd never know.

Strangely enough, television talk shows have become the only popular forum for examining actual human sexuality in public, especially more extreme, explicit expressions of sex. The emphasis in the publicity for these programs is on "real" people, "real" events, "real" emotions. For the most part these people *are* real. There are very few fakes or self-promoters—besides the authors of books—on the talk shows. But with the insistent prodding to spark the interest of a more and more jaded audience, information is slighted in the interest of high emotion and entertainment value. The tone of these programs has changed from controversial to confrontational. The normal people against the oddities, the center of the cultural carpet against the fringes. Those of us in the television audience, safe and anonymous, think we're better than the guests on display, who have become slightly less than human simply by choosing to participate. They are freaks in an electronic carnival side-show. We are horrified, disgusted, titillated—and we eat it up.

The people in this section of the book are not here to get you hot and bothered, or to be pointed out and laughed at. Neither are they selling anything, pushing a particular philosophy or advocating alternative life-styles. In fact, the majority of them are oblivious to the forces that are pushing and pulling, squeezing, bruising them through life. Full of their own prejudices, stumbling along in the darkness of their own blind spots, they are not all "nice" or "misguided" or even sexy. Whether you like them or agree with what they have to say is not the point. The point is, they are like us, except perhaps that most of them are more honest with themselves and the world about who they *really* are sexually, and what they have done and would do, and what they *really* want.

Sex is a funny activity. We all look a little odd in the heat of passion, sweating, limbs akimbo with comic animal noises coming out of our mouths without our conscious control. We all have our secret desires, whether we play them out in real life or not. You know exactly what yours are, and I know mine. All of us have certain words or motions, specific body positions, geographic locations or articles of clothing that can make sex excruciatingly good. And we all know how quirky, theatrical, "dirty," or embarrassing sex can be. Consciousness has made us all freaks of nature.

Although the details of some of these stories are quite bizarre because of some fetish, a twist of fate, or a personal idiosyncrasy, what I find most fascinating is how "normal" these people are. They are not porno-graphic geeks. They are human beings who talk a lot about love, and feelings, about the sights and sounds and smells of sex and of day-to-day existence.

These people have gone to extremes when most of us would blanch and step back. That doesn't make them less than human. In fact, we faint of heart may be the ones with our humanity stoppered up, for better or worse. Using their explorations and self-exposure as a guide, perhaps the rest of us can extrapolate the true depth and power of our own sexuality, gauge the noble and venal limits of our mysterious human condition.

o   o   o

I was born in 1943. I was brought up in a Jewish background in Brooklyn, Flatbush Avenue. Went to Erasmus High School. Conservative upbringing. My sexual ideas were very naive. My parents never mentioned sex to me, whatsoever. I had no sex education. I didn't really even know how it operated, when it came right down to it. At twelve or thirteen years old, I heard the word *scumbag*. That's what they called condoms. I thought maybe you piss into the scumbag, and it went into the woman some way, but I really had no idea how it all worked.

Later on, I started to go out with girls. When I was fifteen, in 1958, we used to dance close; we'd do the Grind. The girls would make believe that they don't feel your dick getting hard on their leg, you would pretend you didn't feel anything, and the two of you would bob and grind.

I always used to come by rubbing on a girl. I would masturbate on their legs a lot. Sometimes they would know. Sometimes they weren't sure, because I would try to cover it up a little bit.

I did go to Forty-second Street to see what was going on. I bought the books. What happened to me, though, which was strange, I always wanted to get the *dirtiest* books, the most explicit books on sex when I was fifteen. I didn't know what I was looking for. When I would go into the stores, there were certain books that were always wrapped, and others that you could look through. I always went for the ones that were wrapped, because I thought they were going to tell everything, instead of a lot of suggestive stuff. But I found myself buying bondage books, not the regular hard-core porn, but TV books—*Transvestite Tales*—only the kinky stuff.

I would read the whole story about some guy getting dressed up in girls' clothes and being dominated, and I wouldn't even know where the punch line was. But I kept on buying these books. I don't know if that hooked me. Eventually, I started to associate these things to my sexual being. Of everything, that would be the only beginning I could see, these books.

At seventeen, I met a woman—not a woman—a *girl* in high school who was fifteen. We started to go steady. For some reason, which I still do not know today, even, I started to ask her to do things for me. I don't even know where these things came from. I had no predilection toward these things previous to that. I started to ask her if I could wear her panties, if she would tie me up. I asked if I could wear girls' clothes. The first time that I tried this it was a thrill. I don't know why it was a thrill myself. And I said, "Well, let's try the bondage thing." I found it just as thrilling. All of a sudden, I was involved.

Now, I felt terribly guilty about this. Don't forget the conservative background where the idea of just being gay wasn't in my vocabulary. Gay is queer and being a fag and a jerk in my mind. A gay guy was a scumbag— "Yuck, a fucking queer, man." The only gay people that I really saw was we used to have screaming mimis, drag queens, doing women's hair in Brooklyn. These hairdressers would be very feminized, very garish and flamboyant. To me, that was gay. What the hell did I know? I didn't really know nothing from nothing. When I started to want to wear panties— heavy conflict! Very heavy conflict. I didn't know where I was at. Number one: I didn't want to be a queer. I looked down in that direction, so why would I want to be that type of person?

I knew I was something, though. I didn't know what, and I didn't know how to ask. I couldn't even ask my friends. It would get around that I wanted to wear panties. I'm there playing football. I was on the swimming team. In college, I was on the wrestling team. I didn't tell anyone.

So for many years, this was a secret between me and this girl. I ended up marrying her, so for thirteen years, the only other person that knew was this girl.

She basically loved me, or said she loved me very much. She got very attached to me. She really did my scene for *me*. I know she didn't enjoy it, or she *might* have enjoyed it if I enjoyed it enough. But it was always a big source of contention. I hate to say this as a joke, because I come from a Jewish background, but do you know what Jewish foreplay is? Two hours of begging. With this particular thing, I really had to like threaten to leave to get her to do my scene, even though she knew this was almost a condition of the marriage. It wasn't like she wasn't aware of this. She knew this was something that I demanded.

Basically, what I liked was to be tied up in girls' clothing, lingerie. Not to be a woman. I'm a fetishist. I have no desire to be a transsexual, no desire to pass as a woman. I don't even like to be in public as a woman, because I have no desire for men. When I'm dressed as a woman, I'm looking towards a woman, so for me to dress as a woman and go *outside,* it doesn't make sense. Even though I don't pass, I imagine I would attract men more than women, even though I probably wouldn't attract either. I look bad in drag. But I like the feel of lingerie.

The primary thing that enveloped me, the thing that really has motivated me most of all in this whole genre, is the ability to convert pain into pleasure. When I was in this type of drag, I would set up an illusion in my mind, and through this illusion and the feeling of being submissive, I was able to convert pain—*physical pain*—into pleasure.

A lot of people who take pain do exactly that, they *take* pain. Later on, they might masturbate to their illusions, but while it's happening, they are not excited. They may be excited before the actual beating, as a punishment, but not from the actual pain. My pleasure came from the *actual* pain, to the extent where I had to be careful. I did not know what was happening to my body. If I would "frenzy"—in other words, I would get totally into it—it would just be total pleasure, so I could really get very, very bruised and beaten, and I wouldn't really know it. "Wow, look what happened over here! This is a black-and-blue. These are two-week marks." After a while you know what marks last, which don't. "This is just a one-day red mark. This is a little deeper. Oh, there's a deep black-and-blue. That'll turn green and then yellow, then disappear. These are two-week marks."

So I decided that I had to keep away from things that could give me really permanent marks. I never really wanted to be mutilated. I was always proud of my body. Even today, I'm in fairly decent shape for a forty-nine-year-old. I can still do a handstand, I can almost do it one-handed. I do a lot of push-ups. I have no scars on my body. So to people who say, "You're really killing yourself, you're really beating yourself up. Look how destructive it is." I say to them, "I'm forty-nine. Take a look at my body. I'm in great shape. There are no marks. If it was going to kill me, I should have been dead already. Football players have broken knees, and fingers, and shoulders that don't work anymore, but because they're getting paid, it's normal. If it's for money, you can kill yourself. But if it's enjoyment, then you're crazy."

Because my scene was the Big Secret when I got married, my wife had it over me. Because I wanted what I wanted, I would almost have to live her lifestyle. I started to associate with her friends. I became very conservative. We used to go over for coffee and cake every weekend at someone's house. I got into antiques. I didn't like the lifestyle. I was always a searcher. She just wanted me to settle down and be a nice Jewish boy actuary. Do my job in the insurance company. Come home. Act normal. That was what was satisfying to her.

The actual physical stuff, acting out the fantasy, she had a lot of trouble with. She did it occasionally, like once every few months. She didn't want to hit me. "Am I hurting you? How can you like this?" She couldn't believe that I was enjoying it.

"Don't worry about it. I like it. Can't you *see?*"

"Aren't I hurting you? This is no good."

"I like it. Don't tell me what it's doing to me." It was constant. She was constantly telling me how bad it was and how bad for me, and I said, "Hey, it feels good to me."

What she did do was a lot of stories. She would tell me stories at night, while I'd lie on her, or if we had intercourse, she would talk to me—"I'd like to dress you up," etc. So that was satisfying enough, and once every couple of months, after a lot of cajoling and threatening, she would go along.

This woman said she loved me. She would do anything for me. I'd come home, and she would scratch my back for an hour. She would massage me. She worked in the daytime, and then she'd do the cooking. She catered to all my needs, except this one thing.

"Forget about the cooking," I said. "You don't have to clean the fucking house! I don't need a massage! This is what I want," and I would slap myself on the chest or arm or somewhere. "You want to make me happy? This is it."

Couldn't get it. I was locked in. She was the only one that was privy to the Big Secret. I told nobody. I was embarrassed by what it was. I knew no one similar to myself. Over the years, even though I saw books at Forty-second Street, I never saw anything relating to this type of action in reality. But I figured, "It's in books. It must exist somewhere."

I was so nuts, I used to try to search out where it was. I looked in French corset shops. "Maybe they're doing something in the back room over there at Madame DuBallet's Corset Shop. Maybe they're changing men into women over there." My fantasies were running wild. Yet, in reality, looking back, it was all fantasy. Nothing was really happening at the time. There were no clubs then. I graduated in 1961, and I got divorced in 1972, so in that time there was really nothing around. I would imagine it, but I never found anything, which made me feel more isolated, more alone, and more stuck.

I don't know what my wife thought. I'm guessing now. It's not fair to her to say that she thought she had me by the balls, that now she could say, "Okay, I've changed you in this way and that way. You're conservative here. You're conservative there. You're acting real good in all these areas. Now, I'm going to pull the plug and bring you all the way in."

But at the end, I wouldn't say that it was the only reason we got divorced, but it was a major reason. As far as I was concerned it was the primary reason. She didn't want to do it anymore. She said, "It's not right." When she pulled back on the S&M, when she pulled the plug, I said, "That's it."

I started to cheat on my wife. I had never cheated. I was a faithful guy from seventeen to thirty. And she was the first girl I was ever with. I started to have an affair with my secretary at work, which was not an S&M relationship per se. It was just crazy, because I was still married. I think I used this woman as some sort of lever to make me feel comfortable outside in order to break up the marriage.

My wife said, "Where were you?"

"I was working." I'd give her the excuses. Like three or four times a week I was with the secretary. What we would do is have straight fucking. The thing with her was, she was seeing another guy, her boyfriend. I really fell for the secretary, and I was always in pain with her. I was stuck with the wife, and then I would see her. Then she'd run off on the weekend to her boyfriend, and it would make me crazy. But I couldn't say anything, because I was married. Yet, I would start putting the pressure on her—"You can't see this guy!" I said I would get a divorce. The windup was that she quit and went to Europe for about two or three months. I did get a divorce, but by the time she showed up again, it just wasn't there anymore. That pain I couldn't convert.

When I say I convert pain into pleasure, there are only specific types of pain that can be converted under certain conditions. I had to have my illusions and my conditions satisfied before I could really get into this. If I went to a dentist and he started drilling my teeth, there's no way I was going to convert that into pleasure. Say, if I was with a girlfriend that I really cared about who was a female dentist, and she tied me up and started to punish me doing my teeth and kept me in a sexual state, there'd be a good possibility that I could convert the pain into pleasure.

After the divorce, I decided that I was going to do *whatever* I wanted to do. No holding back.

One of the first things I did was I found someone on the street. A street hooker on Twenty-eighth Street. I picked her up, and I said, "What I want you to do is just tie me up as tight as you can, and then whip me." She tied me up. She took this metal clothes hanger and made like a whip out of it. The first *whack,* the outline of the hanger was on me. I couldn't convert any of it. Nothing. Nothing. I couldn't submit. I didn't know her. I couldn't *love* her. See, in some way, I have to want to give it up. I didn't want to give it up to her. I couldn't convert.

"WAIT A MINUTE! STOP! NO-NO-NO-NO!" I yelled.

Thank God, she stopped, because I had told her not to stop. I said, "Look, if I scream, don't stop. I like it."

Sometimes, I pretend in my little girl's voice, *"Oh, no. Stop"*—a pretend stop. "Oh, it hurts, it hurts." And moaning. But that time I was like, "OH, NO, YOU'RE KILLING ME!" She let me go, and didn't mug me or nothing. She had me tied down there in this hotel. I was crazy. I was so compelled, I'd even put myself in that type of situation.

That was a good lesson for me. I learned that I couldn't do it at random. It taught me about what I was really feeling. I have to really submit, I have to start really wanting to get into this feeling of being small and loved. Through that method, some way, it works. I still don't know really what the method is.

I went to visit my brother in Illinois. Coming back from the airport, I was rolling down Third Avenue and I see a transvestite hooker standing on Thirteenth Street. I said, "Okay, let me see what this is about." So that's how I first met this girl Dahlia. I call Dahlia "she" even though she wasn't a full sex change. I didn't have that much sex with her. I just fucked her in the ass. I never really looked at her genital area. It was like I didn't want to. I'm basically straight, even though I've had some gay experiences to see if I would be gay, because, you know, dressing up in girls' clothes I wanted to check it out; maybe I was gay, right? One guy tried to talk me into it. I said, "Okay, let's try." But I couldn't get turned on by a man's body. I'm so into femininity that I want to be surrounded by soft skin, soft perfume, nylon. That's what I like. It's not being with a rough-skinned, bearded guy. My turn-on is women and the whole feminine thing, maybe so much that I want to be feminine.

Dahlia was like a caricature of a woman. She didn't walk, she strutted. She wore these really high heels. Her makeup was exaggerated. And that's what I liked. She dressed like the porno book from Forty-second Street.

I'm attracted to that look, the high heels, stockings, garter belt. Who knows why?

I hooked up with her, not financially, even though I did give her something the first night. But then she started to take me to all the transsexual clubs that I didn't even know existed. This is all for transvestites who were out and transsexuals. One of the first places I went to was the Gilded Grape. It was on Eighth Avenue between Forty-second and Forty-third streets. I was in there trying to figure out who these people are. They were transsexual hookers. There were a lot of people of color, lots of Spanish, Puerto Rican. They would dress up, hang out at the bar. Straight guys come to pick them up. What I didn't understand at the time, because I was into my own thing, was that most of these straight guys were getting fucked up the ass by these transvestites. A lot of them still had dicks. Later on, I discovered what all these scenes are. You figure the guys're paying for a blow job or paying to fuck them in the ass, but a lot of them were getting fucked up the ass themselves.

Then there was the Club 220 Houston Street. It was infamous. Four floors, three or four in the morning things would start happening. I've seen rabbis, straightest people in the world, all types of people at these clubs, which opened my eyes.

I was still extremely naive. I had a view of the world when I was married that had nothing to do with reality. Everything had an answer, everything was cut-and-dry. Now I have no answers. At best, I try to take care of myself. That's hard enough. If I can't figure out myself, how could I figure out others? You can't figure yourself out and you can't figure out someone else either.

I didn't have that much dominance with Dahlia. It was very hard for me to get her to do things. She was real self-centered. I tried to get as much information out of her as possible, but not my sexual scene. Once, I fucked her, but she never really dominated me. It seems I needed much more. I really needed to fall for someone in order to convert this pain into pleasure. Love was the key. There had to be this desire to submit to someone.

Now during this time, I'm still working and wearing a tie in the office. I had become a partner in a consulting firm. I was the inside man. I was responsible for the paperwork. The guy who really owned the business —he had all the clients.

Then I met Sally. She was a dancer on Forty-fifth Street, and she wanted to get away from that life in the topless clubs. She was trying to get out of that and back to her daughter. After she got her divorce she'd come to New York from the South. She was blond, pretty, Protestant—all these things I knew nothing about.

At the beginning, we went to Florida. She really opened me up. She would grab my cock in the car as we were going driving. She'd say, "Let's stop here, go into the woods, and do something." I mean, I was still that kid from Brooklyn with this straight view of the world, who had basically only been with a very conservative wife. Sally was open. "Let's do this. Let's do that. Let's have fun."

The first time I told her the Big Secret, it was a big deal for me. For her, it didn't bother her. She didn't care. Sally was so different from my ex-wife. Of all the people in my life, Sally is the one I loved the most to this day. She was unselfish. She didn't demand much. She did my scene with me every day. She used to sew little outfits for me. She used to send me cards in a girl's name. And she did the bondage. She was really in love with me.

But even that I started to abuse. She did care at the end when I became a glutton where I wanted it every day, every moment. As soon as I came home, it became all-consuming. No matter how much was given to me, I always wanted more. If I felt in ecstasy by getting dildo-fucked for one hour, I wanted it for two hours. I'd come, day in and day out, ten, twelve times a day, and yet this girl, I started to push her to much further limits than my ex-wife, because Sally would do everything. I wanted very tight bondage. I got into enemas, even, and dildos, which I wasn't into with my ex-wife. "Dildos are dirty! Yuck!" But Sally would do everything, and I was very compulsive.

She stayed home—she didn't work in the day—smoking pot, waiting for me to come home. Then I wanted her to do the number. Since I can convert the pain into pleasure, she was whipping me very, very hard. I'd get these huge bruises. She would see black-and-blues for a week, two weeks—it would scare her. The whipping was the only thing she had trepidation about, because she saw what it did to me. Not only that, she knew I wasn't going to stop her. No matter how much. I was so in love with her, there was no amount of pain that I couldn't convert. She'd be whipping, and I would be in ecstasy, just screaming with pleasure. I'd be *out there*. She didn't understand it. I still don't understand it. *No one* could understand it.

All of a sudden, I'm not feeling it as pain. It's not tolerating pain. People will tolerate pain just to be with the other person. They're submissive. They say they're into pain. I'm into pleasure. The slap that would give a normal person a pain reaction—I get a pleasurable reaction from it, so I'm into pleasure. People say to me, "What do you mean you feel pleasure?"

"To me it feels good."

"No, no, you're setting up your mind."

"I swear to you, as painful as it feels to you, that's how pleasurable it feels to me. I'm not negating the pain. It's not something I'm putting up with for future pleasure. It's the thing itself, the feeling itself. I'm enjoying it right then and there. You can see I have a hard-on. It makes me come."

I could get whipped and come. I can be in bondage so tight that everything is turning black and blue, and I'll have orgasms. Once I have the orgasm, then it's, "Come on, get this stuff the hell off," especially if it's real tight and digging in. After orgasm, give me five or ten minutes to rebuild, and I can get into another cycle. That was the case. I wanted too much. I always gluttoned myself out. I do it every time.

Sally would go off on alcoholic binges. She'd like vanish for two or three days, even though with me she wouldn't drink. The first time she disappeared, I was fit to be tied. "Where is she, where did she go? Where the hell is she?" Then two days later, I get a phone call, "I'm on Forty-eighth Street. Please come and pick me up."

I'd go pick her up. "Why did you do this to me? I was frantic." I didn't understand this type of behavior yet. Then one time, she went out and she just never came back. She disappeared, and I didn't run after her, and she never called. Then I was devastated. Then I couldn't find her. I looked all over for her. I cried for about six months. I didn't do anything for a year or so.

As time went on, I found out everyone is from a different planet. This one is from Venus. This one is from Korrack. Everyone is in their own world. But I was a seeker. I wanted a cause. I wanted to be honest with myself and about myself. I was converting pain into pleasure and that was a big thrill for me. It was from within me. I was going in this direction no matter what anyone else did. This was part of my being.

I decided to do this extensive interview about my sexuality with pictures and my name in *Hustler* magazine. It put me in a forced situation where I couldn't go back to the old world. In my mind, I knew after doing that article, I did make a break. In some ways it was a deliberate step I took to make sure I couldn't go back to my ex-wife's world.

After that article appeared, I had an aunt—eighty-two-year-old woman —who called up and said, "Did you really put shit on her face?"

"What, Aunt Gladys?"

"Well, I saw the article. Cousin Stanley gave it to Cousin Larry who gave it to Cousin Harold who told me it was on the stand through Aunt Jessica. So I send my friend down—who's seventy-six years old—to go get the *Hustler* magazine article, but they wouldn't sell it to her. They asked her why does she want such a magazine? So she said, 'My friend's nephew is in it.' "

She was a good aunt. The whole family was shocked, but she was interested. She accepted it. Still, that article was very heavy for her. "Did you have to use your real name?" A lot of the family hasn't talked to me since. They didn't talk to me much before that anyway.

Because I wasn't a liar, the next woman I got involved with knew exactly what I was into. In fact, Mary saw me do my thing as a demonstration in this sort of off-Broadway show. We talked and started going out. She chose me for whatever reasons, but she knew what I was. Mary was a beautiful girl and nice to me.

Looking back, I should have married her. But I didn't. Now I wouldn't mind. Now I'm very lonely; my parents both died in the last year. I'm alone and I need someone who is really going to cater to me. I'm not looking for a dominant bitch to beat up on me. I need someone who cares for me, who's going to do what I like for me, do my scene. But I couldn't make a commitment then and eventually I chased her away.

After that point, I decided that I would go out with a different type. I didn't go out with a nice girl. I started to go out with more bimbo types. But also ones that liked me. I could only deal with women who fell for me. Otherwise, I couldn't convert the pain.

It was conquest. I would put out the idea of marriage, the nice apartment. I have money. They would come up, and I'd throw out this temptation for them to do my scene, but at the end I wouldn't come through with the permanent relationship. I had everyone on hold thinking that they're going to score if they stuck in. I went through a whole bunch of women: Pamela, a very nice girl I saw for a few months. Then Gail a few months, then another one and another one and another one. When it came time to get married, they all wanted to. That was my cue to split. I would pull the plug, and I would come out financially cheap, emotionally distraught. Because you pay. You always pay, especially if you want something. You pay more. The scene gives a hook. When you're involved with someone who satisfies your fantasies, the involvement moves very fast. You get hooked into the person faster and deeper.

My scene seems to be necessary. It's something that pushes me right to the core of my being. For instance, there are certain books, certain pornography that I have for twenty years now. The same book, the same story —I could look at the same passage that I've looked at thousands of times and it is hooked into me so much, in one minute I can come. I take a book out with what I like to see, and it goes right into the core—boom boom boom! I'm hot. It's happening for me.

My fantasies are so set. Basically, it's having to be made into a young girl—that's the basis of it, being made into a young girl and punished. Through that scenario, everything is possible. Then the punishment could be whipping, bondage, eating her out, dirty sex. I'm into urine. I'm one of the few who will go for almost anything. I'm an equal-opportunity employer. People say, "Enemas? Anyone into enemas?"

"Yeah, I'm into them."

"How about dirty sex?"

"Yeah, I'm into that."

Anything between heterosexuals I'm into, as long as I feel I'm doing it because this person wants me to do it, and it's part of the punishment or part of what they enjoy, or part of my submission.

I knew in my heart that I was at an impasse. S&M was an impasse. I knew that if I couldn't figure this out, or in some way accept it, or make it work for me, or get through to who I was, I was going to go nowhere. Even if on the outside it could look like I was going somewhere, I was going nowhere personally as a human being until I could bypass this sexuality thing, or incorporate it. Actually, I've spent my whole life trying to figure it out. Unfortunately, I haven't figured anything out. I grew. I feel I grew in the knowledge that people are what they are, and maybe there *aren't* any reasons. At least I accepted what I am.

I learned, number one, that I'm an individual. Number two, there's no cause out there. Everyone is into their own thing. I realized, "Let me just deal with my own problems." What I like to do, I don't like to do in public. I'm a conservative guy, and my scene doesn't lend itself to public viewing. I act silly in the scene, like a thirteen-year-old girl, who is stupid and giddy. I walk around curtsying. It's not something you want to do in front of a bunch of strange guys, or even women you don't know for that matter. It looks ridiculous to them. Then lifting my skirt and getting dildo-fucked. "Ooooooo!" It's my own personal caricature of a scene. It's not reality. Why should people see me like this? I'm not doing a show. People come around at the Hellfire Club, the wankers are standing there wanking off around you. They still wank off around that joint. So I said, "Let me get out of it."

I'm looking for a nice girl. I would like to be married. I'm very lonely. I would like someone to be around if I get sick. I don't mean just to take care of me, but when you have the flu, a friend comes over for a half hour—"Hello, goodbye." I want somebody to sit by me, and hold my hand and bring me some soup. I'm going to be forty-nine and I want that. I don't want to just drag in another woman if I'm not going to marry her. I'm really looking for monogamy—the right one. I don't want to jump in again and get hurt. I can't tolerate the pain of breaking up anymore. It takes a lot out of me, especially if I really fall for somebody and get involved in the scene.

Because I've been alone, I had to make do without women. I got into psychosexual scenes with myself. I started to do a lot of stuff at home. I was getting so intense with it that there came a point where I didn't want to do it with people. A lot of things I have trouble talking about, because it's so crazy that I almost feel if people knew what the hell I was doing, they would like, you know, put me aside. But all in all, I've always maintained. I still have my business. I'm still living decently. I'm not falling apart. It is some sort of controlled craziness.

Not being with a woman for the last several years, and still wanting to get inside myself, I've been doing like these bulimic trips where I would be eating a lot and throwing up. I'd order six or seven dinners a night, throw them up, do the dildoes, right? Set the mirror up, dress up and look in the mirror. Masturbate and make believe I was dominating myself in the mirror.

"If you're not good, you're going to get it!"

"Oh, oh! Stop it!"

"Yeah, I'm going to give you all sorts of . . ."

"Oh, no-no-no."

Looking at pictures and making believe that the pictures are dominating me. If I smoke a little grass, it enhances the feeling and gives me the ability to empathize a little more, create the illusion. Actually try to make it believable, where I actually can believe it's happening when it's really not.

I'm not really out of it in another world, or anything. If the phone rings, and I want to answer it, or I know a call is coming in that I want to get, I can stop immediately what I'm doing—unless I'm all tied up where I can't reach the phone. I can grab the phone, and "Hi, how are you?" I'll just take the dildo out of my behind and talk. No one would be the wiser. Hang up, back into the illusion. So it's more of a controlled craziness. I'm not over the limit. I'm still in control.

Now I want to expose myself a little more, because of my spirituality. I'm not really looking for anything from anyone else. At this point in my life, I'm really trying to give more. I'm not looking to take.

I feel real honest. I don't have an ax to grind. I'm not looking to get into someone else's business. Now that this is exposed, I can expose the other aspects of my personality without fear that if I'm scrutinized they're going to find out about the S&M.

I want to be out in the open. This is what I am. I didn't want to be like this. When it came right down to it, and all these feelings started to pop up, I didn't want this. This wasn't a matter of choice. This was me. Who wants to be labeled as a transvestite pervert? When I was a kid, I looked down on even gay people who weren't doing anything like what I am doing. I'm doing things much more intense. But I was looking down on myself, feeling guilty. "What am I going to do? What is it from? It must be because something bad happened in my childhood."

How come no one ever says, "Oh, the reason you're into S&M is because your mother loved you very much." I've never heard of that excuse. Or, "Your parents were so good to you that you decided that they gave you the ability to even change pain into pleasure, they were so positive." People are always looking for negative reasons for why you're into this. Nothing bad happened to me. Nothing great happened to me. I am what I am. I'm just trying to accept myself.

I want to find a decent girl that I can live with the rest of my life, to fit into my lifestyle in every area, from my work, to going out and having a good time, to being in bed and the sexual preference that I would like. The way I'm going to get this is to offer a woman other things: companionship, loyalty, love, my ability to give and take advice. That's what I have to offer. Sexually if I can get satisfied in there, I'd be very happy. But I'm really looking for more of a lifetime-achievement thing.

My sexuality is something that I'm always struggling with. I hope I won't abuse it next time, I won't be too compulsive. I won't be too greedy. If one is good, two is better. If two is good, six is better. If six is good, let's try for twenty until it gets bad, going on until it turns sour. I can't do that anymore. I don't *want* to do that anymore. I'm just gearing up again for the next bout. I hope I'll come through decently as a human being. Yet, I don't know.

I finally did get a divorce, and I married this other guy. Unbeknownst to me, he was a drug addict and he was a wife abuser. I stayed with him for fifteen years. The first seven years before we had any kids, we partied. He was one of these guys who doesn't like to do drugs alone. One beer is not enough. Two beers is not enough. A case is not enough. If you're doing coke, one snort is not enough, and it progressed through the years.

At first I thought so little of myself that I went along with it. We just got involved in all kinds of things. Sex became a thing with him like his drug habit. The ultimate end wasn't ultimate enough, so he would keep striving for more. He wanted me to sleep with other men. He would just suggest this was something I should try, and then we would talk about it. At first, I was scared, because he's the jealous type. Why would I want to do that?

It all started when we met this guy, and I don't know how or why, but we ended up going to a motel as a threesome. My husband didn't have a bad reaction to it, so I decided this might not be so bad. I had felt really bad about running around on my first husband. After I left, I saw that as something I shouldn't have done—"Look how I've hurt him. I shouldn't have done that." So then I had the fear that somebody would do it to me. But once we were into the threesome thing, I thought, "Now, I don't have to worry about that. I can have my cake and eat it, too. Go out with other guys without having to worry about it."

We used to go riding. We'd be drinking, and we might start in Pennsylvania and end up in Ohio. We might pick up a hitchhiker or somebody, and I'd have sex with him in the car while my husband was there. That's how he got off. We did that for quite a while; then we moved to Florida and got involved with this group of wife swappers and started going to the swingers' clubs.

I did outrageous things. I got involved with an escort service and was a prostitute for a while. He used to take me, drop me off, and pick me up. It was a deal we did together, and he got off on it. "Come back, and tell me what happened." After a while I got burned out. I met a lot of girls who were prostitutes because they didn't want to be who they were, they ran away from home, they had low self-esteem, and all that goes right along with it. The one thing I remember the most about them was how hard they were. They hated men. They felt very used, and yet they kept doing it over and over. I always thought to myself, "I don't want to end up like that. I enjoy sex."

I wasn't being made to do it. I got talked into doing things, and I advanced just like he did into how much more I would do or what else I would do.

At some point we got really strung out. We'd work during the day, and then stay up all night doing speed and going to the swing clubs and doing this escort-service stuff, until it all ran together.

I was getting beat up quite a bit. He was physically abusive—oh, yeah. When he came down off the drugs it was like World War III. I worked, he didn't. I stopped off on the way home and bought submarine sandwiches and came to the apartment. It took me too long—what was I doing, sucking somebody's cock? And the subs went flying out, and the house got torn up.

I got gonorrhea when we lived down there. I went to the doctor, and my husband was so mad. He's the one that's telling me that there's something wrong here and you need to go to the doctor. He wouldn't go to the doctor, but he'd send me. And, yeah, I had contracted gonorrhea. You can take penicillin and get rid of it, but he was so angry. It's like I did it on purpose. I'd say, "We're doing this together. You can't blame me." There was a lot of verbal and mental abuse along with the physical abuse.

When we left that state, it had just about worn me out. I was supposed to be going on calls, and I was supposed to be having fun, and I've got bruises all over. I started feeling like a prostitute off the street. I just kind of tuned out. I was burned out drugwise, sexwise, and otherwise. I had a lot of black eyes. I got hurt. I never ran into any cops. I never had real bad experiences—just businessmen or kids down for Spring Break. It was him who was beating me up.

We moved across the country and didn't get too involved with the sex stuff out there. After seven years of marriage, I got pregnant, and we told everybody, and everybody was supposed to be happy. Then he decided that he wouldn't have a party partner anymore, so he didn't want me to be pregnant after all. He stayed after me and stayed after me, and beat me up once or twice, until I went and had an abortion.

I got real depressed, so four months later he decided that it was time to have a baby. So we had a baby. We ended up having two kids. Things got worse and worse. We moved from job to job and town to town, getting fired because of our fighting and his drug habit. By this time, sexually, don't ask me for sex. If you want it, you can take it, and that's it. If you're not going to be nice to me, then I don't want anything to do with you. But he never understood that. He took it like there's something wrong with him, and of course that made his ego worse. We never discussed much, and I was pretty much frigid by then. I didn't like it, I didn't want it. Don't touch me. Don't talk to me about it. Don't even look at me. Get away! Get away! Get away!

He was smoking crack constantly. When he didn't have it he'd go crazy. All the doorjambs were cracked. He threw a beer bottle and shattered a sliding glass door. I might be in the yard, and he'd be slamming things around the house so hard you could feel the windows shaking on the outside. He'd be calling me a bitch, and the neighbors across the street could hear it. The kids were scared all the time.

He progressed to the point where he didn't beat me up so much as push me around, or he might choke me, or pull my hair. We had two twin beds pushed together in our room and he'd pull this deal where he'd say, "Get your shit out of my room." I had to take the beds apart, take the bed into another bedroom or the basement. Take all my clothes out of the room. And when I'd done it, he'd say, "Okay, put it all back." I was scared to do it, and scared not to do it. I tried a few times to say, "Forget it. I ain't doing it." Then you'd get beat up.

That last day, he'd already thrown the dining-room table and broken a couple of chairs. Right before my older daughter got home from first grade he was yelling at me. He was the type of person if he was yelling at you, he could talk for hours—just go at you and say awful things. You're supposed to sit there and listen, and not get up, don't go take care of your children or anything. My baby girl, I guess, was scared and wanted to go to the bathroom. She pooped in her pants. She came to tell me, and I said, "I have to take her to the bathroom." And I got up. He was so enraged, he ripped up the whole living room. He took our couches and ripped them open, pulled out the stuffing. He took the stereo speakers and dumped everything down. We had this big wooden coffee table. He kicked it over.

I was just crazy by this time. I thought, this is it. He's going to kill us. We had no money. None of the bills had been paid. If I had food for my babies, it was because I wrote a hot check for it.

My older daughter walks in from school. She lost it. She was so mad, she just whirled off and went to her room. When he saw that she was so mad, it scared him then that he might hurt her. He'd never hit them. It was always me. He got up and left the room.

She came to me saying, "I hate my daddy, I hate my daddy. Why'd he tear up our things?"

"Shut up," I said. "Don't you see what he's done? Just shut up." She runs downstairs and goes out through the basement into the backyard. The little one had already snuck out by that time, too, because she was scared to death.

I'm in here, mind you, trying to pick up all the stuffing and put it back in the couch, trying to hurry and clean up before he comes out, or he'll be mad. I just knew in my mind that we would die that night. I thought, "What a fool I am. What a fool. I'll never get this picked up. I'll never get this back together this time." I was always patching holes and fixing things. "I can't do this."

I snuck downstairs. I knew by this time which stairs creaked and which didn't. My youngest's blankey was sticking out from under a pillow on the couch down there. I picked it up. My purse just happened by chance to be at the bottom of the stairs. I snuck out the back door and got both the kids. My neighbors were in their backyard. I begged them to get us out of there. And they did.

I do stupid shit anymore. I sleep with whoever I want to whenever I want to. I fuck with these men's minds on purpose, to see the next day when they see me how are they going to handle it. I get a kick out of it. I do. It's awful. I love it. I work at this bar where everybody in the whole town goes. They come in, and they look at me like I used to look at men, like "What do I say? What do I do?" And it's like, "Yum—the upper hand!" I do have the upper hand. I think I do. It's not what I want at all. I don't want this kind of life. I want what I used to have. No, I don't want that either.

I was married to Roscoe for almost seventeen years, and then he fell off a building and died. I was like, "This shit ain't supposed to happen to me. Not to me, Miss Hardass Dorinda." I was like a perfect wife. I don't know why, because he fucked around on me all the time. But he always came home, always, and treated me like a queen. But he should have. I was a good wife.

I fell in love with him when I was sixteen, and I got pregnant right away. Married the first man I ever went to bed with. Hell, I only had my period about six months, and I was pregnant. I thought we were happy together. I know we were. I knew in my mind that he played around, but I wasn't going to face that.

When we first moved out to the desert from down South, Roscoe got a job right away with this guy Chambers, a big construction company. Chambers was the first man from out there I ever really met. He walked in our house, and when I looked at him I was really awed. I hated him, because I liked him so much, and it scared the shit out of me. Nothing really happened between us. Ever.

When Roscoe died, this man somehow got into my life, and we ended up living together. Chambers physically abused me terrible, I mean terrible. It was like, if you're going to physically abuse me, for God's sake do it on my body where nobody can see this. But he didn't. He did it from the neck up. He hit me big time. There were weeks that I had to stay in my bedroom to keep away from my children, so they wouldn't see my face so swollen up. He'd do this to me, and then the next morning, he'd be in bed beside me, and he was so sorry. "I'm sorry. I love you. I don't know why I do this." And I'd forgive him. Then he'd do it again.

We had some off-the-wall sex, like I'd never had before in my life, ever. Roscoe and I, when we had sex, we made love and that's the way sex was, at least that's what I thought. When I had sex with Chambers, it was nasty. He talked nasty. And I got off on it. But that was weird to me. It was like, "This isn't allowed. This is bad, bad." Did he wise me up, or what? I learned a good lesson from him. Now I do to these men what he did to me, but I'm not violent physically. I'm violent inside of me, because nobody is going to fuck with me. And I could so easily be fucked with.

Finally I told him, "I've got my house up for sale. If you ever do this to me again, I'm out of here." July Fourth, Independence Day, that was the day he did it to me in front of my children for the first time. I had to get my children and run out of this hotel room. We all went up to see the fireworks. We'd been drinking all day. He flipped out and beat the living shit out of me. I mean, I was bleeding. That's what my daughter remembers. My kids were so scared. They were terrified. This man beating me in the face. I don't know what set him off. Whenever other people were around, he didn't like that because he didn't have control. He did it to me in front of my kids, and I said, "I told you. This is it."

I went home from the hotel that night and there was a thing on my answering machine from my realtor. Somebody signed a contract on my house. Everything just came together. I said, "I'm out of here." He was there the whole time. He packed up my stuff. He put everything in the truck. Loaded my whole house up. The day I left, we ended up in each other's arms, crying. It was like, "I can't leave you, but I want to."

He still calls me. Thank God, I'm so far away from him, because I would go back to him in a heartbeat. Why? I don't know why I'd do that. He really hurt me. It was very dangerous. I knew he would kill me sooner or later. In my bedroom the day I left, I looked at the floor when I pulled my waterbed down. There were blood marks on the floor on that side of the bed, because my face was bleeding. My whole face was full of blood. Why would I ever think of going back to him? But I do.

Being a female bartender in a small town, I can have my pick of anybody who's around. That's the truth. Anybody. It's like, get a grip, you guys. You'll never have me. Maybe, if you're lucky enough, you may have this. The men I do this with, they're in their height of glory—"I had Dorinda!"

What the hell is the big deal? I can see it, that look, that stupid look, that stupid, naive look they give me. You idiots.

I'm being an idiot, but I have to do this. I'm being seventeen all over again. It's something I never did. It's not making me happier. I'm not getting much physical satisfaction out of it at all. It's like if I go through all these people, the right one will come along. I'm a very easy person to get along with, but I don't want to be fucked over again. I won't be. I'll fuck you first. Nobody is going to hit me anymore. Don't ever raise a hand to me ever again. That's pain. That's physical pain. I can deal with mental pain, so I'll come back at you and give it to you worse. And I can. To cut a man down is like I've conquered him, and they let me do it. I never had to do that with Roscoe, and I would never have dared to do it with Chambers. He would have tried to beat me to death. But I'll do it now.

I'm sure the way I feel now is a reaction to Chambers, and I hope I get through this. I hope I can overcome this and stop being such a hardass. It's anger. I didn't like what he did to me. When we had sex together, it was nasty. Oh, nasty. Bad to the point where he made me feel like I was a paid piece of meat. Sometimes I would turn to the side and cry. Not sob cry, but tears, because it was like, "I don't like this. I don't like it." He used to talk all this nasty talk, and he got off on it.

Okay, I'll tell you something. After I moved back here from out West— I never had done this in my life—he used to call me on the phone, and we would have phone sex. After I hung up the phone, it was like, "Oh, my God. Let me send you a bill for this." That's the way I felt. The nasty part of me came out. It would excite me, but I would feel, "Oh, man, this is not right."

Hell, I thought he brought out the worst in me. Little did I know how far I'd go. Dorinda, stop! Right now I fuck with these people's minds and I get a kick out of it. I always thought men were the dominant ones. Ha! That's a joke. They're on the same level as me. Sometimes with men it's like their dick makes their mind work. I can coax these men into bed, screw around with their brains, and they don't know what to do about it. You think you've got the power? Give me a break. You have no power!

I went in for breakfast at the place where I was skiing, and this girl was pursuing me. I was so offended by it. She's next to me, she wasn't very attractive, and I wasn't interested in her at all. But she was fishing around for what I did for a living, so finally I said to myself, "I'm going to give it to her."

"I'm a Catholic priest." That shut her up fast. From then on she didn't want to talk to me anymore. She didn't know what to do with it. They can get hostile or turned off. It's very meaningful one way or another to them. Then they don't talk to you like a regular person. They won't talk to you about things they would talk to a normal person about. I find that very objectifying and offensive. I'm no longer a person. I'm an office.

Some women find it very attractive. When I have my Roman collar on, women flirt with me and stare at me. They're very attentive, and I'm an object of mystery. That's not the case—or at least I don't notice it—when I'm dressed ordinarily. I don't know if it's because I'm considered safe or forbidden fruit. I do look pretty nice in a black suit and a Roman collar. Black is my best color. So there must be something there.

Women come across very strangely. They're always hugging you and touching you. They never do that if you're dressed in everyday casual clothes, like every other man. But when you've got that collar on, they think they can take those liberties. It offends me, because I know it's not real. I don't mind being hugged when it means something. I hate being hugged by people who just want to hug me. "What are you hugging me for? You don't mean anything to me. I don't even know you. It doesn't mean anything to you." But women do that. Because they want to make a statement among the people that they're really one with me? Or what?

Taking liberties with a woman before she allows you to or before you should is offensive. I find that offensive when they do it to me.

People fish for things. They try to find out what I do sexually. That's what it's all about many times, what I'm all about sexually. They try to find out if priests and nuns are faithful. I've had people do that. What are they really fishing for? What does my answer mean to them? I answer objectively, and they take it subjectively, and make all these judgments. I hate that. So obviously, I say, "Yeah, I guess they're faithful." It's like saying, "Are you absolutely faithful to your spouse? Does anybody commit adultery?" Obviously, people sleep around, so what do they really want to know? It makes you feel used and exploited.

I don't know what people think. It comes up in subtle ways. People will say, "I don't think the church should force people not to be married." Or, "Isn't that changing about marriage and the priesthood? Don't you think in a couple of years they'll change that so that priests can get married?"

It's on their minds. I don't know whether they're saying, "What a waste!" that I'm not married. Men might think, "How can you just not get laid?" Some people want to know if it's really true that you really do *not* do it.

Things are changing. The seminarians are very feminine these days. They're either foreigners or they look like a bunch of faggots—very effeminate—who never would have been accepted up until a few years ago. So there's a big change in celibacy. The old-timers, the old guard priests were really hard-core, real manly men. The church was very strict about that. Now everything is really *holistic* and all that. But back then you better like sports and meet all the criteria, because they didn't want anything like homosexuality in the seminary. It was really taboo, unthinkable. For men who went in years ago, it was idealistic to be celibate. You were a cut above the regular guy to be able to have that much control. Sex was so put down. It was more like a weakness that you did it. There was a lot of negativism about sexuality.

Now that's not true. People say, "God, why? What's the purpose? Why can't you love God, be a great servant and saintly, *and* have a wife and get laid?"

Celibacy is just a discipline. They could do away with it any time they want. It's economic more than anything else. They give me nine hundred dollars a month, and I have to do everything with that, get my own insurance and my car and everything. Most priests probably get less. Some parishes only give you a few hundred dollars. They couldn't give you a few hundred dollars if you had a wife and kids. They'd have to give you enough money to support a family and a home. That's a lot of money even in a little parish. The economics of it is nothing to be ignored. That's a big thing.

Celibacy has to do with your way to God, not sex. Celibacy has to do with the fact that you have made this commitment to these people, and this is the way God is working in you. So which way is He working? Is He working this way or that way? Make up your mind. You don't become a priest and then say, "Oh, it's not enough. I also need to be married." You should know that before you make the commitment. The theology has to do with service and love of God and love of people, how you're going to grow in love. It doesn't have anything to do with genital sex.

This is not a cop-out, but in a way a priest could go on vacation, and have a wonderful time in Hawaii. Meet a girl and have a sexual experience. She goes back to Omaha, and he goes back to his home, and he didn't violate celibacy. Celibacy means you don't get married. You're not making a vow not to have any kind of sexual experience at all.

When you take a vow, it's a vow of poverty, chastity, and obedience. So then any kind of sexual contact is a violation of the vow of chastity that you have freely taken. You took it, nobody forced it on you. By the time you take a vow for the first time, you should know yourself well enough to know whether or not you can live it out, if you have the psychology to be obedient, if you can live without owning anything of any great value. And that you do have the psychological makeup and sexuality that can survive this vow that you're taking to God as a gift. Celibacy means that you have forgone married life and a family. But you didn't violate your celibacy necessarily when that happened in Hawaii, because you can come home and be very committed, and you're there for people, always on the job, great priest, great servant. This other guy may never have gotten a hard-on, but never can relate to anybody, lives in his own little world, and is just a drain. He might have gone fifty years as a priest and never had anything sexual, but he's far from the people. Which one is more faithful to that vow in its ultimate meaning? The one who violated it by having sex once in a while or the one who never had anything to do with sex, but has become a vegetable that plays golf all the time and is never available? I see that, and it makes you wonder in the broader context of the meaning of chastity, love, and service.

You say that to some people, and they say, "Oh! So you can fool around. You can't get married, but you can have a mistress or be screwing everything in sight, as long as you don't get married." That's going from point A to Z as far as I'm concerned. It's assumed by the church that you're also chaste, but the vow is to celibacy.

I don't feel less of a man because of celibacy. Everybody relates to it differently. As different as each individual priest is different, so the experience of celibacy is different and how he works it out and how he lives it. I'm sure there's a lot of priests fooling around now and then. It's like if you asked me, "Are all married people faithful?" Common sense tells you that's not true. But you can't come out with statistics or percentages. Knowing human nature, you know some priests are having sex. One gets married all of a sudden because some girl's pregnant, so you know somebody's doing something. A lot of good priests have left. A lot of not so good guys have stayed. What does that mean? There's a lot of great priests who've been celibate all their lives and never fooled around. So it works for some people. You just have to make it work. I'm sure they've suffered through it. A lot of good priests who have gone on to be bishops and cardinals have had affairs or relationships.

Celibacy is a message that there is something supernatural, that there is something worth doing it for, and that you can love God.

I was born in a very small town in Pennsylvania. It was very homogeneous. Almost everyone was Catholic. My parents were very devout, so sex was something that was not discussed in the slightest. I don't think I even heard the bed squeaking in my parents' bedroom. I have a brother so I know they had sex more than once.

My mother never told me anything about sex. Here I was in high school, a straight-A student, valedictorian of the class, supposedly a brain, and I knew *nothing* about sex. I did go out occasionally to proms and things. But my father was a schoolteacher, so he would be a chaperone at the dances. He got very upset because this boy was holding me too close. I was a terrible person because I was cheek to cheek or body to body with this boy. The impression I got was you don't touch anybody, you don't get close to them. It is just a horrible, horrible thing. He would not let me take a ride in a boy's car, even if there were other girls in the car. I couldn't even go a couple blocks home from cheerleading practice.

I was very repressed and sheltered. I went to the library a lot. I was reading psychology books and I brought home a book written by Sigmund Freud. My father took it and said, "Nice girls don't read Freud." You don't even read anything about that. I was kept totally away from physical pleasures. I don't read it, I don't talk about it, I don't go near anybody, and that's it.

I went away to college. I was rather unprepared for sex. You were expected to go out all the time. On weekends, since you had a 2-A.M. curfew, you went out and you stayed out until 2 A.M. If you didn't, you were a disgrace, what you would call a nerd nowadays.

I remember a double date with one of my roommates. She and her date were fooling around. The boy I was with was also a Catholic. I didn't really know how to handle this situation. When I did tell him I was a virgin, he stopped everything. On the way home, I really got terribly teased by my roommate. He stood up for me: "She's not that kind of a girl." So it even got reinforced there that sex was something that was evil. I was not "that kind of a girl." Terrible girls have sex, but nice girls, like me, don't. If I had not been a virgin, I'm sure he would have jumped on it right away. It was really very confusing, and sent the wrong messages. Sex was bad. Nice people don't do it.

My first sexual encounter was with an older man, twice my age. I was a premed student, and he was the pathologist for the city morgue. I was talking to him largely about his work. He asked me if I would like to go out for a hamburger. We did go out for hamburgers, and stopped in this picnicky area to eat. I didn't think anything about it. I often went on picnics to state parks with my parents. It was perfectly all right for me to go to a wooded picnic area talking to someone who taught at the university.

He seemed to get rather suddenly aroused. He just jumped on me. I was taken by surprise. I went into a state of shock. I didn't feel anything. I didn't feel pain, I didn't feel pleasure. I didn't even feel like I could move. I just absolutely froze. I really didn't realize what had happened even until after he got off of me. I got up and I was bleeding. At that point, I went into the shakes, and passed into a real physical state of shock.

I'm bleeding so he's trying to calm me down. Then he was pleading with me, "Please, don't tell anybody." So you get more of this, "Oh, gee, don't tell anybody. Sex is awful. What would happen if people knew? You'd be a disgrace." You'd have to call this rape.

So I didn't tell anybody. I was absolutely afraid to tell anybody. I thought if I told my parents I would be disgraced. "No one will ever want to marry you, if you're not a virgin." I'd heard that all my life. This would be a disaster. They would pull me out of school, so I decided just not to tell anybody. I almost wiped it out of my mind. I didn't think about it. Just forgot about it.

This person then brought me a bunch of books on reproduction, on sex. He wanted to continue having sex. I said I wasn't interested. "I don't want to have anything to do with you." In my naïveté, I had the feeling that, "Gee, I've had sex with him, now I have to marry him?" That was not what was on his mind. I would occasionally have to see him at school, but that was like the end of it.

So that was my introduction to sex. It wasn't very pleasant. It was frightening. But I did get some knowledge of it.

After that, I didn't want to have much to do with anybody. But slowly my curiosity began to get the better of me. I realized that all around me there was so much to do about sex. Everybody was talking about it, everybody was doing it. It's even in commercials. It was the sexual revolution coming on, love children and hippies. Everybody was making sex a big deal.

"Gee," I thought, "there's got to be more to sex than what I've experienced, because that wasn't much." So I finally had sex with a boy that I was dating for quite a while. My first orgasm was with him rubbing my clit with his hand. That took a long time. He said, "I was beginning to think you were frigid." Once that happened, I was able to have orgasms in intercourse, and back then people didn't perform oral sex very much. I enjoyed having sex, and we'd have sex quite regularly.

I started having affairs with several of the faculty. I remember going up to the office of an English teacher. We were kissing and he just sort of guided my head down to his groin area and pulled out his penis. It seemed a natural thing to do to put it in my mouth. So he had an orgasm, came in my mouth. There was no problem with that. But I mentioned having done this to a friend, and she was quite appalled by it. She said, "Oh, how terrible! How could you do such a thing? It's like washing out a toilet."

"Oh, really?"

I didn't know what was bad sexually or what was good sexually. I was a clean slate, nonjudgmental. I would try things and if it felt good, it was okay with me.

I met my husband walking down the street, going to a bookstore. He just smiled. When the boy he was with asked him who is that, he said,

"Why, that's the girl I'm going to marry." We met in the bookstore and started going out very regularly. Despite him being Mormon, we did have sex quite often before we were married. It wasn't until we were very much in love that he sprung it on me, mentioned that he was Mormon. Then I tried to convince him of the error of his ways. Unfortunately, I ended up being converted to Mormonism instead.

After we were married, we were very monogamous, but we had a good sexual relationship, pretty much. Except, I have to say that I still had a lot of false conceptions about sex. One being that when the man comes, it's all over, that he can't do anything else. That was a falsehood and that would lead me to be very frustrated at times, just because of the way my particular husband functions. He really doesn't get a good, hard erection until he's ready to ejaculate. Until then, he's sort of semi-rigid. So he would just get really good, and then he would come. I would just be getting orgiastic from the effects of him and it would be done.

We did not talk about sex, even though we were having a lot of sex, just about every day. There was no communication of "I like this or do you like that or why don't you try this?" in twenty years of marriage. Sometimes I would just go to the bathroom and masturbate to relieve the tension of the buildup.

We had eight children, so obviously we got the procreation stuff down right. All the parts worked. Our sex life was very pleasant and fulfilling, but just regular sex, nothing unusual, just the standard missionary position. He did enjoy performing oral sex, so that was fun.

Then the Mormon Church came out for a while with some new rules. In order to go to the Temple, which is like a big deal where you can perform work for the dead and get special endowments that are supposed to guarantee you places in Heaven and Godhead and all that, you had to be interviewed. One of the questions they asked you was, "Are you having oral sex? Or did you perform oral sex?" If you said yes, you would not get a Temple recommend. Being very devout Mormons at this time, it was a big, perplexing problem. Both of us enjoyed oral sex. For years they never asked anybody. Maybe it wasn't popular. But when it became a popular activity, they started asking about it, so we stopped having oral sex.

I would have to say this interfered with our sexual relationship. That really bothered me a lot because, as I mentioned, the way he functions, really it is best for me if he performs oral sex on me first and brings me to orgasm. Then we have sex and I can have an orgasm faster with him. Being brought to orgasm with a not-very-stiff erection is not very likely.

It just got to be too much. After some argument between us, we were patching it up, and he asked me if I would. I said yes. So then we started having oral sex again. The church finally stopped asking people. Too many people were answering yes and saying no to the Temple.

One bishop who interviewed me said he liked oral sex, too, but he'd given it up. "Try kissing instead," he said.

"Kissing my lips doesn't do the same thing as kissing other parts of me."

When I was pregnant with my last child, my husband had the revelation. He received a revelation from God. The Mormons have a priesthood for men. They claim it was restored by Joseph Smith. My husband's revelation was there should have been a priesthood for women, also. The early history of the Mormon Church was quite sexual. There was not only polygamy, but all sorts of rumors going around that there were lots of extramarital sex, cohabitation, and wives passed around. But that was all sort of hushed up and done away with. They became quite respectable, almost as Christian as your Baptist or anybody else.

My husband was very upset by the revelation, in a way. He didn't want to talk about it for a while. Finally, he did come out and say that it would be necessary for me to have sex with other men. This was a big blow to me, having been faithful to him and monogamous for twenty years. I really had to think about it. I'm college-educated, a chemistry professor, but a very religious person. I believed him.

I was not enthusiastic about that idea at first. I thought, "Well, maybe, just one man. Some kind of religious test, like Abraham offering his son, Isaac, as a sacrifice. At the last minute, you expect the angel to come and say, 'No. Since you were willing to do it, you don't really have to kill your son, you know.' " It didn't turn out that way.

Once I agreed, it was, "Gee, who are we going to have sex with? All the people we know are very devout other Mormons." You tend to get in your own little clique. We went to a nude beach and met a stranger. He turned out to be a very nice person. We invited him to a house that my husband used for an office down at the beach. We did not explain to this man that it was a religious thing. We had sex with him. My husband was there at the time. It was such a shock to me. My husband said I looked very shocked when he ejaculated inside me. It was pleasant, and even though this stranger was a good lover, and a very nice person, very considerate, very intelligent, articulate, and just a very ideal person, not a slob, not a sleaze, I was still not able to have an orgasm with him.

I figured that was it, just the one fellow. Then as my husband began to get more revelations, he explained that it would be a priesthood for women where the rituals would be sexual. There was a requirement to become a high priestess that I have sex with a thousand different men before I would be ordained. This was part of the revelation from my husband as well.

So before I had had sex with a thousand, the sex was largely nonreligious. It was just sex. It was done for a religious purpose, but it was not necessarily explained to the person. I mean, where am I going to find a thousand men. I didn't even know a thousand men, let alone a thousand men to have sex with.

I had sex with a thousand men in less than two years. They were really hard to find. Most of our friends had been Mormons. I'm not saying that they all don't have sex, and the divorce rate among Mormons and the infidelity is no lower than in the average population. Still, everybody gives lip service to fidelity, so you don't think about approaching them.

I went to a lot of swing clubs. We went to nude beaches. My husband was very supportive. In the beginning, we were always together when I was having sex. Gradually, as I got more confident, I would be alone with people. When we did go to swing parties, he would occasionally swing. Not a lot, not all the time. But he did have sex with other women, too.

It took me having sex with twenty-five men before I was able to have an orgasm with someone else other than my husband. Now I have orgasms all the time, but it was some sort of barrier. Maybe in the back of my mind this was the thing with me—if I don't have an orgasm, I'm still faithful. I was trying. Once I had that first orgasm with somebody else, then it became very easy. The more orgasms I had, the more I was able to have.

It would be necessary, of course, to have sex with *all* worthy men who were interested in going through with the rituals of the religion. It wasn't picking handsome men or nice men or short men or fat men. Just anyone. So I developed my sexuality by having sex with all different kinds of men. I could respond to a lot of different touches and techniques. I learned a lot more about what is exciting to men other than just being with my husband and knowing what he likes. There's a huge variety of things people like.

Nipples, for instance, men's nipples. My husband's nipples don't do a thing for him, they're just lumps on his chest. But many men find it very exciting to have their nipples sucked on or nibbled on or whatever. Mine are *very* sensitive. I can have orgasms just having my nipples stimulated.

Over the two years, we did write up a constitution and bylaws and all the things that were necessary for incorporation as a religious, nonprofit organization. We did formally write out the lessons. I worked on the rituals. You know, the rituals have to have a specific order, the way things are done and the words that are said. There were lesson manuals on specific issues. The lesson material would change. For instance, the basic form of the Catholic mass is always the same, but the Gospel changes.

After I had accomplished the thousand men and was ordained a high priestess in 1986, then we started holding the official rituals. Since then most of the sex I've had has been in the religious rituals, though I still have sex just for the fun of it.

It was in the beginning very upsetting and traumatic, and nothing that I was terribly enthusiastic about, so I prayed a lot. I read a lot on ancient Goddess religions, too. I realized that the way we are taught in our society, we know very little about ancient civilizations. We start with the Greek history of Western civilization in school. We know nothing about the Egyptians. We know nothing about the periods when the Goddess religion was dominant. We have to go back quite a ways to be able to realize that the way things are now in our patriarchal, male-dominated, antisex society weren't always that way. That's the big hangup that I run into in talking to people, especially doing TV talk shows. They say, "The Bible says *this*."

"We predate the Bible," we say.

"The Bible started with Adam and Eve." They don't know anything about the history of their religion or even when the Bible was written. Ignorance has been the biggest factor in opposition to our religion, I think. People don't realize that this was a very dominant religion, and women were held in high esteem. Women did have sexual freedom, there were prophets and oracles and priestesses long before Moses was wandering around the desert.

We've been persecuted very badly. We believed, in our näiveté, that the Mormon Church would accept this as a priesthood for women. We went on several TV talk shows explaining our religion, and the Church got very upset about it, so they called us in before a court.

We did present our views to the Mormon Church in a Bishop's Court.

That is supposed to be like a trial. There are twelve judges. Six of them are supposed to argue for you, and six of them are supposed to argue against you. But they're all Mormons, so how can they come up with an unbiased opinion? Especially people who had never talked to me about what we believed. This was a trial of the validity of my husband's vision and an excommunication for both of us.

The Court is a mockery. It reminded me of something you would see in the Inquisition. It boiled down to they didn't care anything about our beliefs, or why we had sex, or what the theology behind it was. Finally, the person who presided over it, who was the state president, said, "Well, did you have sex with other men or didn't you?"

"Well, yeah," I said, "I did."

"Then, you're guilty."

We went on to do more TV shows. We did *A Current Affair.* Then we did *Sally Jessy Raphael.* We'd just come back from doing *Geraldo,* and a newspaper reporter asked if he could come over and interview us and see the church. He said he wanted to do an article. We invited him over. No problems. We let him come through the church. At that time, we had a large house on the edge of Beverly Hills that we were using as a church. It had a sphinx out in the front, but we were a very new religion, so of course we couldn't afford the Crystal Cathedral or anything like that.

He came through and took photographs. It was a nice interview, and everything seemed fine. He said the article was going to come out in the Sunday paper. It didn't come out in the Sunday paper. Unbeknownst to us, he had gone to the vice cops and asked them what they thought about our religion, since we had sex. Apparently, this vice cop didn't think much of our religion at all.

He called the church, ostensibly asking for information, saying that he wanted to participate and become a member. So I invited him over, as I do all people after I explain a little bit about the religion to them over the phone.

I explain about our beliefs in a God and a Goddess who are anthropomorphic beings. I explain that sex in our religion isn't considered either adultery or fornication, because the rituals are actually prescribed by the Goddess, sort of like in the Catholic Church you drink wine in the sacrament, but that doesn't make you an alcoholic or a drunk. Neither is a priest considered a bartender. It has symbolic reasons.

I ask if they can accept this. He said, fine, he could accept it, and he wanted to know more, so I invited him over.

When he came over, I took him into our Dedication Room, where I again explained that I'm a priestess. I reiterated our belief in a God and Goddess. I explain that we don't separate our spirit from our bodies. Many religions say your spirit on the one side is good and holy, but your body over here is carnal, devilish, and evil. But we don't do that. We consider the body and spirit to be united.

I explained Confession. In our religion we have something a little more elaborate than the Ten Commandments. We call them the Forty-two Affirmations. In old Egyptian writings they're often referred to as the Forty-two Negative Confessions, but I just don't like the term *negative*. They include things like, "I have not murdered, nor have I bid anyone to murder in my behalf." You can't get off with hiring a hit man to do it. They do include some similar things to the Ten Commandments. Of course, they were written long before the Bible came out. There are more ordinary things in there as well. For example, all Goddess religions were largely connected in modern-day minds with the land and fertility, environmental things, which is probably why they appeal to the New Age people and environmentalists. One of the Confessions is, "I have not fouled the water, nor have I polluted the Earth." We have such nice things that even the Boy Scouts could agree with.

In Confession, I ask the person what their previous religion is, whether they are Catholic, Protestant, Jews, or Moslems. I need to know if they're going to have any hangups from previous backgrounds over whether they think sex is dirty and evil. Is this going to inhibit them for participating in the ritual? Most people say, "No, that's why I got rid of my religion." But some people say, "Gee, I don't know."

"If while we're going through the ritual," I tell them, "your mind switches to this, and you have a problem, talk it over with me, so we can cope with it."

Then I ask them if everything is right with their fellow man, before they continue with the ritual. If you have any ill will, animosity, hatred, if you've stolen something you didn't give back, or any other matter on your conscience, that should be cleared up before you continue.

Usually people say, "Things are fine." I don't know if they're being honest. Everyone says, "No, everything is fine." Occasionally, people will say, "I hate my mother. She did something to me and I've never reconciled it with her." But most people will just say no problem.

The undercover cop is just one of those people that goes, "No. Everything is fine." Not very talkative in the Confession, but that's not unusual.

The next ritual is Dedication. In the Dedication, I explained what the person is doing is putting themselves in the same position that they were when they first came into the world, because we believe the spirit enters the body at the moment of birth. This is in a bit of contrast with some of your orthodox religions, which believe your spirit enters the body at conception. In our religion the spirit unites with the body when it takes that first breath of life. In Egyptian hieroglyphics, this is represented by the Goddess extending the ankh towards the person. That's their breath of life. So we have no problem with abortion. I don't particularly like it. Birth control would be much better, but nonetheless, we don't consider it murder.

So they are to put themselves in that same position when they first came into the world. They're trying to get in touch with their spirit as they were when they first came into this world. This is a mental attitude combined with a physical stance. So I am seated on a chair, and I have a dress on that has slits up the sides, so I can lift the front flap of it. The person puts their head between my legs. This is the priestess representing the Mother of their Spiritual Birth. They put their head between my legs and they're supposed to block all their feelings of the outside world, and just get in touch with their inner self.

The person does perform oral sex on the priestess at that time. The police officer refused to do that. So he said, no, he did not want to do that. He said he just wanted to fuck. I said, "Well, the rituals are done as prescribed. Nobody tells a priestess what to do. You're obviously not serious about the religion. You'll have to leave." So I got up and escorted him to the door.

"I changed my mind," he said.

"No," I told him, "once I end the rituals, they're over. You'll have to leave." I opened the door and he stepped out, but then he grabbed me and tried to pull me out the door. He had not identified himself as a police officer, so I thought he was some weirdo, some nut trying to kidnap me or something. I started screaming, and pushing the door closed on him.

My husband, who is the High Priest, came running out of the library. Another girl who was studying in the library saw the scuffle, so she ran back in the library to call 911. In the meantime, some other police officers from the outside, all undercover cops, finally came up and flashed a badge. It was then that they said, "We're police." So we stopped trying to push them out, opened the door, and said, "What do you want? What's going on here?"

Eight of them stormed in. They said, "You're under arrest."

"What for? Do you have a warrant?"

"No. We don't need a warrant." They grabbed my husband, pulled his hands behind his back, and started to punch him in the stomach. I came up to them and said, "Please, don't hurt him." So two of them grabbed me, threw me up against the wall, and another one held me with my hand in that half-nelson hold pushing up, and I was in really bad pain, so I couldn't wiggle around and see what they were doing to my husband. They had a gun at his head and were telling him to put his hands up. Yet they were holding his hands behind his back and punching him in the stomach, saying, "Don't resist, don't resist."

"I'm not resisting. I can't resist."

They ran into the library after the girl who went to call 911. She told me later they said, "Drop that phone or we'll blow your head off." She dropped the phone, naturally. They put us all in handcuffs and stormed through the whole building without a search warrant, going through all the rooms and through the drawers and everything. Then they took us off to jail.

In the trial we declared it was a First Amendment issue, that we had a right to practice our religion. I got a public defender, because we were not a wealthy prostitution ring, raking in thousands of dollars like the cops said. We were a poor religion living on donations. I could not afford an attorney. My public defender before the trial even started said that she wouldn't use the trial as a forum for my religion.

"If you won't use a religious defense," I said, "then I have no defense." I made a motion in court, saying she wouldn't represent me adequately. The judge decreed that I was not entitled to choose, I was just entitled to an attorney, period. The judge also made the comment to my husband before the trial even started that he should get a job and "stop having that woman supporting you."

In the trial, the police officer testified that I told him I would suck his cock for a hundred and fifty dollars. I never discussed this at all. That was not even mentioned. So he just made something up. It was largely his word against mine.

They found me guilty, and I was given the stiffest sentence ever given to a first-time conviction. A year in jail. My husband was convicted of running a house of ill fame. He served two and a half months. I have seven children at home, so we asked if one of us could go to jail, and then the other one, which seemed quite reasonable. In fact, just recently some rapist who raped a fourteen-year-old girl and beat her up was able to serve his time on weekends only, so that he could take care of his children. They refused to let us stagger our sentences. They would not even give us that much consideration.

I talked to many prostitutes—real ones—while I was in jail, and they couldn't believe that I was given the maximum sentence. Most of them, their first time, they would just be told to get out of town, or they would get a fifty-dollar fine or ten days in jail at the most. They kept saying to me, "You must have done something else. You couldn't have just gotten charged with prostitution." No, this was my first time, I have no convictions of any kind. I'm not a drug user. I'm not an assaulter. Nothing.

As they carted me off to jail they were bent on being degrading and humiliating. It was not even humane treatment. The undercover cops took me there—one of them was a female—and I don't think they expected me to survive. They made the comment, "A little white lady like you won't last long in this place," because it's largely black and they figured I'd get beat up and that would be the end of me. But I survived.

I had the good fortune to be transferred to a more open prison where you do get some time outside. They had a field, so I used to run a lot. Because of overcrowding in the jails, work time, plus good behavior, I actually served five months, which was very miserable. I ran the L.A. Marathon when I got out. I figured, why not? I used to work out a lot, so that gained me respect among most of the prison population, even though I'm a very tiny person. They let me alone.

Since then we've done a couple of more talk shows. We did *Donahue,* we did *The Montel Williams Show.* We're trying to build up again. That's how we're letting people know that we're back. We lost our building, because we couldn't afford to keep it open while we were in jail. So now the ritual is on hold. I have no place to perform the ritual. I wouldn't dare perform the ritual in my house, knowing how hostile the police are. I'm sure they'd come in and drag off all the children if I did anything in the house. Children Services is very vicious.

We hope to convert the world eventually. Right now we are trying to educate people. We have more legal battles that will have to be fought.

At this time, there is no other woman working to become a priestess. The woman who was studying at the church when the arrest took place has been so terrorized by that, she wouldn't be interested unless we had some First Amendment protection, an injunction or something. It's reasonable. I can't blame her. I don't think there's anybody that fervent yet to be willing to risk what I do.

So that's where it stands at this point. We're not able to function completely as a religion. We're probably functioning as much as most Protestant religions do, but we don't have a place to perform the rituals. Ends aren't meeting very well right now. They aren't meeting very well at all. We're living on food stamps.

My sex life has been much better since becoming High Priestess. My orgasms are bigger. They're more frequent. I have many different sizes of orgasms, and some of them are just really earthshaking, overpowering. Where I used to have those only occasionally when I first began, now I have them all the time. It's just easier to respond. I respond to everybody now. My sex life is physical activity, and the more you practice, the better you get at it.

My sexual relationship with my husband was pretty good, but I think jail has affected it pretty much on his part. We don't have sex as often as we used to. He is very emotionally drained by all these legal battles. Court things always drain him sexually, so that has been a big problem. It just takes too much of his energy, and he gets mentally depressed and worn out. To me, there have been no revelations. My husband claims that he is still being given insights and knowledge on things, but as to any specific revelations as to how to immediately get the religion functioning, there has not been any word.

My son in college is pretty nonreligious, though the children were brought up Mormons. His opinion was, "Well, at least you're an interesting person, Mother."

I had a separate and insane existence when I ran this massage parlor. This guy I grew up with wanted to go into a business with this whole bunch of inheritance money he had just gotten. Massage parlors were popping up all over the place at that time, and he thought that would be a good business to get into. It was amazing how sexually loose this country was back then in the '70s. It was just an excess piled on excess. Girls were so loose they'd stop on a dime and drop their drawers for the shallowest of reasons. This is the way women would be if society pushed them that way. It didn't last. Of course, if you read the Bible, it didn't last at Sodom and Gomorrah either. It's got a finite life span, unfortunately, but it was amazing.

We rented a place from a little Greek landlord above a Colombian's coffee shop. Cockroaches would come up from downstairs. We got some guy named Alex who had constructed other massage parlors to build the place for us. We worked with him to save the labor price. We built up these cubicles, and took out ads in the sex papers, and we were in business. I put ads in college papers and on the bulletin boards in colleges for girls to come to work. They just showed up. When it became evident what we were from our signs, they'd just walk in off the street.

My partner was too shy to interview the girls, so I did all that work, but he did put up the money. Coeds were coming in and giving me blow jobs all the time. It was a wonderful year. Because you managed the place, they thought you had some kind of power. They're so stupid, women. They thought that you could get all the pussy that you wanted, so that attracts them to you. They want to be part of the pussy that you get. It works that way with celebrities and professional athletes of all sorts. The way I got on the minor rung of that ladder was to make them think I got so much pussy, that they, too, want to join the line. Don't ask me why. I do not to this day understand how they think.

I've got a tray of slides of the girls from that parlor, if you want to see them. Now you've got me in this nostalgia thing. There's a story behind each one. I'll just set up the slide projector.

I was very fortunate to come of age when I did. I couldn't ask for a better time in terms of wasting my life on sex. This was just custom-made. The time frame was just perfect. It was a perfect window of sexual opportunity. I can't beef.

Click.

There's the place from the street on the second floor above the restaurant. MODELS, we put up on the sign. SECRET LIFE STUDIO. The most valued pornographic book is *The Secret Life,* by some Victorian guy. I'm Mother Goose compared to the guy who wrote this book, a five-thousand-page sexual autobiography. This guy fucked everything that was breathing and was a great chronicler of the horrors of 1880s Victorian life. No one knows for sure who the writer was. He was the inspiration for the parlor. You see how we decorated the place in this terrible little tenement here with purple Victorian curtains and fake wood paneling.

Click.

There it is: the Desk. We spent so many hours there. The nerve center. "Check in for pussy here." The hours of the place as I recall were eleven A.M. to eleven P.M. Consequently, I became a night person. When you closed at night, you take out the used Kleenex and everything, douse the place with antiseptics. In the morning, you just open the door and switch on the lights. There was a scent of sex in the place, sort of a musky smell, a mixture of female scent and semen somehow. It wasn't a filthy place or dirty. You changed the sheets all the time, but there was still a scent. It was an exciting scent. There was also this new furniture that we had. So there was that vinyl smell, and the cork wall, and the cheap perfume the girls wore.

The girls would show up and it'd be slow. These guys would come into the room. We were worried about a bust, so at one point we would ask them if they were cops. We would frisk them for guns, which they didn't care for too much. I would explain to them very carefully that there was no charge for them at all involved in this, so if they weren't enjoying the frisk, I'd be done in a second.

Click.

That's Ginger, the one I fell in love with, a tall, leggy creature from Tennessee. She was a crazy woman. She was beautiful. She had five brothers and sisters, and she said she was the ugliest person in the family down in Tennessee. Her mother and father coauthored learned treatises on literature. She was a bad girl for being up here in the big city being an actress. Ginger was big and tall and full of the devil.

The guy who helped us build this was a cuckolded guy. His partner was fucking his wife. His wife came up to me when we first opened and said, "You know, you're going to fall in love with one of these girls."

I had a girlfriend at the time. "What? Are you kidding? No way!" But I did.

These weren't escort-service girls, which you picture a whore to be today. These were like college coeds, a lot of them were really smart, off on a lark. Some of them just needed money. Basically, they just had to give hand jobs or maybe blow jobs. They didn't have to do that in many instances. They didn't have to fuck you. They weren't supposed to fuck you. So you'd get these girls in there who were extraordinary. Some of them were absolutely beautiful, some of them were just plain crazy, just tramps and whores. There was a mix.

They would sit around the main room. We had three or four session

rooms. They'd do their nails. They'd read magazines. They'd smoke cigarettes. They'd be bored. They fall into little lovebird relationships with
each other, and try to pursue that after hours.

Click.

Here is the one big, black girl who worked there for nothing, and she
was seldom picked. She just liked being around the place. She actually
went and bought the place from us afterwards.

It was boring a lot. I'd go into one of the rooms and read by myself. It
was like flying an airliner, hours of boredom and moments of terror.
Then out of the blue, some girl would come up out of nowhere and she'd
want to give you a blow job, just for the fun of it, or she'd want a job. I
couldn't hire her, and I'd tell her that before, but you'd interview her
anyway for when there was an opening. She'd be a gorgeous blonde or
something, who'd get your dick wet for you and think nothing of it.

Then the hustlers would come in. You get shines coming up there
trying to sell you ski boots in July. Guys would come up with patriotic
red, white, and blue condoms for us, adding machines by the gross, fur
coats. They were just off their track from Times Square. We had religious
visitors. Watchtower people would come up. Salvation Army types, wanting to talk to the girls just to like save their souls.

Couple of mafioso came up. That was kind of scary. One of them
wanted us to "join." But he was indicted the next day, or we would have
heard from him again. I used to joke that I was the only pimp in town
who drove a Toyota. But I wasn't really a pimp. We would charge them
fifteen dollars to use the room and give the girls back four dollars out of
that. So we would make eleven dollars for every session. Then they would
charge for whatever sex took place in the room. They'd make fifty or a
hundred dollars. They'd make in a day what we were lucky to make in a
week. We were a pair of chumps.

Click.

Here I am with the girls. Look at me, the proud peacock, the strutting,
maniacal wop, King of the Cunts, the Hitler of Pussy. *8½,* the one who
cracks the whip.

Click.

Her name was Maria. She was South American. She had that gold tooth.
She goes into the back and makes gold with that mouth of gold teeth. She
was just kind of dumb and insensitive to doing this, until one day when
her brother-in-law walked in as a trick, as a john. They just saw each
other. He bolted out of there. She burst into tears.

Since we had like a family atmosphere, I pulled her off to the side, and found out what happened. I gave her a shot of whiskey I had in the back. I explained to her that he couldn't—no way—go back to her sister, his wife, and say that he caught her working in a cathouse, because *he was in a cathouse.* "He'll know, yes, that you were here. But there is no way he can rat you out."

I was right. I sent her home for the day, and she was back to earning gold two or three days later.

She had rock-hard, Cadillac bumper–like tits, but I didn't like her that much. I don't know what it was. Maybe the gold was just too rich for me. Intimidates me too much in her mouth, but I liked her as a person.

Click.

There's Birdy ready to drag in the Armenian shoemaker from across the street. He'd say, "These guys, they're bums in this neighborhood. They bring in *one shoe* to be repaired." When it snowed he'd be out there with big snowflakes on his head, cursing in Armenian. He'd try to trade. Girls would come down with shoes to be repaired, and he'd say, "How about I fix these for a blow job, huh?" One of those little bald-headed guys with a sharp, aggressive pate. He was nuts.

In terms of customers, the Hasids were dreaded by the girls, because they had irregular bathing habits. They bathe like once a week. Their rules regarding sex with their wives are somewhat unusual. They have to fuck through sheets, and they can't fuck anywhere near the period, because the woman is so impure. They had the usual Judeo-Christian, Western-culture bias against pussy, which extends over to sex and gets the added fillip of their natural fanaticism thrown in on it.

If you get one Hasid, you get them all. They're a terribly close-knit community. "Ach, I got my rocks off with the shiksas over at the Secret Life." Then they'd all go over to our place for whatever they'd want.

They're the corniest guys going. Besides their irregular bathing habits, they are not Tyrone Powers here. We're not talking about any heartthrobs, needless to say. They were kind of funny.

One guy came in, recognized my partner as being Jewish, and he tried to *hondle* on the price. The session price was only fifteen dollars to go into a room. He's saying, "I am your first customer of the day. You must get me." It's a Jewish rule apparently, that the first customer of the day who walks into your store, you have to sell them or your whole day will be shit. They were crazy. They would come early in the day. We did a good trade in Hasids, but the girls weren't too fond of them.

There were a couple of good-looking Italian truckers that the girls liked. There were black guys.

Click.

This white blond college girl, very bright, only liked to fuck black guys. She wouldn't fuck anyone else. She'd do the other stuff, but she'd only fuck blacks to make up for the Establishment's racist inequality to Negroes. She was willing to fuck—for a price—any black guy who came in. She didn't like me. She said, "I don't like pig managers who go for interviews." So I couldn't even interview her, but I let her work.

Click.

This is Bobbi Jo who had the mafia pimp, who fortunately was forced out of town. A vicious guinea, he tells me over the phone, "She's got a bill with me!"

"What do you mean, she's got a bill with you?"

"You're going to have a bill with me in about two minutes. Rationalize that! I'm going to be on your ass." Then he never came by.

Click.

She was kind of a glad girl. Here she is talking on the phone. Looks like she's talking to her fiancé, doesn't it, with the smile and the head tilted coyly to one side? You know who that is? That's some jack-off on the line saying, "Tell me what your tits are like. Describe your cunt to me."

She's going like, "Oh. Well, I'm about five-six . . ."

"Bobbi Jo," we'd have to go, "hang up on that guy." She did this all the time. To say that Bobbi Jo was a pushover is to do a disservice to pushovers. She was beyond the valley of the pushovers.

Click.

This one was great. She was about forty. She wasn't attractive at all. She had a dumpy body. But she was a literati. She could talk about culture, literature, music, and she did. They came in there and sunk their tired, middle-aged heads on her chest. They didn't even want to fuck her. They just would say, "Give me some solace."

She hated my partner. He was a fucking wimp, and he made me fire her. Afterwards, we'd meet at the Museum of Modern Art and have lunch. We got along famously. We were friends even though she was very crazy.

Click.

This one I liked very much. She's Polish, bubble tits. She had a great sense of humor. She was dating this big, good-looking black guy. We'd chant like little kids, "Vicki is dating a nigger, Vicki is dating a nigger."

We were in love. She offered to fuck me. I never fucked her. Everyone was fucking everyone there. After I wouldn't fuck her, she loved me more. Sometimes when you wouldn't fuck them, they'd fall more in love with you than if you fucked them and made them come like no man ever did before. They're sort of more high-minded about this stuff than us men.

Click.

That's the guy next door. He's an Italian from Brooklyn, in case you couldn't tell from that pasta puss. Him and his wife were social workers. He was a photographer on the side. His wife liked me. She came in one night about eleven, when I was closing up the place. I'd sent the girls home. She said, "Do you think I could be a masseuse? What do you have to do to be a masseuse?"

I was getting a lot of nookie there and I didn't need any trouble from old Vito next door, so I sent her home.

He came in about a week later, ran into the doorway of the place and looked all around. I said, "Hiya, Vito." He didn't acknowledge me. She wasn't there, but she had told him something to make him crazy, like she was going next door to make a few extra bucks. I don't know what.

Click.

There's the Armenian again. "Give me a blow job, and I fix them nice for you!"

Click.

There's the lawyer who incorporated us. "Pay your taxes," he said. Nice Jewish boy.

We had the Board of Health cops come in to try and shake us down for pussy or fine money. I said, "Okay, I don't care, give us the fine." The Rat Shit Squad, I'd call them to their faces. I thought I was cool then, too. I was a different person than I am. I'm lucky I survived.

Click.

Here's another girl I loved, Grace. Her father was a police sergeant in Queens. Grace was beautiful, very sensitive, on drugs but tolerated by the rest of us. She'd come in on four or five Tuinols. She was a wreck.

Click.

This girl here, an Army brat named Claire, she could talk the ears off a brass monkey. She could drive me nuts. She was about four-foot-six and had enormous tits. She would talk in this soft, mesmerizing Southern twang about the worst fucking shit. She just was a whore right through to her ovaries. Every fiber, every molecule of this woman was born to be a whore. The guys liked her, because she had big tits. But she was terrible.

Practically all the other girls we had there were on a lark, or if they were whores they had the class not to act like whores. Claire would talk about her lowest rate and her best price, and this customer did this and that one did that. She was repulsive to me. She was a veteran parlor girl, but I never thought of having an interview with her, get her to give me a massage or mooch a blow job out of her or anything else. It was the furthest thing from my mind. I wanted to strangle Claire.

My favorite moment with Claire came when this real spectral, middle-aged guy came in. He had a sneaky look about him. Went with her. He fucked her, and was going to pay her afterwards. But he jumped into his clothes real quick and walked out of the room. She was nude and wouldn't come out. He said he left the money somewhere in the room and split. She came out, half-dressed, and ran out into the hall. You've got to picture this four-foot-nothing, but with tits wrapped in half her clothes, screaming down the stairs, "You stiffed me! He stiffed me! Hey, you come back!"

My heart soared. But then she turned around to me and said, "All right, that's it! No more Mr. Nice Guy!" She's already squeezing their blood out, just so they could shoot their measly little spoonful into one of her orifices. These poor marks, but no more Mr. Nice Guy.

I had a problem with a customer one night because of Claire. He was the janitor of the building across the street. Big, beefy Irish guy with maybe a double digit IQ. He went to the bar next door, got loaded, and came up. Being a man of low taste, he went with Claire. She just probably tried to charge him too much, which I had no control over. That was their business. The guy stormed out of the place. He said, "I can't do anything with her. Give me my money back."

"That's between you and her," I said. "I can't give you your money back. I got to give her part of that." He stormed downstairs, busted the hall light on his way out.

About an hour later, we always had like a wine-and-cheese fest at the end of the day. The public wasn't invited. We'd smoke, and drink a bottle of wine after eleven, hang around and talk. Especially I did this with Ginger, because I liked her.

When we got downstairs, my car was out in front. This guy was watching in the window of the bar. He came out, charging across the street. I knew I was in trouble. I told them to get in the car and lock the doors. He comes up to me and he says, "You got to give me my money back, or I'm going to hurt you."

I'm a lover, not a fighter, so I gave him his money back, which is humiliating, but he bought me a drink after that. In retrospect, he was right. But I got them locked in the car, and they were safe. I really wanted to kill Claire after that one. I drove her home. Then Ginger and I went into Central Park. That was the night I made love to her twice in Central Park. We had this hot and heavy thing for a couple of months at least. And I was in love with her. My little whore girlfriend.

That ended rather abruptly. The parlor lasted a year. My partner ran out of money. We weren't making any money. The thing folded. The most fun-filled year of my life.

Click.

Whores. I enjoyed them actually. I still enjoy them in theory. Of course, it's a different ball game today. I've got enough problems in my life without having to wake up in the morning and feel around on the floor to find my dick, because it fell off. With that being a fact of sexuality, I don't frequent whores much anymore.

I liked hookers. Why did I like hookers? Why do plenty of men? Women are amazed when they see good-looking men going into strip shows and whorehouses, men that they think wouldn't be attracted to going to whores. Women in general don't understand that about men, how they could be so indiscriminate, so insensitive. It's naïveté.

With a whore there is no responsibility whatsoever. You can do whatever you want. It's fun to play the game of treating a whore like a lady and a lady like a whore—that was my clarion call through a whole period of time. Playing the game with a whore, but never having to do anything, just being able to order her automatically.

It wasn't that, though, because I was doing that anyway with women who weren't whores. So it's something else. A lot of it was just the idea that they were there, and they were available. The thing that you scuffle for and fight for, that pussy that's in your genes and your crazy mind that drove you all the time, you could just give them a few bills, some filthy lucre, and you could just have them. The idea of that has always fascinated me about whores. Always! You could just have them, this thing that you tried on all those dates that you went on when you were younger and you didn't get anywhere for whatever reason, you just didn't hit it off with her, you didn't like her to begin with, you did like her but she didn't like you. All the scuffling, all the jumping through fucking hoops to get pussy, and you didn't get it. The idea that they're just standing there, and you don't have to talk to them if you don't want to. You just say, "How much?"

I've been told it's a woman-hating thing, too. If it is or it isn't, I'm not sure. I don't think it's that simple myself. It's tied up with you don't have to be anything, and you *can be* anything. In fact, you want to be something else when you're with them, and they want to be something else, too.

They're interesting. Sometimes they break your heart and make you feel like the lowest thing alive for adding to their misery. Others just delight and amaze you, even terrify you. These are women on the edge. I've had whores recite great poetry to me. Others can barely read or write. In dealing with them, almost invariably I found it to be true that the poor things try to impress you on the first date. They don't even *want* you after the first time, but I've had so many of them that you would think they were in love with you that first time. They'd do anything you'd want. They were the most charming women alive. Until they were sure they got you, convinced you and got you to talk that, "You know, you've got to give this shit up. You're too nice a girl. What's a nice girl like you do-ing . . ." That's their reward in a way. Then they have tricked you. Then you *were* a trick. Then they have beaten you as a female to a male. They're fucking you.

But you know you're going to get this great performance from them the first time. It's wonderful. It's like a dream date in a way. You get what you want, *exactly* what you want, when you want it. They're great conver-sationalists. You have fun. You like each other. You keep in touch. Some-times they even give you a kiss when they leave. The tough ones, like the lesbians who I am very fond of, will give you the thumbs up sign, which is their version of a kiss to a male, after sucking your dick and performing whatever sex acts you asked them to perform.

So although I've always had a love for civilian women, I have cherished a love for whores. I've always had this desire for them, no matter how much the sky was raining cats in pants. They never did any harm to me, or my little dick.

What terrifies me is looks in their eyes, things they've said, their stories. I've been terrified by things they've told me they've done to others. Not that I was afraid that they would repeat it to me, because I knew they weren't going to do that, but it made me aware that I was around real danger. One was just proud to show me scars where someone fucking tried to stab her, and she took the knife off the guy and plunged it into his heart. She got off with the police. She was not telling me this to try and intimidate me in any way or form. She was bragging about it, but sort of reporting how steady she is, what exciting things have happened to her.

One girl's story was how her uncle, when she was fourteen years old while her father was in jail, sodomized her to the point where she had to go to the hospital, tore her asshole open when she was fourteen and forced her to suck him off. Raped her and got away with it. Stories like that.

The one who was eight years old and was raped by her father repeatedly and identified it on a body doll. The father was arrested and served seven years.

"Where is he today?" I asked her.

"In Puerto Rico. I'd love to have him killed. In fact as soon as I find out where that motherfucker is down there, I'm going to have the motherfucker killed." Talking to a woman who is twenty-four years old and to hear her tell you that she's been brought to the point of wanting to have her father killed after he served seven years for fucking her, and have her say these things to you in Puerto Ricanese, which is kind of corny. Then she does her hard-boiled imitation of an innocent girl: "Some of the other girls say, 'At fourteen, I *gave myself up* to Hector or Tony.' But I could never say that, because I was raped when I was eight." Her face just clouded over. She was a terrifying one in that sense. But because she was so tough, she was less sympathetic than she might have been.

I get them to tell the stories, and I always listen to them. They leave you feeling shitty, because you've just taken part in something. Or you get someone you know is a dope fiend—I've been with a few of those—and you're just contributing. You're no less guilty than the pimp or anyone else. So the dark side comes out of that.

Most of them aren't that sympathetic. You don't have to get all involved with them. It's using them like it is a shoeshine guy or a barber. I've always sort of thought about it that way. Until I found myself boxed into a situation where I couldn't score regular pussy. Then you get a little resentful about it.

But always over the years I never felt it was lame in any way to use a whore. So I used them throughout whatever periods of sexual access I was going through, without too much of a problem.

I don't drive, so that's always been a problem when I travel. I was staying at the Mondrian Hotel on Sunset. Going to the office every day, I kept seeing this strip joint, so one night I decided to go in there for starters. I was the only woman in the place. I was all dressed up, full makeup, lots of cash. I just sat at the table by myself and watched this strip show. That got me really turned on. I went backstage to meet the girls and find out if there was a gay club nearby. They sent me to a place "around the corner." In L.A., around the corner is about a mile, and finding a taxi is impossible. So I just walked to this place anyway, because I was determined to get laid. I'm going to get laid and that's the end of it.

When I walked into this club, I didn't really know what was going on. I thought it was a straight gay club with a drag show. I didn't know that a lot of the women who were customers were transvestites. I saw this beautiful, beautiful blond woman. The best description would be Grace Kelly in her heyday, with the platinum blond, perfect hair. She had on this Donna Karan outfit, rich, expensive, the black gloves. I found out later transvestites and transsexuals are the worst thieves. She stole everything. I thought she was a millionaire. Unbelievable tits, and I have a major tit fetish, *major* tit fetish. Perfect waist, and the whole look. I was pretty drunk and feeling pretty cool, because I was away on business. I had a very cool job, and made lots of money. When you're anonymous like that, you got balls. So I went over to her, and I said, "Hi, my name is Mary Ellen. Are you gay?"

"No," she said, real flirty.

"Well, will you sleep with me tonight?"

"Yeah."

I was like, "Thank you, God! *Yes! Yes!*" Her name was Maxine. It was unbelievable. I couldn't wait to leave. We watched the show a little. We go out together, get in her car. It's a sixty-thousand-dollar job, one of those sleek black sports cars, stereo for days. Just her driving it was like a fantasy, the whole thing.

I didn't think she was, but I said, "You're not a drag queen, are you?" Just in passing.

"No, no," she said.

"Okay, fine."

We go back to my hotel and up into the room. We're making out. Her shirt is off. The most beautiful breasts I've ever seen on a woman to this day. It's getting a little hot and heavy, and she stopped me. "I got to tell you something," she says.

"What?"

"Something bad," she says.

"Did you kill anyone?"

"No."

"Then it can't be that bad." I'm like my father, pretty forgiving.

"Remember what you asked me in the car?"

"Yeah."

"Well, I am."

"Oh, okay. That's all right." I continue to kiss her and suck her titties. I wouldn't go near her penis. I couldn't deal with that. Except she did penetrate me a little bit with it. I let her one night, because I was really drunk. She loved it; she was crying.

I think it was my Catholic upbringing that made me prefer women. I was always attracted to them, but I never felt guilty after sleeping with a woman. I always felt guilty after sleeping with a man. When I'd sleep with men, we'd never have intercourse, everything but. I guess I'm still a virgin. In all my travels, I've slept with and picked up a lot more people than I've had sex with. I'm more into the score than the actual act of sex. I don't relish going down on someone, unless I love them. I don't really like women going down on me, unless I'm fucking drunk and crazed. Really for me it was just getting the person. Having sex with them was a whole other issue, which I would see through if I had to, but not really what it was all about. I get off more like humping them, masturbating on their leg, or whatever you want to call it, than actually having sex with people. At this point, I'm pretty set in my ways, and to me it's normal to be a gay woman.

So Maxine and I continued to see each other my whole trip to L.A. She was my lover and my companion. I loved going out with Maxine, man. We'd go on the town. I'm tomboyish. She'd say, "Put a skirt on." She'd make me all pretty. But she looked so million-bucks-Rodeo-Drive, not a hair out of place, that when we'd walk out of the hotel, literally every man that worked there would be opening the door for her. She would look at me and go, "Service. Isn't it wonderful?" I love this girl. The joke was on them. We went all over the place, and if there were red carpets to be rolled out, just by looking at this girl, they would be rolled out. She also had lots of personality, just fun.

What happened, which was a disaster, was she fell in love with me. When I left L.A., she was saying, "I can't believe I went through all this trouble to be a woman, and now I fell in love with a woman. I'm in love with you."

I had a female rock-and-roller back home who was fucking me over left and right. Anyway, Max and I had a phone relationship. We planned for her to come to Chicago, and she did. I met her at O'Hare, and the second she got off the plane, and I saw her, I knew it was gone, the fire was gone. She was so happy to see me. She came over, and she tried to be intimate with me. I froze up. I broke her heart. She left early.

Now, we're friends, and we talk, but it was really sad because I couldn't see it through. I thought I could. In L.A. it was great, but she was in my territory, where my family is—and I pride myself on being very open to all kinds of people—but I got real cold feet. It was a little too much for me to handle. That saddens me still to this day. I'm glad we're still friends.

Anyway, she went back to L.A. and got involved with this woman who is changing into a man named Jimmy. Jimmy had her tits removed and still had a vagina, but was getting a penis. Jimmy was making passes at Maxine, but she ignored them, because she had me in Chicago. But when I rejected her, she called Jimmy and Jimmy picked her up at the airport. They had a relationship for two or three years, and I was glad.

Isn't that wild, though? I saw pictures of "him." You cannot believe that this man has a vagina. He has a beard, he's a man. So this was Max, the most beautiful woman I ever saw with a penis and this girl—a man with a vagina—and they were fucking. It's kind of an interesting thing. It's kind of romantic how it works out.

Max breaks my heart, because I don't know if she'll ever be happy. Now she's a religious fanatic. You call her machine, and it's got something from the Bible on it.

The part I never admit to people when I tell the story is that I fell in love with her, too. That's the part I don't admit, that we continued a love relationship. Not because I'm ashamed to admit it as much as it turns out that people can't handle that.

At the time I was thirty-nine, and this girl was twenty-three. I fell in love with her. She looked perfect, acted perfect. This girl made my life a living hell.

In my relationships with women, I've been cautious. I'm not a fast, smooth mover. With this girl, it was like instant. We were involved and seeing one another constantly. I was sleeping three hours a night. We were sitting out in the car until three in the morning, just talking. Then she would call me up at home at seven A.M. to talk to me. We went window-shopping for an engagement ring. I bought her one the first store we went to, because she wanted one.

I've never met anyone like her. She always looked good, always wore nice clothes. Then two seconds later, she would be a raging lunatic trying to kill you. The next minute, she's apologizing, sweet as can be. She'd start scenes in restaurants and public places. She didn't care. She wasn't afraid to make a scene in public. I took her to one of my favorite restaurants. She says, "I hate this place. I can't stand this place! We have to leave now."

We've got drinks in front of us. "Wait. Let me pay for this."

"I have to leave now," and gets up and walks out the door. All of a sudden, I realize she's nuts. We went out to dinner with my mother. She started a major scene in the place about something small. When we got outside, I took her home. I was driving my mother home, and my mother said, "I don't want to say anything to you because you're getting married, but there's something seriously wrong with that girl."

"What do you think, Ma? Tell me the truth."

"I think she's a schizophrenic by the way her personality changes just like that." A couple of friends told me something was wrong. My own alarms were going off. These snap changes were a giveaway.

Then I started not wanting to see her. We broke the engagement, and after that we started having sex. We were members of this born-again Christian church, and we weren't allowed to have sex before marriage, but when I stopped wanting to see her, we started having sex. I know how weird that sounds. But young born-again people I know, they have sex. They get guilty behind it and they pray about it, but that's exactly what happens. It's hard to deny the flesh.

Her idea of sex was very foreign to mine. She wanted to be tied up. She wanted to be beaten. She gave me a belt, so I wouldn't hurt my hand. "Here, spank me with this, so you don't hurt yourself."

She wanted to be degraded and humiliated and abused. From talking to her about her childhood, her mother beat her. It began with a hairbrush. She didn't go into it a whole lot, but I get the idea her mother hit her a lot, that she equated love with pain. At least, that's what it came out like.

I did a lot of stuff with her. A lot of it was things I'd read about or seen in movies or fantasized about, but that I'd never done with anyone. I couldn't pay anyone to do these things, because I was too embarrassed to ask anyone. I could never ask one of my girlfriends to do that, because it was kinky. No one I had ever met had tried any of this stuff. I was tying her up, beating her with a belt, spanking her. Doing anything she asked, plus everything I had ever fantasized or read about or seen in a movie and said, "Hmm, maybe I'd like to try that." We did it.

And I didn't like any of it. I don't know how she could enjoy having that stuff done to her. I didn't like hitting her. I found it difficult. She would do stuff to provoke me and make me angry. Then when she'd get me angry, she'd say, "Hit me." I could only do it if I was mad. If she walked up to me and said, "Here, hit me," I couldn't do it. Even if I was angry with her, as soon as I started, I'd want to stop. I'd start feeling sick.

For sex acts, everything she wanted to do was either painful or degrading. I kept thinking, "How can you do this to someone you love? I can't do this. I can't do this with my heart." It was ugly and embarrassing. I was supposed to love this girl, and even when I stopped loving her—I didn't even *like* her—I still didn't want to hurt her.

I told her I didn't want to see her. She wouldn't leave me alone. Like I'd come out of work, and she'd be parked down the block. She'd follow me home. I used to do evasive driving maneuvers, like go down one-way streets the wrong way. Drove over curbs and across someone's lawn one time to get to another block, because she was following me.

She came to where I worked and attacked me. She hit me like I was fighting with another man. She was throwing uppercuts, roundhouse punches. She fought like a guy. She kicked me in the nuts. When she kicked me in the nuts is when I hit her back. I punched her in the forehead. She went down, lifted her head up, and she smiled at me. I said to myself, "Now I'm in serious trouble. I hit her as hard as I could, and she's laughing at me. What do I do now?"

While I'm trying to defend myself, I'm thinking, "I have to stop doing this. She likes this. She enjoys this. This is better than sex for her." Two guys I worked with, bigger than me, got in between us and pulled us apart. They took her out to the street. The one guy was saying, "He doesn't love you. Why don't you go home?"

"But I love him, the stupid prick," she's saying. "I love him."

"I don't even like you," I said. "Why don't you go home? I don't love you."

She's standing in the street going, "I love you, I love you, I love you. I'll love you *forever*."

"I should die."

She's in the parking lot and she says, "All right, I won't hit you, if you'll just come outside and talk to me."

"Okay."

"I love you. Come over to my house tonight. I'll make love to you. I'll do everything you want me to do. I'll make you feel so good." She's going on and on.

It was Wednesday. We had Wednesday-night Bible service at the church. I said, "Okay. You go home and get cleaned up, and I'll call you later." I went to the church. I got the pastor, sat down and told him what had happened. He knew there were problems. I said, "What do I do?"

"You're supposed to call her?" he asks. So he calls her up on the phone. "Hi. I heard what happened with you and John today. I want you to leave him alone." She starts cursing him out over the phone. He hangs up and the phone rings. It's her.

"I'm sorry, I didn't mean to say that. I apologize." I know her routine. She does horrible stuff and then she apologizes. That's how she gets away with it.

I'm whispering to the pastor, "Kick her out of the church."

"If you want to continue to be a member of this church," he says, "you have to leave him alone. I don't want you to ever talk to him again."

Thank you, thank you.

So she starts coming to church and whatever row I'm sitting in she sits across from me and stares at me the whole time. I don't like going to church anymore. Everyone in the church I've known for two years now is looking at me like I'm a lunatic. I'm no longer asked to be an usher. I'm looking over my shoulder all the time.

Finally, she comes to my house. I live in a basement apartment. One of the windows is above ground. She marches up to the window wearing a dress. She knocks on the window. I look up at the window and she pulls her dress up. She has no underwear on. "Let me come in, please. Come on. I'll take care of you."

This goes on for months. She attacks the pastor of the church when he throws her out of the church because she's bothering me. I'm not happy going to the church anymore, but I still go there, because it's the only place I feel safe. They won't let her in.

I have a couple of friends who are cops, and I say, "What should I do?"

"File a couple of reports on her. Get a restraining injunction, and if she keeps bothering you, then you can kill her. But they'll know that you've tried to get rid of her. That's the best way to get rid of her." So I filed on her. She'd still come to my job, she'd come to my house. She wouldn't come to the door. She'd come to the window, knock, and pull up her skirt. She wouldn't go away. She'd just stand there.

Of course, I didn't sleep well during this period; you could understand that. I pass out one night. The lights are on and everything. I wake up the next morning and I've still got my clothes on and the lights are on. I go outside, and there are bad vibes. I see the screen is ripped off the window. It's all bent. I had the window locked. I look and there's cigarette butts—the type she smokes—three of them on the windowsill. She's been sitting outside my apartment banging on the window, tearing on the screen, trying to get inside.

She calls up one day. I answered the phone, because I was expecting someone else. It's her. *"Leave me alone!"* I hang up. She calls back, and keeps calling back. I'm ready to pull the phone out of the wall, but I said, "No, I'm going to do something. I'm going to talk to her."

I pick up the phone and I said, "Listen, I don't love you. I don't like you. I don't want to have sex with you. I don't want to talk to you. If you don't leave me alone, I'm going to take a razor and cut your face to ribbons, and no one is ever going to want you ever again!"

That was the last I heard from her. I've run into her twice. One time she was just on the street. She started cursing me out, calling me names. Another time, she just stared at me. But she's never come to my house since then, and I don't think she's followed me since then.

I grew up out in the country in the Pacific Northwest. Five children. Very domineering, charismatic father. My father is basically German, very cold, very distant, very, very unaffectionate, no touching. He said in later years that the reason he never gave any affection to us was that he was desperately afraid of pedophilia and incest. Because these things were such horrible, detestable ideas to him, he never wanted to do anything that could be mistaken in any way for incest. Oh, yeah, Dad, so now we know, you wanted to fuck us. Great, Dad, you were such a moral man. Thank you for being moral and not getting anywhere near us. What it did for me was to make me just sexually obsessed. That was a way to get emotional needs met.

When I was about five years old, the children across the street took me into their clubhouse and drew a diagram on a blackboard showing me what people do. This is really disturbing to me because my parents had told me the vague fantasy that when a man and woman are in love, and they lie in bed together at night, a seed from the man goes to the woman. The seed goes in this egg she has, and she gets pregnant. So I imagined a seed with little legs wandering across the sheets. I went home and told my mother about this lesson, and she said indeed what I had been told was true. I knew that early on.

I also saw animals having sex. That was very exciting to me, and I've always been excited by animals having sex with each other. I love the old forbidden porn of animals having sex with women, because you got to see the passion in animals. We had a dog when I was ten years old. We had again moved, and I was particularly new and unloved in the neighborhood. The dog used to jump up on everybody and try to hump them. He was a fairly big dog that took some effort to push away. For instance, I would see him doing this to my mother when she was stooped down gardening. It was very exciting to see, so I got the dog out behind the doghouse, got down on my hands and knees, and he did it to me. It was exciting but shaming and guilt-producing, but at the same time one of the most important factors was that the dog was very loving. The dog would be licking my face. There was this strong feeling that the dog loves me. I never actually had sex with the dog. God knows, the idea entered my head, and it has figured in fantasy. In truth I'd look at it and go, "Yuck, you're getting me dirty."

When I reached puberty, I was about twelve or thirteen years old. I started going to bed early, so I could lie in bed and fantasize. I was able to have orgasms without any kind of masturbation—I didn't know women could masturbate—just vague fantasies. They began with Robin Hood, who was one of my heroes. I would be stranded in the woods and Robin Hood would come and sweep me up onto the horse. That would be a very exciting moment, mistaking romance for sex.

As it went on, it developed into something that I know is very common, which is the idea that if anything was forced, then it was okay. You're not allowed to have sex, but the childish manipulation sex—"They made me do it!"—was okay.

An early dream was I was kidnapped into some kind of harem. There were people who worked for whoever the "Harem Dude" was who were going to prepare me for this guy. They had these Bakelite appliances that had to be inserted into my vagina and opened up, because this guy was going to be so big. But I never even saw this man; the whole dream and the whole exciting thing was that these people, in this pseudomedical setting, were holding me down and strapping them on and forcing me to wear these appliances which opened me up in this way. Gee, and my dad's a doctor. How about that?

It moved to having fantasies about anything that was forced, even disgusting people. I liked bikers. I liked the idea of a big gang of dirty guys, even the fat ones. I didn't idealize the way bikers were. I'd like to be gang-banged, but forced into it. A war situation, bring on the Nazis.

I was a very gawky, unpopular child. I was very tall, very thin. We moved a lot, we had a funny name, we ate funny food. All the things having to do with my parents' eccentricities made us outcasts. I was very, very securely an outcast in my peer group by the time I reached puberty. The butt of all school jokes, humiliated, very unpopular.

Therefore, I had no access to the normal young teenage dating activities. I may have had crushes on boys, but it was never reciprocated. It was used against me, if they found I had a crush on somebody. There were incidents where they'd leave a note in my locker supposedly signed by this person—"Oh, yes, I like you. Come and meet me behind the school." Naively, I'd go and do that. There would be a bunch of girls waiting to laugh at me and tell me how ugly I was.

So my early experiences were very bad. But I also learned early, at about thirteen, that older men did find me attractive, because I was mature for my age. So I found that if I could go take long walks at night, the guys might pull over in cars and talk to me. I didn't have the nerve to get in the car yet, but I used to force my dog to walk for miles in the evening, so these sorts of things could happen.

When I was fourteen, my mother, sisters and brothers, and I took a trip to California. I was just in full youthful horniness by this time and also desperately in need of attention.

We went down the West Coast in a car. We'd be stopping in places like Coos Bay, Oregon, for the night, all little logging towns. Every night, I would leave the motel after everybody went to sleep and wander through the town to bait people into stopping in their cars and saying something to me. This trip, I did indeed get into cars with a variety of ungodly people. A fat, middle-aged man in Coos Bay, I remember, who started fondling my breasts. We were pulled over by the cops, who knew him and told him that they knew I wasn't his niece as he was continuing to fondle me. They forced me to get out of the car.

Each town was a different adventure. I wasn't having sex with these guys. I was just exploring things. In Ukiah, California, I got picked up by a couple of race-car drivers who took me back to their house. One of them just got me in the bedroom, got up on top of me and tried to make me have sex with him. I began sniveling and crying, telling him I was a virgin. He was saying, "Well, I can take care of that for you." But I kicked around enough that in disgust they let me get up and leave. But all of these things then made wonderful sexual fantasies for me. I then left their house in the middle of nowhere and went out and hitched another ride with some other guy who tried to do the same thing. But I managed to get myself back to the motel.

I met a murderer in Willows, California, who took me out on a dam and was very respectful as he told me all the gory details of how he killed his father when he was twelve years old.

These things got back to my mother, because she woke up in Willows, California, that night and found out that I was gone at three o'clock in the morning. When I did arrive home in the pickup truck with the young, half-breed Indian murderer, the cops were all there. So when we got back, my father had a talk with me. He told me that women have these urges for love when they are young, and they seek it from men, but men do not feel love until they have been married to women for many years. Before that time all men feel is sexual urges towards women. Women will mistake these sexual urges for love, but when women have sex with men, the men will never love them. Therefore, women have to hold this in check until we meet a man we can somehow trap into marrying us, so he can begin this long process of falling in love with us.

My father could use his voice to make it sound warm, but there wasn't any warmth in it. He was a good actor. I wasn't very socialized. I was aggressively passive.

I did, however, begin having sex. The first time was when I was fifteen. There was an old man artist who had a gallery studio down under the public market, which was the hippie place to hang out. I used to go there, because I was attracted to outcasts of any stripe. I had identification with them. This old man was a true beatnik. He had the little goatee, the beret, and the black turtleneck. He'd get irritable with me for hanging around there sometimes, and then he would taunt me. "What is it you want?" One time he kissed me and yelled, "Is this what you want? Huh?" And he would tell me I was too young.

But one of his friends didn't think I was too young. He just very casually had sex with me there one day, so quickly that I didn't even know that it had happened. I was menstruating at the time. Back then we didn't wear tampons, so I had a pad on. He was just sort of fooling around with me, and suddenly he pulled this thing out of the way, stuck his penis in and came. I was like, "Huh?" Actually, I already lost my hymen before that in a struggle in a backseat with somebody without having sex, so I really didn't realize for about six months that I'd had sex, but I had in fact.

Following this, I met my first boyfriend at some sort of hippie concert. I thought he was a hippie. I didn't know the difference between a hippie and a bum, but it turned out that he was just a bum. He was a thirty-two-year-old bum who lived with his father in a flophouse in a bum section of town. He was a romantic bum, played the guitar. He was a hod carrier, itinerant hod carrier. He and his father would travel around from town to town, trying to get work and drinking themselves into oblivion, then move on somewhere else. We actually did have sex. I know it was very confused with the idea of love, because it felt so good, and he was just paying so much attention to me. It seemed like just the greatest thing on Earth.

At this point, I was about sixteen, and it just made me want to leave home. It made me want to go away from this miserable situation where I was going to high school, an outcast, made fun of and picked on. At home I was without affection or love, having to live with these strange dictates of my family and their rigid eccentricities. I disappeared for a week with somebody else besides the hod carrier. I simply went home with this guy and started smoking dope and having sex. I knew I'd stayed too long and was going to get into a lot of trouble if I went home, so I just didn't go home for a week. I was very afraid of my parents' disapproval.

I go to a shrink. I saw her yesterday, and she was talking to me about sex before I had done drugs and alcohol. I said, "There was no time before that. It all came at the same time. Sex and drugs were always linked together. Drugs and alcohol were foreplay. No proper man would attempt to have sex with a woman without offering her drugs or alcohol. That was the natural lubrication."

When I came back from being gone for a week, the cat was out of the bag. I really couldn't hide the fact that I was sexual from my parents. And I just didn't want to. The high school suggested that I shouldn't be allowed to come back, because I was sexually active. As they explained it, because I had experienced sexual pleasure, I would contaminate the other students, who they assumed were all virgins. I said, "Fine." My parents simply allowed me to move out of the house around my seventeenth birthday.

I moved into the center of the hippie district, went to a public school there, and worked at night. I began indulging myself in sex and drugs. I was very promiscuous, and thankfully the hippie movement was there to say it was okay, so I could handle the guilt about it a little better. I was also certainly drinking a lot and smoking a lot of dope. I felt very ruled by my sexuality. I would still say, "Gee, I'm horny. I've drunk a bottle of wine. I think I'll go take a walk." The old way still worked. I'd see who would pull over in a car. When one that looked interesting pulled over, "Yeah, I'll take a ride. Let's see where it goes. Let's see what happens."

I was fortunate in that I really did enjoy sex. I was orgasmic. I found it very easy, but I was also very shamed. Finally, after about a year of this, I felt very guilty about it. When I counted up and realized that I had, in fact, had sex with more than twenty-five men, I knew I was definitely going to go to hell and no one was ever going to marry me. "I'm almost eighteen and my life is ruined."

So I met a man who wasn't particularly interested in sex. That made me think he truly loved me, so I married him. Turned out he wasn't really interested in sex because he thought he was a woman trapped in a man's body. He liked to wear my clothes. "Oh, great, this is a secret that we can share, and it will bind us together." I helped him. I let him. He wasn't much bigger than me, and we would go shopping together. I'd try on shoes that were a size too big, and then buy them for him. I indulged his transvestism.

It was very destructive, because he was very solo sex–oriented. All he wanted to do was dress up and masturbate. He did not tell me at the time that he wanted to be a woman. He told me just that he liked the feel of women's clothing and that was the extent of his peculiarity. I should learn to masturbate. That went further and further until it was, "Women are smelly and wet, and I really don't like to get near it."

We did manage to have a child though. He was very jealous about the child. It was a horrible phase. He would attack the child. He would attack me. Physically abusive, psychologically abusive, but also I had been raised with the understanding that a woman's number-one reason to live was to serve her husband. After that came the children. So he'd say, "Okay, we're going to put the child in a foster home." And I'd say okay. I tried to get help from my parents, but they would not help. My mother in particular was adamant about the fact that my husband was there to take care of these things for me. They didn't really listen. So the child went into various foster homes. Would come back, and it would be the same.

My husband convinced me that if we moved to the South, where his relatives lived, they would take care of the child. We moved to a tiny town in the Deep South. I did not realize that a tiny town in a Southern state was not going to allow my lifestyle. It was real educational. The family was an alcoholic grandmother and a couple of identical-twin Faulkner characters. So there was no help. It was down there that he finally convinced me to put the child up for adoption. I did and went on my way.

I was emotionally dead at this point. We weren't having any sex or sex maybe once every three months. I had been completely convinced that I was utterly sexually undesirable and that was the problem. He was more and more into transvestism. He would go out at night and was picking up boys. He liked to expose himself to children. Or try to get children to expose themselves to him. He was into corruption of innocence, either male or female. If he could get a twelve-year-old girl to touch herself in front of him, that would be great. He would try to get one child to suck another child's dick; that would be exciting to him. He was always trying to get me into his fantasies—"What if we waited in this alley until a girl came along and we'd pull her into the alley, pull her pants down, spank her and then let her go?" That never quite happened. I was willing to say, "Here, we'll wait in the alley and see." I went along.

I'm very ashamed about the way I was then, but I know it came from my upbringing. I was so absolutely passive and such a victim.

He did succeed in getting me into masturbation though, which I had never known was possible. It did turn out to be a great thing. I was very glad to learn that from him. He was very intent on teaching me to masturbate, so he could free himself from having to have sex with me.

When the child was actually put up for adoption, we were practically stoned and run out of this small town. We retreated to where my parents had moved in Maryland and worked in a hospital together as nurse's aides. He had an affair with a receptionist and flaunted it in my face. Thankfully that allowed me to end it. But also it took a toll on me, because it had been so long since we had had sex, that when I actually began an affair of my own, I found that I couldn't just come anymore. It had worked on me when he told me I wasn't sexually desirable. I remember bursting into tears when I had sex and realized that it wasn't the same anymore, it wasn't like before the marriage.

But I continued being promiscuous and smoking a lot of dope and drinking a lot of alcohol and having fun in a way. Sex felt very gratifying. Okay, if I didn't come, I could always masturbate later, and it would be great. I could think about what had gone on, so it was like setting up my own masturbation scenarios, acting them out in real life, and then masturbating to them to get satisfaction later. Strange pattern.

I liked seeing a lot of men at the same time. I liked seeing young men, men younger than me. I was proud in that period of just collecting them for their attractiveness and dick size.

But then, after a couple of years, I would feel shamed again and wander back into a monogamous relationship. The promiscuity would be fun, but I would always feel guilty. This was not the way it was supposed to be. You were supposed to have a relationship. Then I would form a relationship with some really inappropriate person.

The person I chose at this time was the one who got me into my present career in the world of pornography, who was probably the worst one I've been involved with. A really fucked-up misogynist who actually hit me. My first husband was mean, but he didn't actually hit me. I learned that it was fun to hit this guy back. He was extremely sexually compulsive, where he had to have orgasms eight, nine, ten times a day. If you got into a cab, this guy would want a hand job in the back. If you got into an elevator, he would want you to suck his dick. It all had to do with appearances. It had to do with the idea of it, not the fact of it, to make him feel good, to make him feel he was alive.

He was very promiscuous, a liar, violent. But I learned to enjoy being violent back. He'd hit me, and I'd hit him harder. Then it got to where I'd hit him first.

We were in a restaurant eating with an author who was a friend of his. He was trying to impress this guy and being an utter asshole. He was stealing my food and telling me what to order, humiliating me. Finally, I'd just had enough. I just turned around and said, as I was doing it, "I'm going to hit you." I hit him right in the jaw, knocked him over backwards in his chair in the restaurant. That did impress the author, who just burst out laughing and was utterly thrilled with it. The guy got up and punched me in the stomach, kicked me in the shins, so we had to leave the restaurant.

This relationship was a turning point. We got so bad that we got into therapy to fix our relationship. I was finally told, "Get away from this man, he's a lunatic." What finally happened with this guy was that he was trying to choke me as I was leaving him, and I kicked him in the balls. Seeing him writhing on the floor, weak and in pain, gave me a sense of my power. I got away from that. I can't say that I became absolutely healthy overnight, but it was a big leap forward.

I went back to being the jolly, promiscuous person, indulging in the New York City sexuality of that period, which meant that I went to Plato's Retreat, I went to the S&M clubs. It was a wonderful thing to have been able to do, and I'm very glad that I got to live through that period of history and survive. The ability to walk into a club on a Friday night, and there are six hundred naked people. Take my clothes off, put them in a locker and walk around, shoot pool, swim in that wonderful warm pool, and engage in whatever peculiar sexual whim came up. It made me feel very healthy.

There are so many images, just visuals to cherish from that time. Sitting at the S&M clubs while naked old men sucked our toes and brought us beer. The guy who used to stand outside the women's restroom door at one S&M club with a stack of cups and five-dollar bills. He'd hand you a cup. Then when you came out with it full of urine, he'd give you a five-dollar bill. Then he'd sip on it while he waited for the next one.

It was a strangely invigorating time. When I got home, I felt good. It's shocking. It was the feeling of pure indulgence, of being a complete hedonist, drinking and smoking dope and doing coke and indulging in sex and still young enough to be immortal. I was in my late twenties by this time. I never got a venereal disease. I survived.

At the time it was happening, I would have said I was just immensely enjoying my sexuality. But when I go over it in my mind, how much of the time was I actually having orgasms? Almost never. I would go home and masturbate. I never thought about it until I got into therapy. When I walked in, the therapist asked about sex and I said, "I have no problems with sex. I love sex. I'm a very sexual person. Sex is great." And yet I have to look back and say, yes, I was doing all these things, and it was very psychologically, visually, sensually, intellectually exciting—I am very voy-euristic and this was just filling up the old voyeur bank with incredible material—but in the way that we're supposed to see sex as satisfying, no, it was not satisfying.

As usual, I came to the point of feeling guilty. I was going to be thirty soon, and "Oh, my God, no one is going to marry me if I go on like this, so I'd better find somebody." Whenever that thought would enter my mind, immediately someone would present themselves.

I met a man. We had our first sexual encounter at Plato's. We'd all gone as a group. We began living together three months later. A year later, we were married. Gee, once again, I had married a man who didn't like sex, or seemed not to like sex. The problems were more complex than that. He was an alcoholic, and his self-image was so bad that while he had to flirt wildly with women and was very sexually compulsive, he didn't feel worthy. So once he was actually settled down and married, he didn't want to have sex. I repeated that pattern, feeling what I had been taught as a child: If a man wants to have sex with me, it means he does not love me. If he does not want to have sex with me, it means he does love me. But I couldn't figure that out at the time. All I thought was I must make men want to stop having sex, or there's just something very fucked up in me that I pick guys who don't like sex. Certainly I blamed it all on them.

After trying to be monogamous with this for three years, I began having affairs, feeling very, very angry towards my husband. He wouldn't talk about it, wouldn't deal with it. But I know now that it didn't really have to do with sex. At the time that's what I was focused on. My problem was that my husband doesn't want to have sex with me, so I must have sex. Sex is very important to me. I must find somebody to have sex with.

Now, I think I just felt rejected. I defined myself through sex and had been raised that way. The only affection I ever saw my father deliver was in sexual form to my mother. He was forever sticking his hands up her dress or feeling her tits in front of us. The only way he felt comfortable expressing himself was through sex, which was why he couldn't give us any affection, because he saw all affection as sexual. I grew up with that idea in my mind, too.

My occupation is a sexual occupation. I have defined myself entirely through sex and through being a highly sexed woman. It's very important to me to be perceived as a highly sexed woman. After being the geek of all geeks in school, I learned to dress sexy. I wanted to walk down the street and turn every head, have people see me as a sexy woman.

So I left that husband for another person, who I thought I was going to have great sex with, a younger, dumber man. I then repeated the pattern. He then got into his alcoholism and got into drugs and didn't want to have sex with me. I was pushing for sex all the time. He was rebelling by not wanting it. So again, after two or three years of this frustration, I began an affair with someone else. God knows, if I'd left this one for that one, the same thing might have happened.

Fortunately, I was getting fed up. I was saying, "This is something that's not going to work. Maybe I'm just not going to have a monogamous relationship with somebody, because they'll all quit having sex with me." It drove me into therapy.

Therapy has totally destroyed my sex life. I'm in a transitional phase. What I finally learned is that I really wanted affection. I mean, it's so trite, so female, I despise it. I hate it. I can't deny that I had a great time with all the sex for all those years, but I was getting all my emotional needs met through sex. I would make sex a really important thing that I would look forward to tremendously and initiate it whenever possible. Now I learned that, indeed, I have affectionate needs and needs that have nothing to do with sex.

The trite thing is that I actually want affection more than sex. I'm actually just a regular woman, and it sucks the big one. I would much rather admit to you, "Hey, I'm a hot-to-trot babe, who is sexually compulsive," than to say, "I'm a regular woman with a regular woman's sex drive. It's a little hard to come, and I have to masturbate with intercourse in order to come, and I don't really want to have sex more than anybody else. I want to be loved and cuddled."

I hate it. I want to be a man. I have great envy for male sexuality. I want to be able to look at someone on the street and throb. But the truth is that women don't work that way, and I don't like it. I don't like it a bit. For sixteen years, I've read letters from men about their sexuality. I do sex magazines. I have seen the extremities of male desire. I'm particularly interested in the fetish areas. Fetishes are incredible drives. Men can be obsessive about sex the way women aren't. I envy it. I know it's male hormones. I know women who take steroids. They get horny. They drip. Their clits get big. They get sexually aggressive. I don't have penis envy, I have sensitivity envy. I don't want a dick, I just want what I see as the easy fun that goes with it. Of course, I could take testosterone, but I'm much too vain to do it. I want all my feminine attributes. I want to be Super Woman.

It's been real hard for me the last couple of years. I am in a relationship, a very good one, the best, healthiest monogamous relationship of my life. My sex life is unexceptional. I have problems like I've heard other women whine about for years, when I would always smugly say, "I don't have those problems. I'm not really a woman."

FOUR

REALITY CHECK

1. DATING

Dating conjures up anachronistic images of prom night with Ozzie and Harriet Nelson stirring the punch bowl at the dance, or perhaps a movie and ice-cream sodas; an evening ending with an innocent kiss on the cheek and the certainty that father does know best. Today, teenagers still embark on their first forays into sexual socializing with awkward telephone conversations and sweaty palms, but almost everything else about dating has changed radically in the last twenty years.

Dating—the unchaperoned, open-ended congress of men and women as isolated couples—is a relatively modern phenomenon, acceptable as a social institution for only a generation or two. In the early part of this century, a proper, class-appropriate young man would woo a respectable young woman under the watchful eyes of her family at cotillions and church socials, on front-porch swings and at taffy pulls. This was courtship, not seduction. The idea was to find a mate. As late as the 1950s, a young man might be asked about his "intentions" after a few weeks or months of dating the same woman.

World War II is ultimately responsible for dating as we know it today. The disruptions of class and caste, along with the independence women gained when they were impressed into the workforce of the war machine, led directly to what would be called the sexual revolution twenty years later. Along the way Hollywood whipped up the confectionary cultural ideal of the immediate postwar period with Rock Hudson and Doris Day, the rich, eligible playboy and the squeaky-clean but sexy working girl. He chased her until she caught him. The game had changed, but the result was still the same. They got married before they had sex.

The social upheaval in the late 1960s, combined with the introduction of the birth-control pill, seemed for a while to make the date superfluous. College students could now have sex without fear of pregnancy. But free love—"If you can't be with the one you love, love the one you're with"—turned out to be mostly exploitative hype instead of the herald of utopian sexual equality. Free sex without guilt or strings attached never made it into mainstream American culture, although there *are* a lot of home movies in America's attics of hippie weddings full of flowers and flowery vows.

By the 1970s, the passionate idealism was gone, but the new sexual freedom added an element of sport to the dating scene. With the de-emphasis on marriage, dating became primarily a way for adults to find sexual partners. Although the search was still vaguely tinged with expectations of finding a lifetime commitment, many men and women simply became sexual predators, and they fed greedily on one another's physical and emotional vulnerability.

Today, their vision blurred by the confusing crosscurrents of rapidly changing male and female roles in modern society, bloodied by the head-banging of sexual politics, many men and women in America have spent the last twenty years or more "dating" one person after another in a quixotic fishing expedition for "the right one." The dating game has become just that—a frustrating game that often subverts and overwhelms the players, because there is no clear-cut endgame. Dating is no longer an activity only for the young. Men well past their prime and running to mental and physical pudginess and women beyond their biologically reproductive years stand in the singles' bars, cynically critiquing the members of the opposite sex at their elbows, despairing of ever finding a soul mate.

With so many marriages ending in divorce, hundreds of thousands of people every year find themselves back on the market for a partner at different stages in their lives. Few couples manage to survive divorce amicably. Serial monogamy without the formality of documents and sacraments is no better. By definition, it implies multiple breakups, each of which can be as agonizing and antagonistic as legal divorce. So more and more people bring the bitterness engendered by their earlier disappointments with the opposite sex to the search for a new partner. Instead of the playful exploration one might expect to find, dating is often typified today by an edge of anger and retaliation. Men and women approach each other full of suspicion.

The field of play for the dating game has moved. Although people still flirt and talk in bars or dance clubs, meet in church groups or at dinner with friends, economic necessity forces most people to spend their days and, often, part of their nights at work. That's where people meet as leisure hours disappear in hard times. However, the recent emphasis on sexual harassment on the job has disrupted the office romance as well. Dating your boss or someone who works for you or with you is more complicated than ever for both men and women.

If dating is a dangerous game emotionally and socially, physically it can be downright deadly. The specter of AIDS infection haunts every sexual encounter with a new person. Getting to know one another better means exchanging sexual histories and maybe HIV test results. Never before has the condom been as integral to dating as the charge card. So sexually active adults playing the dating game have sweaty palms and awkward telephone conversations, too, these days. But unlike the teenagers' basic fears of rejection, adults' anxieties are a mixture of a gut-level distrust of the opposite sex and an acute sense of their own mortality.

o   o   o

After my first marriage when I became single again, I eventually was able to figure out how to pick up women and seduce them. I'll give a few tips for the readers.

Eye contact is very important. That's number one. They like a little intensity.

Physical attractiveness helps a lot. When you listen to girls talk, they talk about the way guys look. Guys don't dress or pay as much attention to physical looks as women do. Women are interested in fashion, and they do notice when you dress nicely.

It also helps if you have a lot of money. Doesn't hurt a bit. If you're not good-looking or rich, you just do your best to keep neat, stay trim, and look prosperous.

They like you to talk to them. Women love to talk. They are always looking for someone to talk to. If you are really interested in them and want to listen to what they have to say, they will let you do that. There is nothing so pleasant in my mind as sitting in a bar with a new woman that

I'm just beginning to get to know, gazing into her eyes, and letting her talk to me for hours on end.

They will let you know when they are ready. They send out signals. They will reach over and pick a piece of lint off your lapel, or somehow give you the signal that it's okay to invade their space a little bit.

It's important to breathe in their faces, because it's an exchange of pheromone. Scent is extremely important in all aspects of sex, something that modern people don't appreciate as much as they should. There is nothing—oh, God—like the scent of a woman. Um-um-um.

Oh, I left out an important step. Before breathing in their face, you have to dance with them. Women like dancing. It's some sort of primitive deal. That's the attraction of nightclubs and bars where they do dancing. Women like it, and it's a lot of fun. Dancing with a strange woman, there's nothing like it!

There's nothing like meeting a woman in a bar, spending some time getting to know her, dancing with her for hours. Then at the end of the evening, have her take a matchbook, and jot down her name and number in a nice feminine hand. That is great. You take that little souvenir home, and look at where she's written out her number in this lovely cursive scrawl, and it's something to treasure. I wish I had a shoe box full of little slips of paper where women have written down their phone numbers for me. How sexy!

I have never slept with a woman on the same night that I met her, although, Lord knows, I've tried. I'm of the understanding that in the late '60s and early '70s, you could go down to a bar, meet a girl in her twenties, say, "Hey, let's go home, get stoned, and fuck," and they'd say okay. I never did that, but I understand it was doable. Maybe people just say that they did that. It happened at least enough to become an urban legend.

I've heard guys say, "I wouldn't want to go sleep with a girl on the first night I met her." I don't believe that for a minute. I'd love to do that. Or they say, "That's not the type of girl you'd sleep with."

"Nonsense," I say.

When you do get a chance to have sex with them, you have got to pay attention to their breasts. They all like that, invariably. I have found that once you have gotten a woman aroused, there is a point that they cross over. You can get them turned on, make out, and you can feel them up. Then it's like they just snap. When they get turned on, and the juices start going, they're ready and you can talk them into almost anything.

Those are a few of my tips for getting along with the fairer sex. This represents original research based on countless hours of trial and error.

I probably slept with ten or twelve different women over a three- or four-year time span, one every two or three months. I found that tremendously exciting. I was in my late twenties, early thirties. The girls were in that age range. They were all bitter about men at that point, because every one of them had been in at least one relationship that had gone sour. It was like dating the walking wounded. They were all in this little shell that you had to chip away at, earn their trust.

I did not find any women looking for sex just for the sake of sex, the same way I was. I ran across some women who only sleep with guys they don't like, sort of a self-protective thing. I ran across a couple of women who, after we'd go out on a date and had come back to my place, it would be like, "Okay, what do you want me to do?" They were not particularly interested in romance. They knew that I was interested in sex, and they let me know that they were willing to put up with it. They were not all that much fun.

Thinking back on it now with a little bit more maturity, I could have done some things to bring them around. Maybe say, "Why don't you lay down on this couch, and we'll turn the lights down low. You drink a glass of wine. I'll give you a foot massage, while you tell me all the bad things that happened to you today." Now, that would work. Back then I didn't know. I was very selfish and didn't know what women's problems were. I was just looking out for myself, learning stuff as I went along.

Some women really did like sex more than other women. There was this one girl, Carol Young. She was the best sexual partner I ever had. I could just make Carol have orgasm after orgasm. She loved it, just ate it up, wanted to do fun things. She was the only woman in my life who would actually buy sexy negligees just for my benefit. It's such an ego trip to have a woman really concentrate on giving you pleasure. My experience is that it doesn't happen very often. Those are rare and valuable women if you can find them.

Since I was recently divorced, the last thing in the world I wanted was another relationship. I would tell that to women, pretty much. Consequently, I was not as successful at finding them. I tried to be forthright and up-front. I didn't go out of my way when I met a woman to say, "Listen, I don't really want a relationship, and I'm *definitely* never going to get married again, so if you'd like to go talk to someone else, please do." But I made no secret of the fact that I wasn't quite ready to settle down either. I don't believe in the notion of letting it all hang out. I believe in politeness and giving people respect. Sometimes people don't want to know everything about you.

It was very up and down. I'd fall in love and it would be great. Then I'd be heartbroken and in the depths of depression for a week or two. Then I'd be in love again, and on a mountaintop. I've heard a lot of people say they didn't like being single, because they didn't like the roller-coaster ride. I really enjoyed that roller-coaster ride, although people tell me I'm just glorifying the past.

G oing back to being single after having not been single was very interesting, mainly because of my own disappointments. When you're tied up with someone, you always imagine that thing that's happening outside the relationship is what you're most eager for. I thought, "Man, I'm verbal and attractive. I won't have any problem."

It was really grim. I didn't really have anything to offer. I'm not somebody who allows relationships to remain superficial. I like to get right into it. So superficial fucking isn't that attractive to me except as sort of an exercise. I'm not too crazy about postcoital comedowns where you just go, "Why did I do that?"

So I found myself in a weird position where I didn't have anything to offer, *just sex,* and I couldn't pretend it was otherwise. I couldn't bring down the mask, the pretense, and say, "Listen, I'm just going to screw you, and then we'll go our own ways," because when I'd meet them, I'd be operating on a program to try to get to the deeper person. Maybe I was being manipulative, but I was miserable. I wasn't macho enough to use their bodies and get the hell out of there. At the same time, I wasn't able to signal enough need.

Friends of mine who were getting laid all the time were doing it because they were incredibly needy, and it was obvious that they were needy. They *needed* the company. Women related to that and felt very useful. I don't know how they did it, but I was amazed when I was comparing notes with my pals. The ones who I thought were just hopeless, pathetic, and neurotic were getting all the dates.

In the sexual courtship and dance, it's very hard to figure out what you're supposed to be supplying. Are you supplying strength? Are you allowing the other person to know what they're supplying? I just didn't have a need except for the physical one. I wasn't really looking for anything, and women can see that.

It's like the old thing that I've found is true: If you're having lots of sex, it's sensed, like pheromone. People sense it, and they want to get in. If you're in a period of very low sexual activity, it's sensible for some reason. Our antennae pick up on this stuff.

When I was going through dry spells when I couldn't make contact with a woman for love nor money, and then finally I would make it, suddenly I was very attractive. When you're married, women want to talk to you. You get hit on when you're happy.

I generally found that it didn't pay off to be the sensitive guy. Friends of mine who are more macho and brutal and insensitive in general always scored better than me. They always got more women. So when you come into this theory of are we being rewarded by women in a sexual way for being sensitive, caring men, I would say categorically, no, we are not. At a certain point when they decide to settle down, that issue may become more important, the desire for strength, shelter, and finding a strong man, but not while they're dating.

My whole college career was taken up with talking a good game, and still losing to the Neanderthal bass player who could barely talk. Days later I would still be going, "I can't believe you went with the guy in the microbus. That is like so juvenile. I can't believe it!"

They say now that one of the most important elements in a man's makeup to a woman—after honesty—is a sense of humor. I have a *great* sense of humor. It got me close to women, but it never got me anywhere sexually. Ultimately, they were still going to go home with Bonehead Number One—the handsome, unfeeling individual would constantly win out.

This stuff about, "Who are you dating now?"—heck, I'm not dating anybody. I haven't had anybody call me for a date in so long I don't know that dating happens anymore. Do people date? You see magazine articles: WHAT DO YOU WEAR ON A DATE? I don't know what you wear on a date. Shit, you don't wear anything, because you don't go on a date.

I have a jaded and tainted attitude towards men, but I have hope. Maybe that sums it up. I'm scared, but not so scared that I won't try again. Men don't really understand what women want, because women don't know what they want. We're all confused. I was brought up to be June Cleaver. Then all of a sudden we had all this free love, then the women's movement, then there's Madonna. I mean, I've been dragged through all kinds of stuff. It's amazing I can figure out which foot to put in which shoe in the mornings. Do you wear a bra, or do you *not* wear a bra? Do you date, or do you *not* date? Do you sleep with them, or do you *not* sleep with them? There aren't any rules anymore. You make them up as you go along.

My experience with men is they want to control women. They want to have one set of rules for the women in their lives and another set for themselves—it's okay for them to fuck around, but it's not okay for her to fuck around. There's this "I'm up here as a guy, and you—woman—are down there."

They don't understand that here's this woman who is a human being, a person with needs and feelings. They can't comprehend that. Maybe they don't comprehend what their own needs and feelings are. I can't speak for all women, but I know that's not what I want. I want someone who will not always be looking for some other woman to sleep with, just because it's new and different. I don't understand why they do that. It undermined my confidence in men. I felt used. This man says he loves me and respects me, then he turns around and does something that is so opposite to loving and respecting somebody. Why should I trust him?

I broke up with my last girlfriend three years ago. I haven't gone out on a date since then. Oh, a couple of blind dates, set up by friends, but never for more than one date. Never a second date. I've never called them back.

I've thought about this. In my life, I went out with three girls who really wanted to get married to me. Whether they were wrong or right for me, I could have been married three times. Yet, I've never been married once. I like children very much. I enjoy my friends' kids. I don't have any kids of my own. When I think about this stuff, I say, "It ain't them. It's got to be me." When I had them standing right there in front of me, and she said, "Do you want to get married to me?" I said, "No."

The thing I like about women is sex. The things I don't like are: They need constant attention, and they want to talk about stuff that just doesn't seem to matter, or they want to talk about stuff too long. I miss women, or I miss parts of them. Some parts. When I think about it, what I miss is sex. I sit there and say to myself, "Gee, I'm horny. I haven't gotten laid in what? I can't remember how long. What am I going to do about this?" Then I think about what I have to go through to have sex. I don't intend to pay a hooker, because there's too much disease out there. I'm not a smooth talker. I'm not going to a bar and pick someone up. It's not me.

So the way to have sex is I got to have a relationship. When I think about meeting some woman and doing the whole thing, and how long it's going to take to get laid, I say, "I don't want to do this." It's not worth the effort now. I don't know if it will be in the future. I'm hoping I change my mind on this.

I'm in my early forties. If I want kids, I got to meet someone who's not past the point where they're afraid to have kids. That's substantially younger than me now. I've got to meet someone who's compatible and who's willing to take on a forty-two-year-old blue-collar worker. That's when things get strange out there.

I work in a restaurant some nights. The girls in the restaurant, they're all twenty years old. I'm not compatible with a twenty-year-old girl. They're cute. I'd like to go to bed with them, but they're not worth the effort. I don't have anything in common with them.

For the last couple of years, I haven't done anything except get turned off by strangers. This one friend of mine, his wife set me up like five times on blind dates. She thinks everyone should be married. Only one of them was anyone I would have gone out with. The others were definitely not my type from the get-go. There was one girl, though, who was smart as a whip, fun to be with, and I didn't turn her on worth two cents. We've become friends; I see her at family functions. We sit next to one another, and we have a great time together, because she's got a very sarcastic sense of humor, but I don't thrill her. Of the five girls I was introduced to, this is the only one I like, and she's not interested.

She set me up with another woman, who I haven't talked to since. She's left messages on my answering machine. One of them said, "I need to talk to you. I need to talk to you. Call me back as soon as you can." I don't like that message. It sounded desperate.

The second message was, "Oh, hi, it's Sunday. You know, I get every-body's answering machine, and I always feel like they're sitting there listening to me and not wanting to talk to me. If that's not the case, call me back whenever you want to."

I came home and I saw the answering-machine light on. I listen to that, and I say, "Do I really want to go meet this girl? She's already paranoid that I'm screening her out of my life? I don't want to meet her."

I don't know what I'm going to do. I don't know if I want to get involved, or just stay the way I am. I have my friends and members of my family that I like. I live alone, and I have on and off since I left my parents' house. I have my books. I have my movies. I have the stuff that I want to do. I don't know if I want someone else to come into that. I think about having a relationship. If I get involved with a woman, that means I have to clean up my apartment if they want to come over—which is going to be a monumental task in itself. If I invite my friends over, I don't care if they see that I'm not a big whoop-de-do housekeeper. So what? When one of my married friends comes over, he says, "I hate you. You're my only friend I have whose toilet seat is always up. You don't have to worry about women being here."

I've come to no conclusion. It worries me. Most of my friends are married, and the ones who aren't married have girlfriends. I'm talking to this one guy who doesn't, and he's saying, "I want to find a girlfriend, I want to find a girlfriend."

"What for?" I'm thinking, "They're nothing but a pain in the ass." Then I get home and think to myself, "What are you saying, 'They're nothing but a pain in the ass'? What about that *love* stuff? Sex, love, spending time together, someone to share your thoughts with?"

Either I'm going to forget about this, and just make a life without women forever, or I'm going to have to get off the fence on this one. I've thought about putting ads out—"Looking for physical relationship, and nothing else"—just to see what would happen.

I miss sex and not just sex. I miss the intimacy that goes with being with a person you are *intimate* with. The overall feeling, the little "in" jokes, the things just between the two of you. There's intimacy to just sitting on the same couch and reading different sections of the same newspaper at the same time.

The other stuff? Is it worth the trouble for that? I've been living without that for a while, and I say to myself, "I can live without this. At least, it's not killing me. I may not be real happy about it a lot of the time, but I'm not fighting with my wife or my girlfriend like I see some of my friends doing constantly."

I went out a couple of times with this lawyer on dates. He's a real nice guy. I just didn't know what the problem was between us. Finally, he told me, "Margot, you're too modest. You've got too many morals. I'm just going to tell you, I find you very attractive, but the things I like, you wouldn't do them."

"What do you mean? I don't know what you're talking about," I said.

"You're perfect. And you'll be perfect for some other guy. But I want a chick who will be into it if I have a fantasy, and I want to see her sleep with four or five different guys while I stand there and watch. You wouldn't do that."

"Hell, no. I'd probably kill you if you asked me to do something like that."

"But today," he told me, "men want sleaze."

"Who wants to marry sleaze?" I said. They can say, "Oh, she's cold as ice. She is strict." That's not true. I'm a very loving person. I'm a very affectionate person, but I refuse to be dogged out and know it. So many women are easy, they just tolerate the men, put up with them.

Men today, they just don't have any morals. There is so much sex out there, and that's the only thing they know. I don't even go to the clubs anymore. I've been in clubs where a man walked up—didn't know me from Eve. The first thing he said was, "Oh, you look so good. I would love to eat you out."

Doesn't know my first name! I said, "Uh, excuse me. Not tonight. Call me, maybe we'll work it out tomorrow." That's the way I talk to them—just crazy. They don't have any respect to come out and say that to somebody. I don't know if it's because they run across a little trampy, no-caring woman that they can say that to, and they think it's funny. I don't find it very amusing. What do you figure I am—dessert?

One of the biggest men in this town wants to date me. We talk. He wants a fool. I'm no fool. I told him, "First of all, you've got a woman. She comes over to your house when you tell her, on Wednesdays, I believe it is. She does whatever you say to do. You've got the wrong chick here, bud."

"You're too independent, Margot," he says. "You're too headstrong."

"No, you want me to be a fool. You want me to come over there and give you a piece of ass when you want it. You've been dating that girl eight years. You bought a house with her, but all you use her for is a bed partner. You think I'm going to help you out on that? Wrong."

"You just like to punish men."

"No, and just because you took me out to dinner, don't think you're going to get a free piece of ass."

A man likes a woman that's ignorant, that doesn't have sense to talk up for herself, not enough sense to do anything but work and give him her money. And he doesn't want her to say shit back. The fact is that I'm not going to let anybody use me, and men today will use you real quick. I mean *real* quick.

I want to tell you all about my friends John and Marsha. They are a couple that have a very good relationship; at least, I thought they had a very good relationship. They're both in their mid-forties. He had never been married. He is what you would call a confirmed bachelor. She is divorced, and has been divorced for eight or nine years. They have been dating for the last four or five years. Each has their own separate house. They see each other, they date, they have a good time. But they both have their own very distinct lives. I never thought either one of them was particularly interested in marriage.

This was a good deal. This could be a '90s type of relationship, where she's got her own house and her own family and her own thing. And he's got his own thing. This was really cool.

I found out this weekend that they are broken up. The reason is that she wanted more out of the relationship, which I found very typical. Marsha, like most women, wants a man that she can rely on, who will be there when she needs him. When the dog dies, she wants someone she knows will be there to comfort her. John, on the other hand, he wouldn't even have a dog to begin with. And if he did and it died, he wouldn't need anyone to comfort him. He's very self-reliant. You go out, dig a hole in the backyard, bury the dog, maybe cry a few tears, say a few words, and that would be it. Most men if they have a problem would just as soon be left alone.

For him to get more involved with her would just be added responsibility on his part. He'd have to take care of her in times of crises, and be with her. He didn't want that. That's what marriage is all about, having someone that you are responsible for. He's got a job and a house and adult responsibilities. Most men don't particularly want the responsibility of marriage.

That's the difference between dating and marriage. Dating is the fun part where you go out and do things together. You have sex, eat dinner, and go to the movies together. There was more champagne and roses in John and Marsha's relationship than the average couple has to deal with, because they *were not married.*

Typically, she says she doesn't want to get married, *but* she wants the relationship to evolve. To me, it seems that women are always wanting relationships to evolve, and guys would be perfectly happy to have a relationship that's just static, that stays the same all the time. Perpetual dating that doesn't go anyplace.

I survived the sexual revolution relatively unscathed. Right now I'm forty-nine and back on the streets, divorced and single again. I did not want to be there.

I had a blind date just this past weekend. This lady was attractive enough, but within hours of meeting her, she's talking about all the girls who must be running through my apartment and all this shit. About the only women in my apartment are my daughters. I finally said to her, "There are no women running through here, but what if there were? What would it have to do with this date?"

She was full of this, "I won't ever hear from you again," and on and on with this shit. I'm thinking about being close, about maybe getting laid, but—oh, shit!—have I kicked the tar baby here?

This lady spent the night with me, and we did not have sex. I go to sleep. I don't know how long it was, but I'd been sound asleep and woke up, because she is playing with my dick—roughly, like someone might milk a cow. I'm thinking, "Now, that hurts, but at least she seems interested."

"No, no, I'm sorry," she apologizes. "I shouldn't have done that." And she turns me down again. She did that a couple of times during the night. I can't get rid of her in the middle of the night. She's from out of town. I managed to get rid of her the next morning, but then I just sat around all afternoon and shuddered. "Oh, goddamn, what was that?"

My point is that this is the kind of shit that's left. This is what I have to look forward to, culling through the culls. That is not a pleasant prospect. It makes celibacy look more attractive.

These days I either want sex with no complications at all—let's get together and do something mechanical and take it for what it's worth—or I want to have a relationship. I don't want any of that in-between stuff which we used to get in the late '70s. You could be in love for a week with somebody, and then somebody else next week. It was all pretty easy. It didn't take a lot of mental effort.

Primarily, I'd like a relationship. I don't want to sleep around with all the bullshit that's out there now. I don't want to die.

I wish we could talk in public about what is appropriate and not appropriate. If I could say something to the women of America, I would say, "You need to be a little more aggressive in letting us know when you're really saying no and when you're really saying perhaps." But, goddamn, that sounds insensitive. Maybe I should put it a little differently: "Let us know when you are saying *yes.*"

I'd say, "Lighten up. Let's find some common ground." Tell the women of America that I'm tired of male-bashing. I know there are a lot of complex problems, and I know there is too much unwanted sexual attention. I can't help it. Give us a hand here. Good negotiators try to find common ground where both sides can win. That's what I want to hear from women, not what assholes men are. What can we do to get together on the right track? Men need a better dialogue with women and they need to recognize that we are different animals. We do like to get laid. Our sexual response is different than theirs, but that doesn't mean that ours is right and theirs is wrong or vice versa.

I would never rape a woman. I'm not at all turned on by a woman who is not interested in me. I find "No" is a real turn-off. To me, the whole positive experience of seducing a woman is getting her to want to say yes. This slow, drawn-out game. But most of that game is played in non-verbal clues and innuendo as the woman lets you know what you can and cannot do.

It would be what you call date rape, but I call it rape. I was with somebody who was a friend of mine, kind of. I really was friendly with some other people and this guy was around them. I never was really sure about this guy.

This was also in the time when people experimented with drugs. I didn't, because I was never a big drug user, either. On this occasion the drug was Quaaludes. I remember doing them, and I remember vague things. I remember going with this guy in his car, but we were going somewhere for a purpose that we never got to. The guy's father owned a trailer park, so I remember ending up in this trailer, one of the furnished show trailers, complete with all the furniture, and in this bed, with no strength. I remember trying to get this guy off of me. I couldn't get him off to save my life, and I'm pretty tough.

Then, I don't remember a lot until I woke up. I must have fallen asleep or passed out. But when I woke up, there was blood everywhere, and it was not my period. The guy had just mutilated me. I was hurting and in pain and plus hung over as well. I felt terrible. I was sick.

I had to get over that whole thing, because I certainly wasn't going to say I was raped by good old Joe. We all knew him. Anyway, at that time, there wasn't this big date-rape thing. I wasn't even sure what had happened. But I'm sure of it now. I've hated the guy ever since. I *do* blame him for it. I *do* feel I was trying to tell somebody no. Maybe I didn't have much strength, but I was certainly vocal enough for any normal person to understand what I'm saying.

I wound up pregnant. Oh, God, what a mess! I had an abortion and was really sick after that. I had one of those abortions where they don't get it all. It was a nightmare. I had to go back and repeat the procedure.

Then my fever kept going up. I was getting really whacked out, and I couldn't think straight. They finally found out—the son of a bitch—I had gonorrhea, too. I mean, can you imagine? This is all from one guy. Through the abortion and all that, the infection had spread all up into my tubes and created pelvic inflammatory disease and other things. They took out most of my tube and some other part. I didn't have a hysterectomy, but I can't have kids.

I've been in more situations like date rape in the last three years, never in high school. I was able to talk people out of it. There have been two particular situations, both of them a little bit different. One of them, I went to an office Christmas party with a friend of mine. She had a crush on this guy who worked at the company. We hooked up with him and his assistant. Somehow, I ended up leaving with the assistant. We got back to his apartment, and his roommate was up there watching the news. This was the night of the crash of Pan Am Flight 103. I was really upset about it, and he was trying to be incredibly sensitive, thinking that it would get my pants off more quickly.

We were fooling around a lot. We'd both been drinking a lot. Alcohol seems to come into these things very often, and it was a good Christmas party. I'd slept with people on first dates, but I'd never actually picked somebody up and gone home with them. It always was somebody I knew for more than two hours, in other words. I just decided that I couldn't sleep with him.

"I can't do this," I said. "I changed my mind."

"You're going to do it!" was his attitude.

I talked him out of it. I said, "Okay, I'll stay, but I'm not having sex with you." He was pinning me to the bed, that kind of stuff. He was getting violent, so I said, "Okay, fine, I'll stay. I won't leave, but I don't want to have sex with you." I can't even remember if the next morning we did or not. I don't think I'm blocking it out from trauma or anything like that. I just was on pins and needles to get out of there.

I actually heard later that the other guy asked him if he had a good time, and he said, "Oh, yeah, we had a really nice time." I had told my friend what had actually happened. I couldn't understand why he couldn't just say, "No, things didn't work out."

If in fact he *had* raped me, and if I'd hauled him into a court of law, I'm not even sure I wouldn't put some of the blame on me, because I was there, I had all my clothes off, he had all his clothes off, we were fooling around and I just changed my mind.

Now there was a guy that I did pick up in a bar maybe six months ago. The thing that scared me the most about that was we did go back to his apartment, and I thought, "This guy is twenty-seven years old, picking up women in bars. He's a doctor, he doesn't have any condoms, and he seems like he never has any condoms around."

"Yeah, I don't have any, so big deal," he said. The thing that scared me so bad about that was not that he could have raped me—and, thank God, he didn't—but the fact that if he had raped me and had been HIV positive, it would have pissed me off that I let myself get in that situation. Rape is not fatal.

There is a lot of date rape that goes on, but women don't take enough responsibility for that kind of stuff. I know there have been times when I have said, "No, no, no—*yes!*" Now, that doesn't mean that a guy should not take no as a no, but a woman has to take responsibility for it, if she's going to go home with the guy, that this guy may not be an understanding, sensitive male who takes no for an answer. If you're not going to take responsibility when you're drunk, then don't drink.

I've made life miserable for guys who have slept in my apartment that I really wanted to sleep with, when I've crawled into bed with them. There was one guy I had been having a relationship with somewhere else. We discussed it before he came to town, and he said, "I'm not sleeping with you." I was going fine, fine, fine. Then the minute he got over here, I was devastated that he wasn't going to sleep with me, and was crawling into bed with him, and making his life miserable. Basically, I was acting like we accuse men of acting. A lot of women do.

There's a lot of creepy guys out there who get kind of loose and externalize some weird part of their mentality against some usually innocent woman. Women have an equally bizarre background, but they don't react in the same way. They'll tend to drive themselves crazy, whereas a guy will tend to do something to another person. A million women going quietly insane inside their apartments with their cats doesn't sell magazines. Date rape sells a lot of magazines, and Sally Jessy Raphael will have you on her show. So it's good copy and a good sound bite, especially if you're a celebrity.

But I don't think it's anything particular to men. This overt manifestation is particular for men. The guy ought to be pitied as much as the woman ought to be pitied. The fact that it manifests itself to the harm of some other person means you've got to do something about it from the social-justice standpoint and put him away. At the same time, you can't just say, "Isn't he horrible, isn't he just a monster?" any more than you would say that the million women going quietly crazy—sitting by themselves going nuts—are monsters. There's five of them, I guarantee you, in this apartment complex right now.

Date rape is a major problem. I can point to it in my own background with my buddies where we misbehaved and treated women abysmally out of insecurity. We were so afraid about sex, we didn't know what it was about. It was so mysterious that we really misread the signals. Instead of trying to figure it out, we'd just try to dominate.

I know that I've had sex with someone without having as much of her permission as I should have. I'm deeply humiliated by that. It's real painful to think about what I did. It wasn't forced, but she says that she was saying no and I was too drunk to pay attention. I can't rationalize that I ignored her permission. Apparently, I was out of control. I don't know that I trust the woman's relation to it, because I think that she was operating out of pain and overdescribed it, but it was the least consensual act that I've ever been involved in. If I'm capable of that, then I know other men are.

How big a problem is it? I don't know. Women are often pretending to be less responsible than they often are in these circumstances. Women think they can drink at the frat house till four in the morning. Are they asking for it? No. They're not asking to be punished, but they are not being responsible enough. It's like walking through Central Park at night. You've got to know not to do that whether you're a man or a woman. It doesn't alleviate the situation when you're hurt, it doesn't change it, but everybody has to be educated that this is a possibility and men will act on that. You can't apply one standard to all men, because we're all different. But men will act very ruthlessly when you excite them sexually and then deny them sex. Women do that, and they do it in a manipulative sense. It can be a power trip for them.

I once sat at a bar and was fed drinks by a gay guy who wanted to blow me. I felt what it was like to get drinks out of somebody who wanted sexual favors that I had no intention of giving. I can laugh that off as my own little reverse psychological experiment, but it was really kind of despicable. It was disgusting, but one of my rationalizations was, "That's what women do."

On the other hand, rape is inexcusable. I hate to sound like a liberal, but it's outrageous, and I don't know how we cope with it. Men have to learn not to be as frightened as they are, lashing out at the wrong things in trying to cope with the intense confusion and fear they have about how they behave sexually.

Men are pretty fucked up. We can complain all we want, but we dominate the situation. We really don't have a right to complain. Women are systematically taught that they are secondhand units in this system. Men know it, and they get off on that. It's fucked up. You can like man's animalistic nature, and there is a joy in recovering that. Conversely, there is a lot of that which is just stupid selfishness from men who are unable or unwilling to learn and grow.

You feel like you're arguing for turf sometimes. They say no, but they don't really mean no. When does no mean *No?* I've been in a situation where a girl has said, "No. Gosh, no, I don't feel like it." But that wasn't a no. Sometimes "nice girls" say no and they don't really mean it. They want you to run the red light. Is it red or is it flashing yellow: "Slow down but don't really stop." It's mixed signals and cross-communication. If every guy stopped when a girl said no, there'd be a lot less romance in the world.

Men want to be suave, aggressive, and impressive, but on the other hand you don't want to step over the line and, God forbid, come across as this offensive jerk who's got no sense of the boundaries.

It's like when you're at the amusement park and she says, "No, I don't want to go on the roller coaster. It's too scary."

"Come on, come on. You'll really enjoy it." And you talk her into it even though she's saying no. And then she says, "Okay, that was great. I'm glad you talked me into it." People get talked into things all the time.

"I don't want to go out tonight. I'm really depressed."

"No, no, come on, we'll go out and have a great time."

When that kind of back-and-forth gets applied to the bedroom, suddenly it becomes a very complicated and difficult thing. It's part of the experience of pushing the edge of the envelope. What should I do? Maybe this is just like the roller coaster, and I should just say, "Come on, come on, come on." Then she'll get over her fears and anxiety about it and end up enjoying it.

I said this to a couple of friends of mine. He said he understood what I meant. She got really mad. Her posture was, "You can ask. Okay? If you don't know where the line is, you can ask."

That makes some sense, but on the other hand it doesn't work at a certain level. It's not so human. It doesn't speak to a spark that we all have when your heart's pounding while you're flirting with someone. "Where is this going to go?" That's really scary, exciting, fun, and invigorating, appealing, and anxious—all that mixture, that elixir of emotions that is very tasty and narcotic.

The line is a blurry one, increasingly blurry and hard to deal with. Is it like Outward Bound, they just need a little push, and in the end they'll be happy to have taken the chance? Or is it coercion, therefore wrong, and too aggressive, and too powerful and male?

I'm one of the few women in my office. This one guy was going on and on about what does a woman expect if she sits there with you at a bar all night drinking and saying, "Come hither, come hither," and then says no to sex.

I told him, "No means no. Don't play the game, if it is a game. Get up, put on your pants, and leave. Give her some of her own medicine. If she wants you, it'll happen, believe me. You can bench press three hundred pounds. She's not going to rape *you*."

I'm an assistant vice president. Let's say one of the directors, a woman, good-looking, sultry, short skirts and all, is coming on to me. Now being a male, I'm going to take that, on the one hand, as a badge of honor. On the other hand, I'm going to be a little scared about that. Do I really want to sleep with my boss? But it's not going to be that much of a problem for me. Now, if she uses that sexual come-on to put weight on me as far as my work goes, buddy, it would freak me out. This doesn't happen much women-to-men, so I'm just trying to put myself in the shoes of a woman who would be in this spot. "If you don't sleep with me, you've had it." Good God, I wouldn't know what to do.

I was relatively friends with the chairman of the board of directors for the project I was working on. One night after a meeting, he came up to me and asked if I wanted to go to his room and watch dirty movies. He was sort of a cowboy, but this was just out of the blue. He then went to my boss and said he didn't understand what I was doing in my position, and that I wasn't following directions. I said to my boss at the time, "I'll tell you what directions I'm not following. I didn't follow his directions to his room."

I once knew an architect who moved to another city. She was just out of college. She was all alone when she got a job with an architectural firm.

After she had worked there a few weeks, a guy asked her out. After they went out twice, she went to bed with the guy. Next morning he said, "Thanks. All the guys in the office had a pool on who was going to fuck you first, and I won."

It's really hard to harass guys in the office. "Come on, harass me. Harass me some more." I was always real careful to avoid affairs in the office. I always kept just far enough away. I always tried to pick up chicks who worked for other companies on other floors on the same elevator bank.

The problem is, if you're over the age of thirty and a professional, you really don't have much of an opportunity to meet people outside the office. We're forced into making contact at work, because if you're there nine or ten hours a day, the time you have to spend on other activities is very limited. That is your social framework. And you're at work and the women are usually looking pretty good, you know?

I see it more in terms of power than sexuality. But with men and women those two things can be very close cousins. The difficulty is how you deal with power, how you deal with being the boss. It's a complicated and seductive situation. "Gee, it's nice that every time I talk to her she's very responsive and friendly. Hey, she really likes me." Then the guy gets carried away and loses sight of where the lines are drawn. The woman in the subordinate position is thinking, "I don't know how much longer I can keep this stupid smile plastered across my face at everything he says. What a jerk."

If you are supervising people, you cannot have relationships with them. They are off-limits. You can't have sex with your siblings, your aunts or uncles or some of your cousins. There should be a social taboo on sleeping with people you supervise. People don't know that? Where have they been for the last ten or twenty years?

I've had relationships lately with guys who cannot handle it, because we talk about sex a lot. I haven't had to go through my entire sexual history with somebody, and I hope I don't. I can't remember all their names. But

I'm a great believer in talking about it, and guys have a horrible time talking about sex. The men who know my sexual history when a lot of it has come up were actually scared.

They would never in a million years look at their own past, sexwise, and say, "I've slept with thirty women, so I might give her something, too." If I ask somebody to use a condom, and I always do, it's not that I'm scared that they're going to give me something, it's that I'm scared that I'm going to give them something. I wouldn't want to do that to anybody.

The thing that scares me is the average bear who's dating is pretty stupid about this stuff. Most guys say, "I haven't slept with any men, I haven't slept with any women who would sleep with men who slept with men, I don't have a history of IV drug use, so I'm okay." Most guys think that they're not going to catch anything from the woman, because the risk of transmission is so small. But last week, I don't know how I did it, with my ring or something, I cut my lover when I was sleeping with him. It would have been easy for him to get something through that cut. If you're not going to worry about anything else, then worry about that.

Most men, if they can get you to sleep with them, they will try to get you not to use a condom. Some of them seem to feel like it's attacking their manhood to ask them to wear a condom. "I wouldn't sleep with a man, so of course I have not gotten the AIDS virus!" After they get over that, they say, "Why? Are you sick? Oh, no, you're going to give me something, you're going to give me something!" The thing that is scary is that there can be so many men out there who are so blasé about condoms that they obviously never have them in the house.

On the other hand, I slept with this one guy, and I thought I was going to have to call the nut house to come and get him. We were using a condom, and it broke. I was like, "Okay, fine. No big deal. Nothing we can do about it now." The guy was running around the apartment going, "Oh, my God! Oh, my God! I can't believe it broke!"

"Come on, this is not the end of the world. Well, maybe, but chances are that it's not. Besides, there's nothing we can do about it." But he was really freaked out.

I'm not as careful as I could be. You make an informed decision. There's nothing that's one-hundred-percent safe. It's a decision that you make every single time. I'm somebody who's smart about it. I know how AIDS is transmitted. Even with that, there are times when I've made a conscious decision and he's made a conscious decision not to use condoms. If I don't square my behavior with the facts, I don't think about it. That sounds like I'm being flip about it, but I'm not trying to be flip.

Men are going to lie about it, if they can, and a lot of women would not take responsibility for it. If she caught something, she would say, "It's his fault because he lied to me."

I slept with a guy on vacation and didn't use a condom. We spent several nights together, and we would have run out of condoms anyway. But it was a conscious choice—I'm doing this and he's doing this with the responsibility of what it means. If he gets sick, I don't blame anybody but myself. Which is a thin line, but I think it's an important one.

You do what you can. You can't be panicky all the time. To me that's pretty much it. You can't live in constant fear.

In this day and age, something is going to get you. I would never go out and have sex indiscriminately with fifty thousand people without using condoms, and ninety-nine percent of the time, I use them. Then there's all sorts of other stuff. Like giving and receiving oral sex. You shouldn't do that either, if you're going to be one-hundred-percent safe about things.

I've run into several guys who won't perform oral sex anymore, because they're afraid that they'll catch something. That seems to be where they'll draw the line. Men seem to be far more concerned about their mouths than their penises these days. You can quote me on that. I really think some of the same guys who wouldn't perform oral sex on you would probably have sex without a condom. Men feel far more threatened by that than they do just having plain old straight sex. People seem so uptight.

I'm not real worried. I'm not stupid, but I'm not real worried. I've probably had sex with at least one hundred men. That's high. Is that right? Who knows? So many, I can't remember them all. It's been fun. When I look at my population, it's never been with a homosexual—that I've known about—never with an IV drug user. They're usually white, educated, middle- to upper-middle-class men. I realize that AIDS happens to white, educated, middle-class men, so that doesn't protect me, but I haven't dipped into the high-risk pools.

I am having less sex. But I can't pull it out and say AIDS is the primary reason for that. It's not guiding my behavior, but it's a factor in my behavior. I've slowed down mostly for emotional reasons.

What I do now, like with the guy I had sex with the other night—we were sort of getting hot and heavy. He said, "Oooo, we need to have the AIDS talk, we need to talk sexual history."

"Come inside me, let's have sex," I said.

"No," he said. "For several reasons. We need to talk about our sexual histories when we're not standing naked in front of each other all ready to go. I want to go slow. I want to build up. I want us to make each other a little bit crazy. The older I get, the slower I go, because then when it finally happens, it's absolutely wonderful." Smart guy, which makes me like him even more. So there are discussions like that going on.

It may be blind foolishness or blind faith not to worry about it. I'm going to be aware of it, and alter my behavior a little bit, but it's not going to rule my life. The same thing as with crime. I'm not going to bolt my window shut every time I leave my house. I know I run the risk of somebody breaking in, but I refuse to live that way. I'm aware of the risk and I'll take it. I'm also aware that with AIDS I may have been at risk in the past, and I may be at risk now. God only knows how many partners my friend has had. He said he's been just as active as I have in the past, and I swallowed his semen, you know, but for some reason I was willing to do that then. I'm more cautious, but I haven't shut down.

When did we start calling them condoms? Rubbers. Men wear rubbers now. I hate rubbers. I hate them. You can't feel them come inside you. They pull out right away, because it'll shrink up and come off. For the record: I hate them, I hate them, I hate them. And there have been a few times in the heat of the moment when I'm all worked up and I've said, "Oh, don't put that thing on," where the man has gone, "Yes, I will. I must."

Thank God. Now I'm insisting on it more and more. I hate them, but they are necessary. I'm not fond of a seat belt in my car, but I see them as necessary. I hate health insurance and some of the other ugly responsibilities of life, but you got to have them. So I can hate it, and still do it. That's where I am.

I ended up meeting this woman who was just stunningly beautiful, gorgeous and very "downtown," very clubbish and of the street. She wasn't working nine-to-five. A little weird. We ended up going to bed together very early in what was a very short-lived relationship. When we went to bed the first time, I went and got a condom. It was my house, after all. Her response was, "Oooo, I hate those things."

At this point, it began to dawn on me that this wasn't going to be a very long-term relationship. The emotional and intellectual investment was going to be minimal, but in my brain, internally, my posture was, "Jeez-Louise! I'm glad I don't hate them." Her implication was, "Let's not bother with that." And my implication was, "What? Are you crazy? We don't know each other." I don't care if she was Little Miss Petit Fours from prep school. My assumption was that she'd been with lots of men and lots of drugs and lots of sexual experiences. I didn't want to be in any greater jeopardy than I had to be. It didn't dawn on me that she wouldn't think the same way.

As terrible and sad and miserable as it sounds, why would you want it to be an experience that puts you in jeopardy? To look at a condom and say, "Oooo, I don't like those things, ugh," just struck me as peculiar. It was in and of itself enough for me to rule her out as someone I wanted to spend a lot of time with.

Sex has been a real problem the last three or four years because of AIDS. Now you can't explore that avenue so blithely as one did at another time. There was no fear, no dark shadow. It was just a part of life and it was good. In fact it was the real bright spot in being a fatalist. I could die tomorrow and sex is all part of it, so I'm going to go for it!

The worst thing about AIDS and not knowing is that our rate of suspicion is just growing like crazy. The barriers between individuals, between the sexes are building beyond our reach.

I had this run-in with a man that I met. We met at a friend's party, so I figured, fine. He was from another city and had a girlfriend down there. We went out a couple of times, when he was staying here. We came home to my apartment to make love. I brought out the condoms. I didn't think I was going to have to do a sales job on them or anything. The whole situation changed, because he was so ignorant. I mean, the foreplay was fine, but then I insisted, "If we don't use condoms, we don't have intercourse."

"How can you switch off just like that?" he said.

"This isn't a switch off, this is part of the process. This is what sex has become. There's an area of responsibility that I feel we must share here, or otherwise I can't have sex. It's just too dangerous for me."

The thing that was most amazing was that he saw this as a big city thing. AIDS only happens up here and rampantly. He won't admit to there being any problem in his own neck of the woods.

"You've got to be kidding me," I said. "I feel ignorant about AIDS, but I know ten times more than you do. I just look at this as my survival."

Then it came to, "I have this girlfriend back home, and I have a cut on my finger." I wasn't meaning to put the demons in him, but he said, "Could I get it?"

"I can't tell you one hundred percent if you could or not," I said. "But that's the thing about this disease. It's not defined. You have to take precautions. You can get it from the five bodily fluids, so is there a possibility you could get AIDS if I had AIDS? Yes."

The man went lunatic. That was it for the sex. But we now have conversations over the phone. He wants me to take a blood test. I said, "I took a blood test six months ago, just because I believe in doing this. I don't have AIDS. I'm not HIV positive." Trying to explain to him.

"But that was six months ago," he said.

"Then, I guess what it comes down to is this: You're going to have to take my word for it. In six months' time, you can go have a blood test." I said, "You think I have AIDS. You're learning a hard lesson. If you think that way, and you're going to be responsible, then you can't have sex with your girlfriend." He's stepped off the deep end, he really did. He's this macho man who thinks only people in these eccentric places get this eccentric disease.

What it did bring up to me is that the bedroom has become this war zone between trusting and not trusting. Therefore, sex with someone without protection is crazy.

Sex now for me is episodes like this that are just crazy. I'm realizing that I can't do that anymore. I can't go through this accusatory type of thing.

On the good side, sex is more constant. It's forced me into hanging on to some very old friendships. Not that I wouldn't anyway, but the friendships are even more valuable. There's sex, and there's knowing each other, and there's a fear of AIDS. So there is being absolutely honest about this. In one way, it's opened things up. These are men that we've learned about sexuality together anyway, but discussions have occurred that wouldn't have occurred in the past. More fatalistic discussions about, "If you ever thought that you had it, you'd let me know?"

Having sex with someone these days is almost like roulette. I used to have nightmares when I was a little kid about King Kong coming after me, something dark and evil trying to get me, and I was hiding under the house. AIDS is my adult King Kong. There's no defense, and I feel defenseless. I don't want to be like Howard Hughes, always afraid of my shadow, but fear is the shepherd pushing me to change. Sex sure isn't as much fun when you're scared about your own mortality. It was a hell of a lot more fun when you were just worried about not getting pregnant.

I had an IUD that worked for me in terms of birth control. But I decided to have it taken out, because I knew I wouldn't be as careful about using condoms if I had it in. So for me the issue was disease control and not so much birth control. I should have done both, but I knew I can get sloppy. You think, "Oh, he's all right." But you can't do that anymore. So I put myself more at risk for pregnancy to make sure I wouldn't risk getting infected with AIDS.

Just recently I got a call from a woman I went out with before I started my present relationship. She was somebody who...how do I explain this woman? She could get herself into trouble. My first thought when I heard her voice on the other end of the telephone was that there was something wrong, like, "How are you feeling?" Turns out, she just wanted me to help a mutual friend get a job. But when an old girlfriend calls you after a long absence, my first thought is, "She's calling to tell me she has AIDS, so watch out."

I'm thinking that the convent looks awfully nice. I'm giving up. I've had it. I feel like I've been dating for twenty years now, and it's just gone downhill. Now what's the point? Honestly, sex isn't going to play as pivotal a role in the early stages of my relationships, which is probably good. People will be less blinded by the physical crush, the overwhelming physical attraction. Hopefully, I'll still feel that, but I'm going to have to put it into perspective, and let it wait. But sooner or later, you're going to have to be a gambler whether you like it or not.

There is no moment where you are more in a state of reckless, careless abandon than when you're lying in bed with a woman, turned on and ready to have sex. To have always in the back of your mind, AIDS AIDS AIDS AIDS DEATH, that's sad and terrifying.

2. IS THERE SEX AFTER MARRIAGE?

"I don't know how much sex married couples are supposed to be having, but when I read things in magazines, I think, 'I'm way out of normal here.' I read this survey in a women's magazine that says married couples my age are having sex an average of once a week. I look around and say, 'Okay, who's lying?' They've got to be lying. Or somebody's skewing this survey by having sex a thousand times a week." These are the words of one woman approaching forty, the mother of three children with a full-time job.

"Originally, I thought marriage was a means of procuring a steady sexual partner," says a forty-year-old philosopher, motivational speaker, and career counselor, twice married and the father of four children. "Many men see it that way. In fact, it's completely the opposite. Sometimes, in spite of the fact that you're married, you have good sex. If you're lucky."

These could be the voices of all married people. Marriage is hard. Two people staying together for life is improbable. Just reconciling your differences as individual human beings is a perplexing task, complicated by the nagging technicality that you are different sexes as well. Even in the best of relationships, it is easy for the daily tug-of-war over minor disagreements to escalate into a battle of wills, complete with shouting matches and door slamming. Staying in the same room for five minutes can be impossible at times.

Sex?

Married couples are harried by financial responsibilities. With jobs burning up most people's lives, bills and more bills, home maintenance, and the IRS, there isn't a spare moment. When there is a little time, there is no energy left after work.

Sex?

And children—one of the more common results of marriage, if not always the cause—can wreck a couple's sex life. They continually break up meaningful communication between their parents, sucking up their attention, patience, and vitality, not to mention destroying their privacy.

Sex?

What separates human beings sexually from the other animals may not be so much our awareness of pleasure as our awareness of sexual ennui. People like change, the excitement of the unknown—a new body, a new voice, a new touch. Marriage means sexual fidelity, even though you know every move he'll make, every emotional blunder, every flick and turn from foreplay to consummation. Sex can become so limited, so repetitious, so numbingly monotonous. As a forty-year-old schoolteacher, recently separated from his wife, explained, "In long-term sexual relationships, we eliminate so much in a physical way, especially the early stuff like the making out, the exploration, and the kissing. That's probably the best part. Or at least has the most excitement involved with it. The actual sex act is anticlimactic. Some people actually find it difficult to retrieve any of that and employ it in their long-standing relationship. They see making out as silly." Never mind the dearth of inventiveness, familiarity can kill the basic intimacy between two people.

Sex?

Even when couples have a good physical relationship and continue to enjoy sex with each other, it is rare if they have the same appetite at the same time. Married men claim that they must always be the aggressors to have even minimal sex lives, but in many cases it turns out that the voracious male sex drive is more cultural posturing than it is real. As a forty-four-year-old actor admits, "I find myself being the aggressor in sex a lot. If I'm not the aggressor, it usually means I fell asleep. If it's the other way around, it's hard for me to admit that I'd be the one who says, 'Not tonight, honey.' But a lot of times I am. A lot of times I'm just too fucking pooped to really be that giving."

Sex?

Women suffer the loss of romance and mourn the passing of courtship, cuddling, and foreplay. They claim they'd have sex more often if men weren't so abrupt and selfish. But for some women the unconscious vestiges of old-fashioned cultural conditioning also are shaping their behavior. The idea that women might like sex is relatively new in American society. As a woman in her sixties explained it, "Women in my generation were told, 'Sex is wrong, sex is wrong, you don't do that,' and on and on. All of a sudden when you get married, you're supposed to say, 'Oh, it's okay now. Am I supposed to like it?'

" 'No, it's still not okay to like it. It's just a duty to your husband.' I was told I wouldn't enjoy it."

Sex?

And this is only a superficial sketch of the impediments to having a satisfactory sex life that are facing men and women in good marriages, who still love and respect one another, who enjoy the male/female dialectic, and who try to maintain sexual fidelity. The fact that about half of all marriages end in divorce is not so amazing as the fact that any of us stay together. What is amazing is that more people aren't popping down to the corner for a loaf of bread and never coming back.

Men's and women's egos are inextricably twined with their sexuality. Thwarted sexual expectations, perceived slights in bed, inadvertent schedule conflicts can quickly escalate from minor disruptions in a marriage to all-out war. In those marriages in which there is no real commitment, in which the dialogue between male and female never existed or has degenerated to backhanded compliments and continuous sniping and scolding, marital sex becomes merely a bodily function, a chore, at worst, a weapon. Once again, this is the schoolteacher on his way to getting a divorce: "Judging by my wife and me, married couples use sex as a weapon. If you're a good boy or a good girl, you get it. And if you're a bad boy or bad girl, you don't get it. 'Until you start seeing things my way, you're not going to have sex with me.' Instead of sex being a healing act, it becomes a weapon of retribution or punishment, when you withdraw or the other person shuts you out."

Good sex is essential to a good marriage. Mutual sexual satisfaction heals the wounds inflicted by the outside world on the private planet two people build for themselves. The opportunity to reveal yourself, to share the vulnerability that absolute passion demands under the protection of the bond you have with your spouse restores self-image, revitalizes body and soul, and repairs the delicate strands that connect us to those we love. There is nothing to compare with the total intimacy of sex in marriage at its best.

The trouble is it's just not going to happen that often. In all but a very few cases, the consuming sexual passion of first love must wane to a hunger pang. That's life. Sexual attraction can pull people together, but it cannot hold them there. Luckily, sex isn't everything. We have love to compensate. Here's a woman in her early thirties, a successful entrepreneur, who is preparing to marry a man almost twice her age. For her, their sex together is only adequate, even at this early stage of their relationship:

"Sexuality is just another part of life. It's not all about sex. My mind-set for so long was to be active sexually, to be 'good in bed.' That's what it's all about. That's the answer. Multiple orgasms and you've achieved what you're supposed to do in life. But that's not true. I've not been this happy or relaxed or fulfilled, ever. That's why I've decided to marry this guy."

o   o   o

Gradually as the years have gone by, sex is just less and less important. It is important, but it's a thing that I fit in when I can. I know that's not the best way to do it, but my focus right now, my priorities are on my kids. I'm so whipped most of the time when I get home from work that I could go to bed at nine o'clock every night and be completely happy.

I really am the one who decides. I pretty much pick and choose the time when my husband and I have sex. We have sex maybe once every two weeks—maybe. Maybe twice in three weeks, and that's a lot. I mean, having an orgasm is not my motivating force in life or anything. It's nice when it happens, but I could just as well go to sleep. I still have to get up at five forty-five in the morning, not that it takes that long. Once I get into it, once I'm well started on sex, I say to myself, "This is great, and I'm glad I did this." It's the getting motivated, it's getting past the, "Oh, shit, I really don't want to do this. I don't want the effort. I don't want to have to get up and go to the bathroom."

For the man, it's easier. It's not messy. There's nothing that they really have to deal with like you do as a woman. Okay, quick, get out of bed, so your bed isn't wet. That sounds dumb, but it's true. Diaphragms? I hate those things.

Sometimes, I just don't have enough emotion to make it *all* work. I already feel there's not enough for me in marriage just alone, that self is kind of sublimated and probably will be for a while. Sometimes there's just not enough room for anything else. And that kind of goes along with the whole sexual feeling for the marriage, too. Sometimes you just feel like your cup is too full, and you just really don't want to deal with anything else. If someone were to tell me, "I just don't think that we're having sex enough," I'd just have to say, "Too bad. I don't really care."

Amazingly enough, my husband has never said that to me. He's really been very accommodating. He lets me go through my phases, my moods, and whatever. I feel that he really wants our marriage to work, and so he will do what he thinks he knows is best to make that work.

We ended up getting married in '77. Had our first child in July of '79, a year and a half later. We had Christopher in '81 and the third in '85. I haven't had sex with anybody else except my wife since we got married. I've been tempted a few times. Never real strong. Never had a real great opportunity. I'm sure it's just what every normal male goes through.

People I'm around a lot, like the people that I work with and see every day, I end up from time to time thinking, "Hmmm, I may be getting a little attracted to this person. I want to get a little bit closer with them." I just kind of write that off as normal male behavior, just hormonal influence on my body. I've never had a situation where it would be real easy to have an extramarital affair. I don't know how I would hold up under such circumstances. I'm sure it would depend a lot on my relationship with my wife right at that moment, whether we were getting along. My sexual desire is cyclical. If it caught me at a peak, I don't know what I might do.

I've always been a pretty responsible person, whether I really want to be or not. I think about sex quite a lot. I think, "A lot of guys run around. There's lots of pretty women out there. I finally have a little money and position. Maybe I should run around, too." Women always look at you more when you have a wife. They give you the come-on a lot more. I guess they feel safer since someone else has found you responsible, so maybe you are. I write it off as normal.

The hardest times is when my wife goes through periods of just asexuality, where she just isn't turned on. The seven-day headache. I get times when I'd really like to have sex and she doesn't. I get pissed off.

"Goddamn it, I'm busting my ass making money, supporting this whole family, and all I want is a piece of ass!" Most of the time I tolerate it pretty well—maybe I'm just getting experienced at it. But you get angry, and that makes it worse. Then you *really* aren't going to get a piece of ass.

That's when I'm most tempted to say, "Maybe I ought to go out and get some pussy when I want some. And if she says anything about it, I'll say, 'I had no choice. There wasn't any here for love nor money.'"

Somehow masturbation seems a more acceptable alternative than risking my marriage. I don't really like to masturbate that much either. I still have weird guilt feelings about that, too.

Anytime I have problems, I sit down, and I think, "I'm a very average person, very typical. Probably, most married people go through what I'm going through. I'm sure they do. People are so much alike it's pathetic." That's a little solace, but not much.

When you hit forty, things really speed up. A whole week can go by without you knowing it. I don't mind being forty. I've always liked the age I was, but I'm also at the point now where I see that there is less time than there was for me to live an active life. We are at the pinnacle right now. In ten or twenty years, I might not want to have sex every other night. I might not even now, but I'd like to give it a try.

How many times does any husband say how desirable his wife is? If they would just go on and say that for the next twenty-two years—even if it was a lie—men have no idea what that would mean to women. Just to say that they were pretty. That is such a turn-on, and it really fills a need. Everybody needs strokes. Men think, "Oh, she knows I think she's desirable, or I wouldn't reach out for her." But if you don't say it, then women *don't* take it for granted. They don't automatically think, "He cares for me because he's here." That doesn't quite make it. Many men seem to say, "I'm here, aren't I?"

You're too lazy to leave, that's why you're here!

Sometimes I have sex as much as I possibly can, and sometimes it's fine if I get it once a week. I'm okay. If it goes longer than that, I become aware that a whole week has gone past, I haven't gotten laid, and there's no reason, because there is a woman I do find attractive laying right next to me. It's just that I'm too tired, with our schedules being what they are.

Women don't appreciate it when you just jump on them. Even after all these years of marriage, still, there's got to be all this foreplay. I can't believe it. You'd think they'd let you off the hook at least once in a while and admit that they just want to be popped, just like you do. But no, no, no.

I like foreplay, too, if I can, like, just stay awake for it, man. It usually adds to the whole sexual experience. It does.

I met my current wife and just fell instantly in love and continue to be. Our sex life started off real good, that and everything about her personality. We just fit together well, because she allows me to pretty much dominate the relationship in my space. She doesn't want to dominate. She doesn't want to be out front. She's real shy for the most part. So we balance each other. I never thought opposites attract, but they really do. She's not the kind of person I would have imagined myself being with.

A few years ago, after my first marriage, I thought, "I really need to get somebody who fits me better, not that I'm just like, not that has this mind thing the same as me, but somebody who fits in a different way, in a lifetime kind of way that you just know this is going to be it."

What's so wonderful about my sexual relationship with my wife, and I know it's got to be what tortures a lot of men, is my wife knows how much I have to have sex. She takes care of that. She just takes care of that. If I want head before I go to work, all I have to do is say, "Huuunnnnyyy." I'll put on a tape of *The Wizard of Oz* for our little one, after the other two have gone to school, and she'll take care of business behind locked doors. That's great. A lot of people have good sex, but that's a missing part in so many relationships—it's so neat to have a woman who understands. There are plenty of times when I know her attitude is, "Go ahead. Do your business." And that's okay. There are times when I say, "Just show up. And I'll be a happy camper." She's not offended by that, and she doesn't get tortured by it. There are plenty of times when she has more fun than I do, I'm convinced, if outward signs mean anything. She says she does. But then there are plenty of times when she just couldn't give a rat's ass what happens, but she knows that I do. That's the difference between many men and women, that men have such a voracious, steady sexual appetite. It's not something that goes away or that is easily squelched. It's a real, living, organic need.

Last night after we finished having sex, I told my wife, "That's probably some of the worst work I've ever done in my life." It was really pitiful. It was just pathetic. I barely got to the Heaven's Gate. She didn't care. It was my trip, but I had to work at it. For some reason, there was something last night. I was tired, I wanted to escape work, and I was even less ready than I usually am, but I still wanted to have sex. I just did. There are some times when even a bad trip is better than no trip at all.

I used to beat off a lot in my first marriage. I just don't. Right at the first with Molly I did, because you have to get used to not doing it. I still do occasionally—every once in a while it's kind of fun to ride the pony around the ring yourself—but I don't have to. I usually don't, because I know I can have sex anytime I want to. If you're not getting it, you're going to have to do *something,* or you're going to be tortured and not be able to concentrate. I'm not. If more women understood that, the world would be a better place. Men and women would get along much better. That's not something that a lot of women understand to the degree that my wife does.

How can a person sleep with only one other person for ten or twenty or thirty years? I've been sleeping with this woman for ten years, and I just can't imagine that the rest of my life this is going to be *it*. That's all there is?

They talk about men in their forties going out with younger women when they dump their old wives. If a younger woman came along and really wanted me, I don't know what I'd do. But I can't imagine that circumstance happening to me. I'm getting older and fatter and losing my hair. I've never had a woman run after me. These guys who go out and find younger women, I don't know how they do it. It can't be a passive thing where they just get entrapped, unless they have a lot of money.

Sometimes I think, if I can't get my wife interested in sex, it's my fault. There's no sense whining about it. I should be able to talk her into things. One advantage of a wife is that anything you can talk her into doing, you can talk her into doing. If for instance you want to do a threesome, you could maybe make a good enough pitch for it where you could accomplish that. I go back and forth on how real that is. Now I'm thinking, "No, you just can't. There's a natural limit that you hit." However, you'd think you could get some of the underwear that you wanted. But for some reason it just hasn't worked out that way.

Back when we were having sex like once a month, we went to a marriage counselor. Part of the problem is that she does not like to have sex when she's depressed, or when she's stressed out. That includes when she has a death in the family, or when she has a test coming up in her night courses, or if things are tough on the job, then she's not interested in sex at all. This is an attitude I don't like, and it's almost exactly the opposite of me and most men.

To me, sex is a reaffirmation of life. It also is distracting. It feels good. It is this hormonal chemical rush. It is a stress-relieving depression escape.

The other thing I can't understand is why we don't have sex more as pure entertainment. When we go someplace on vacation, it's always a problem. We get to a new city someplace, and she doesn't want to have sex. She wants to go out and have fun. She just wants to have a good time. She's not interested in staying in the hotel room and having sex. In fact, when we're at home, she would rather go watch a movie on TV, go read a good book, or go do some fun stuff rather than having sex. It's just not a high priority for her. For me, it's the big, number-one priority. I would do it just for the plain old fun of it.

I don't mean to put her down so much. It's not her fault. The worst thing about the whole deal is, it's really not her fault. She wants me to be sexually satisfied more than anything in the whole world. She wants to be doing a good job. Everyone wants to do a good job as a spouse. She loves me. She wants to make me happy more than anything. But she just can't. It's just not her nature. It's like some people are real good at laughing at their boss's jokes, but some people just can't make themselves pretend to laugh. She just can't make herself pretend to be sexually interested when she's not. That's the way she is, and she can't help it. It's not that she doesn't realize that there is a problem here, and it's not that she doesn't want to fix the problem, but she can't make herself be something that she's not. She's just not going to do a striptease for me with high heels on. She doesn't like to wear high heels, because they hurt her feet.

Now I'm about to marry a fifty-eight-year-old man. He's twenty years older than me. He's got three kids from a previous marriage. I'll have a thirty-two-year-old stepdaughter, a fifteen-year-old stepdaughter and a twenty-eight-year-old stepson. The man I'm going to marry is a wonderful person. Sexually, eh, not the greatest; I've had much better. But he's so loving, so wonderful. He makes me feel so good, so secure and happy. I enjoy his company so much that the sexuality in the relationship is secondary. Although for him it's primary. He thinks it's fantastic, because he's been with only three women in his life. I've been with—I won't even count them.

I feel like I've sown my oats. I've done every form of sexual behavior I can think of, and I don't feel the need anymore. He satisfies me sexually, makes me feel comfortable. It's not particularly creative, it's not particularly wild or long-lasting, but it's really fine. Sexually, I feel satisfied, and he does, too. He's with this young woman, so he's happy as a clam. It's good.

I met him on a blind date. I didn't think I was going to be able to go through with it when he came to the door that night. I'm used to being physically attracted to the person I'm with. But we proceeded to have a fantastic night. He was hilariously funny, had an amazing sense of humor, very warm and compassionate, a great listener, had wonderful stories about his life, his past wives and his divorces. I fell for the guy. I tried to keep him at bay for a while instead of jumping in with both feet like I usually do. And he just wooed me. After a couple of months, he asked me to go to Paris with him, and I did. We've had several honeymoons, and we aren't even married yet.

I worry about sex down the line. I worry about when I'm fifty, and he's seventy. What will our sexual life be together? But I'm going to take it one step at a time, be happy for what it is now, and worry about that later. I might want to take a lover someday. Hey, life is short. I make him very happy, he makes me very happy now, so I won't worry about things like that. But it could happen. I like to look at men, and I like to think about men. Sometimes I fantasize about other men when I'm making love with my man, but I still don't feel the need to go off and find somebody else.

What I would like from our sex life now is for the dynamics to change. I have become very passive, and he becomes very active. He likes it like that. He's kind of straight, so he doesn't really understand, and it's hard to introduce new things into the relationship. I'm used to being more aggressive in sex and more creative. But what I do he likes, so if it's not broken, don't fix it.

It is strange. Every morning I look in the mirror and I say, "You're with a fifty-eight-year-old man, who's no great hunk." He's tall and skinny. There's not a muscle on his body. Not the stud of yesteryear that I'm used to. And yet, I love him, I think about him, and I miss him when he's not there. I'm crazy about the guy.

So we're getting married next month. A thirty-eight-year-old bride in white—*pure* white. I said to this dress designer, "I want the whitest white we can get. I want a dress so white that you need sunglasses to look at me in this dress." No problem.

I'm more or less bored by sex now. I'd much rather read a book. But I've been with the same man now for two years. He's not boring, but we have very different work schedules during the week, and when the weekend finally does roll around it seems like I pass out, because I'm so tired from working all week. You have to plan sex to do it, and to plan it takes too much time. I just don't care. I could go without it except for about once a month. It's lost its attraction for me.

So my girlfriend thinks that's weird, that this is the age where you're supposed to be blossoming. I already blossomed. Maybe I'll blossom again someday. Not now.

This is a man I really love and care about. I want to have him as my companion forever, but that six months and then straggling on for a year of having sex all the time doesn't really hold much interest for me. After a while you get to be such good friends that sex seems funny.

If he pressed it, and was to come to me and say, "We don't have sex enough. We've got to start having it more!" I'd start thinking about it, and trying to do what I could do. Although, I might resent that. At least somebody would have told me.

I'm always amazed by people who are all interested in sex and read stuff. If I saw a book about people's sex lives, I'd think, "I don't care." I'm not interested in reading about people's fetishes. I don't care about erotic literature. I don't want to watch these fucking fuck films. All that just doesn't do it for me. The overexertion it takes to make sex different when it comes to this S&M is just beyond my imagination. God, how could you get that much energy to even want to go through all the stuff you have to go through to create that esoteric sex life. I find that weird. It seems more like a play than real life. Maybe I'm just lazy.

I went to a wedding back home. After rehearsal dinner with four guys along, we went to a bunch of strip joints. This was the bachelor party; however, we could not talk the groom into coming with us, so he was in for a round of hazing by the rest of us for that evening, and for the rest of the weekend. In fact, probably for the rest of his life he won't be able to live this one down.

We started off at this place called the Men's Club. It was small and well lit. I could tell the place was going to be okay to begin with, because they had valet parking. This is pretty upscale, not dangerous downtown with winos and serial killers. We are probably the most prosperously dressed group in the place. It was kind of blue-collar, casual, and the crowd was men in their twenties and thirties. It was not a motorcycle-gang bar.

Okay, we went and sat at a table right up front by the stage. Apparently, the way this deal works is they have these girls up on stage, you can go watch the girl, and you can tip her. There must have been about thirty guys in the place, and eight or ten girls there. The girl on stage would dance for two or three numbers. Then someone else would get up there and dance. Meanwhile, the rest of them would circulate around. For ten bucks, they would do what they called a table dance. They would come over and dance for you right at your table. I liked that notion.

Sure enough, this woman who must have been in her early twenties, young enough to be my daughter, came to our table. This woman is dressed in high heels and underwear. She essentially asks me if I would like for her to take off her clothes for me for ten bucks. I say, essentially, "Yeah! Great!"

I'm sitting there turned slightly away from the table. What happens is she very seductively and very wonderfully starts doing this dance in front of me. I'll tell you, it was great. It was like the best sex I've had in years, and we didn't even have sex. She would put her hands on my shoulders, lean over and breathe in my face. Let me look at her naked breasts and stare into her eyes. She would brush up against me and kiss me. She would whisper in my ear. She turned around, bends over, takes off her underpants, lets me look at her pussy. Then she stands up and leans backwards. I'm sitting down, so she's just a little taller than me. She lets her long hair fall into my face. She moves her head around and lets her hair brush against me. It was just this wonderful, fine, sweet-smelling hair. I really got off on this.

Then the music stopped. She was very nice, she told me her name and smiled at me. I think that she really enjoyed it. I know she's doing this for money. But I've been around. I know when someone is kissing up to you, but she seemed to enjoy giving me the pleasure of watching her. I clearly enjoyed it. She went off.

I just wanted to kill all the three guys I was with. They were in this macho bullshit thing. "Oh, these girls are *ugly*. We need to go to this other club. This place is so bad. The girls here couldn't be waitresses down at the Platinum Club. We need to go to the Platinum Club." Finally, they dragged me out of this place. I wanted to stay. I wanted this woman to come and sit at the table with me. I wanted to talk to her. Hold hands with her. I was just totally in love.

The point of this story is—I started thinking about it afterwards, and the thing that struck me was, I don't understand why my wife doesn't do this for me. My sex life at home is not that good. As a matter of fact, it's pretty bad. After we got married sex gradually tapered off until we were only doing it about once a month. Now we have sex maybe about once a week, because I finally put my foot down and said, "Look, this is ridiculous. We need to do better than this." So we increased the frequency. But the thing is, it's nice, it's very warm, it's loving and sweet and tender and all that, but it's not like *fucking*. It's like lovemaking, and I want to do some serious fucking. I want to have some *sex*.

To me it would be very easy for her to make me happy. If I were a woman, I could make someone like me happy easily. But I could not get my wife to stand up in front of me and dance and do a striptease. I could maybe talk her into it, but it would be like, "Are we finished yet? Can I take off these shoes now?" She would make it very clear to me that she does not enjoy this. What she really enjoys doing is having me play with her breasts, which is nice and it gets her going and stuff, but that's it. We have this formalized, ritualistic lovemaking, and it's really not that much fun.

I have always been obsessed with sex. I don't know why this is. I wish I wasn't obsessed with sex. My wife says that her number-one problem with life right now is economics. We're not broke or anything, but we don't have as much money as she would like to have. She says, whenever she's not doing anything else, she thinks about our indebtedness. Whenever I'm not thinking about anything else, I'm thinking about getting laid. I have pretty much always been that way.

Sex has always been a big deal to me. That is, I like sex and if I look back at my life, I've built a lot of my life around creating situations where I can have plenty of sex. In my first marriage, for example, one of the issues that led to my unhappiness with that situation was when I realized that our exploration of each other as sexual beings was going to be fairly limited in scope. That really means that my first wife, having tried it a few times, really wasn't interested in sucking on my dick. There I was, twenty-seven years old, thinking, "Jeez, you mean, I'm going to go through my life without having my dick sucked anymore?" That wasn't a really happy prospect. I know that itself led to my openness to having affairs during that marriage, which really was a part of the communication breakdown that we experienced, that drove real wedges into our intimacy, which then led to us not being in the marriage together, not being partners in it, not really having a relationship where we could tell each other everything and share openly. We ended up in different camps and not on each other's side. Hence, we split up.

I would say right now my relationship with my present wife is better than it's ever been as an overall rating—openness, communication, caring, love, etc.—but we just have a minimal amount of sex. That's a problem for me. I think it's a problem for her, but we don't really discuss it. Although, it really is coming back around the priority list of things to talk about, we've never been able to discuss it in the past in a way that didn't reek of blame and defense. She felt blamed for it. The problem is that I probably did blame her for it, so she really fought against even the open discussion of it, because it was somehow always her fault.

Our relationship has been strewn with extramarital affairs, really to the point where it broke our relationship down completely for a while. It looked like we weren't going to be together anymore. We came back together again with a sort of truce around the sexual issue. But it was a truce, not a resolution. A truce is, "We're not going to fight about it anymore. We're just not going to fight about it."

Part of what has happened for me is to recognize that while sex is high on my list of desires, sex is a luxury and not a need. At times, when I'm really horny, it starts to be more like a need. I've done two things with that. One is masturbation. The other is extramarital affairs when the opportunities have surfaced, and I find the woman sexy. So when those things have happened, I have not protected the sacredness of our relationship, or however you want to say that, by abstaining. I have in fact had the affairs. Simply the knowledge that this is possible is one of the things that prevents me from being in despair in our relationship.

I live in a place where I don't know if our relationship will ever become what it once was and be a real source of sexual satisfaction for me. Yet high on my list of things I want in my life is sexual satisfaction. I made a value decision that my relationship and my family—at least for the time being—is more important than my sexual satisfaction. I actually had to make that distinction, and be aware of that and stay conscious of that distinction in order to have a good relationship with my wife.

Being committed, I had thought, would feel stifling, boring. I would get restless and hate it. But during the period of time when he and I were committed to each other and living together, it wasn't boring at all. It became so private. We could rely on that privacy. It was the most wonderful sexual experience of my life ever. So I hold that kind of intimacy as much more exciting sexually, instead of boring. Not to mention it makes for a lot deeper and better friendship. This is for me. I don't think other people feel that way. But that's what I want and have not yet found.

Most people would regard their boyfriend or girlfriend, husband or wife, as somebody they can lie to. That's just accepted, a given. This is probably the toughest thing for me to deal with. I would be less likely to do something to hurt my lover, if I were going to hurt anyone. Aren't you supposed to be closer to somebody that you're intimate with? Obviously not. The man I'm living with at present, I know he has a completely different idea about sex than I do. To him it's just physical. It's something to be lied about, and he's lied to me about it. We've had some pretty bad problems. What started out as a relationship I thought could—and may still—blossom into something very powerful, has been incredibly stunted in its growth, because he has lied to me and betrayed me and didn't think much of it.

Maybe he's a late bloomer. Maybe he'll never feel the same way as I see it. I don't think it's a difference between men and women. He believes that it is. I've heard him say it. A lot of people believe that. But I had his attitude at the age of nineteen. It's just an immature way to approach things. That's a judgment that I'm making, and I'm aware that it's a judgment. Maybe that's not fair, but that's what I really believe. It's really immature to lie to someone that you're close to. If you want to have a lot of relationships with other people—I even see that as being a silly attitude—but if that's what you want to do, be up-front about it. Period. And go do it. Hey, have fun.

I know that I'm pretty black or white in these areas, and it's not always realistic. My mother always talked about sex being very loving, and the importance of strong relationships, but I saw her in various relationships that, although they were monogamous, they were serially monogamous. My dad did the same thing dating. To me, at first, relationships were sort of like disposable razors. You got one, they were good for a while, then they lost their edge, and you got rid of them. That might be right to some extent. Everything is temporary, and we all die. But what I've discovered now is I really long for a lasting relationship that I can depend on, count on. Not depend on in a needy way, but just know that it will be there. I can relax and not have to think about it. That would be great.

The social taboo on having different sex partners in marriage has to do with jealousy. That's probably the main thing that messes it up. It's too bad. I just don't understand jealousy at all. I think wife-swapping would be fun. What's the big deal as long as you come up with some social rules? You and some friends of yours get together once a year—New Year's Eve or something—and if not actually switch partners, it would be fun taking turns having sex with your own partner in a round-robin sort of thing. You watch us do it, and then we watch you. Or just play sex games—make out with each other for certain, set time periods. Why can't people do that, especially people who have grown up in the '60s and have a little bit more liberal attitude about sex, and are supposed to be free-thinking? It doesn't seem to be a national trend. In fact, it's just the opposite. Monogamy seems to be in and on the upswing.

Occasionally, you read in the newspaper where couples do a little wife-swapping, and then the cross couples fall in love with each other, or someone in the group gets jealous because he's not getting enough attention. The next thing you know there's a gunfight. Someone gets shot. But it would seem to me, if you could make it socially acceptable and figure out some rules, you could make it work.

We have all these national holidays where you have customary behavior you only indulge on that holiday. Like Thanksgiving is just gluttony. You stuff yourself with turkey. New Year's Eve you go out and get drunk out of your mind. Fourth of July you play with fire. It seems like they should have one night a year where you could go out and have some different sex partners, and then have Monday off. But for some reason you can't.

Institutionalizing the occasional naughtiness wouldn't be bad. If you don't want to have wife-swapping where you actually are fucking, maybe you can do something just a little bit naughty—mutual masturbation with friends, sort of like Hands Across America. It seems like we ought to be able to find something to spice things up here in America. We've always been the leaders. Maybe the young people will come up with something.

One of the things that happens in marital sex is that you finish having a family, and the need and desire to procreate is no longer a driving force. For men that is a driving force in terms of dominance—"I'm going to (pardon the language) knock you up so you can have another kid by me, therefore expressing my supreme sexual talent by producing a perfectly healthy child again." When that desire is no longer there, you sublimate that stuff into your career, your hobbies, your other friendships. You find your physical energy is going in other directions, and as you get older, you only have so much physical energy to put out. You're falling asleep at ten or eleven at night.

One of you goes to bed at ten, the other one comes in at midnight. The next day, "Oh, I came in at twelve, and I thought we'd have a night in bed, but you're always asleep."

"I work hard all day. If I don't get my sleep, I'm miserable."

"What? You don't love me anymore? We're never going to have sex again?"

All these little dialogues go on. They start building up into things that they are not. You start taking all this stuff personally. "You're falling asleep early *purposefully* because you're trying to avoid me."

"No, I'm doing it because I just can't stay up. I have to be up at five o'clock in the morning to travel two hours on the train. I have to work all day in the hospital, or with the kids, and I'm just spent, used up."

So married couples' sex becomes an occasion. You have to plan for it. Put it on the calendar. Show up on time, bring a gift. You're all the way back to the beginning again. You expected a free ride for the next thirty years, and instead you end up back in the same place. To get to first base again, you have to make the phone call and bring the flowers. "You doing anything Saturday night? Would you like to get together?" Hopefully, on Saturday night, the kids don't wake up.

Unless there is an openness and dialogue that goes on in marriages, and problems are worked out in a dialectic between the man and the woman, then it's very hard to maintain the sexual attraction. It's very difficult to maintain it when you have all these other issues coming up all the time, issues about how to raise the kids—"I want to do it this way."

Where is the money coming from? All these issues start becoming deterrents to love. They become so overwhelming that they start camouflaging or burying love. That life that was so preeminent when you first got married and had your first children, and you're watching them grow, that light begins diminishing as the realities of being a family close in. That's my experience anyway. For some relationships the people involved have this experience, too, but to them all these filters serve another purpose. "We don't *have* to have sex anymore. We've already had our kids, and we're a very happy family. That was really for when we were younger." Some people look at it that way.

My marital experience has been awful, so I speak of the whole institution rather cynically. In marriage, it becomes very hard to maintain the sexual attraction. Is that sexual attraction something that's *supposed* to be, or is it something that our culture imposes on us—that we're supposed to be sexually active for the rest of our mature lives, to have this sexual party like Jordache jeans or Diet Pepsi presents to us? This is supposed to go on forever? This is paradise because we can still do it? I don't know.

Thinking about these things doesn't drive me crazy, or impose itself upon my daily activities. Otherwise, I wouldn't be seeking to build another relationship at this point in my life. There are certainly questions that I ask myself in terms of how we present ourselves sexually as we get older. How do we attract each other, husbands and wives? What modes of attraction do we use? Does it have to be that we listen to a certain kind of music or walk a certain way anymore, or do we just *become* attractive? Are we supposed to be attracted to different kinds of elements in men and women as we get older? If you're with your spouse and having problems with sex, is it because she is no longer sexually attractive as she was fifteen years ago, or do you expect yourself and her to stay that person, frozen in time and space?

What I'm finding out in my present relationship is the thrill again of the goodnight kiss. Saying goodnight to someone, getting in the car, and going back to your place. The thrill of things to come. The more you can hold the thing to come at bay, the better off you are. She and I talk about this a lot. We complain to each other, we make a lot of sexual-innuendo humor with each other, but it's all part of the foreplay, part of making out. We say all the time that it's just better not to make love, because it can be the make-or-break thing in a relationship to have sex with someone you're trying to build a relationship with. You could blow everything. Maybe that's what happens in marriages.

The first place my husband and I made love was in a motel room—Motel 6, room 210. I swear to God, I have the receipts. I forced the man to spend money on me, and I was worth it. Or so I thought then.

It was not great. I guess I had bigger expectations than anything. I'd just gotten out of another relationship, and I didn't really want to feel anything for my husband. I just refused to. So it was not a great thing until the third or the fourth time. By that time, I knew him a lot better. He started getting more gentle and let loose, instead of being so macho. He was fun after that.

And still today, it's a lot of fun. I nudge him awake in the middle of the night and say, "Did I wake you? I'm sorry, baby."

"It's four o'clock in the morning!"

"Oh, is it? C'mon, jump on it." So it's fun. We have great sex. We have three wonderful children and still have great sex.

I told him, "I don't ever remember having an orgasm before you."

"That's because they didn't love you like I do. They were all selfish men, baby. That's why you never had an orgasm. Nobody ever let you have an orgasm."

"Really? If I'd known it was this good . . ."

"I'm glad you never did. I'm glad nobody ever gave you the satisfaction before me."

When we were first together, we would have sex every chance we got. *"Yes! Yes!"*

"Okay, let's go to the beach."

"Yes, the beach. Let's *do it* at the beach."

"Yes! Yes!"

We'd do it everywhere. He would be getting ready to go to work. Breakfast time? Yes! Lunch time? Yes! All day. All night. Yes!

"Damn, you're going to kill me," I said.

"I think you're going to kill me, too."

Today, we still make love four or five times a week, and we've been married seven years. He says to me, "Baby, do you think we're going to make love like this until we're about sixty?"

"You better. I'm going to be a horny old lady." If we don't kill each other by the time we get that old, I think he'll be a horny old man, too. "They died from too much sex." Put that on our tombstone.

3. ADULTERY

Adultery is an old-fashioned word, but Americans are often old-fashioned people. Despite the mutations in the public perception of sex and in personal sexual practice begat by the Baby Boom generation during the sexual revolution, adultery still means something. The proof is evident in the plots of most television soap operas as well as our tabloid-headline approach to electing presidents. Adultery is wrong, a sin, and you shouldn't do it.

The cynics see adultery as the penultimate stage in the natural entropy of human relationships. Love, marriage, adultery, divorce. Disloyalty, followed by dissolution, is the organic end of love. Those who don't reach this experience have put their sex lives in some sort of suspended animation, out of exhaustion or timidity.

I'm not exactly a romantic, but my personal experience with life and love prevents me from holding either of these negative and narrow views of adultery. I am lucky enough to be married—truly mated—to a person I love, respect, and continue to desire. That doesn't mean I haven't thought about sex with other women, even given the idea serious consideration from time to time. So I can't condemn adultery out of hand. In fact, I'd have to agree with the cynics that anyone who *hasn't* thought about sex with someone other than his or her spouse is as good as dead or at least sexually deadened. My problem is that in the last few years I've talked with many, many men and women, and a goodly number of them have had sex with someone other than their spouses for a variety of reasons in any number of situations. Being human is very complex.

For some individuals, adultery is a way of life. A forty-five-year-old building contractor working on his second marriage explains his behavior like this: "It has always been a constant thing with me. If I see an appealing woman and she shows any interest at all in return, I will pursue her, and eventually it will culminate in a tryst somewhere. Don't ever mistake that I'm proud of everything I've done, but it's just a part of me. I have always envied men who have a relationship with their wives where they are totally satisfied and committed to her, so they can resist any kind of temptation. I, unfortunately, have never been able to resist any woman who has ever flirted with me. I've been extremely flattered, and affairs have become a complete pastime."

It is not the accepted ideal, but plenty of marriages survive constant adulterous sex by one or both partners. Stereotypically, it is the wife who gives tacit complicity to her husband's discreet affairs. But obviously his lovers must often be married women as well. As the building contractor explains it, "I *only* have affairs with married women, because thay are just as interested and have just as much to lose as I do. They make no bones about it. Let's do it for the sake of it. Don't carry any extra luggage home with us."

More often, adultery is an anomaly in people's lives, an indulgence in physical passion, a refreshing plunge into danger, a desperate grasping for companionship, for comfort, or for an ego boost. In a few cases, it is simply the manifestation of the death of an old love and the beginning of a new one.

At its best self-centered, adultery is often selfish and mean.

Discovering an unfaithful lover is devastating for the unsuspecting partner. Few relationships survive the attendant guilt and disillusionment of divided loyalty. Adultery can cause great pain and lingering anger.

But what would sexual and emotional fealty mean if there were no temptation to be unfaithful? There cannot be steadfast love if there is no threat to that allegiance. What joy would there be in true love if it took no discipline, like opening flat champagne every anniversary?

Adultery is as good a compass to direct us to the true nature of love as unwavering devotion, maybe better since it turns in many directions in the way human emotions do. Adultery demonstrates how love can sneak up on people, how they can be duped by counterfeit affection, how men and women are capable of loving more than one person deeply. Sometimes the great risks that accompany sexual deception point to courageous selflessness or desperate escapes, not reckless appetite. The very real possibility of the loved one having sex with someone else puts tension in the spring of love and gives commitment a special passion, just as the taut excitement of engaging in illicit sex can put such an addictive fever into an affair. There is a certain wild beauty in the stamina of sexual desire and the fervent need of the body, like some great, admirably healthy animal, riding rough-shod over our veneer of civilized rationality. Adultery speaks plainly of the human condition—the frailty of our resolve, the emptiness of words and reason at the fulfilling caress of warm flesh, our willingness to wound someone we love merely for a fleeting pleasure.

But there is the touch of human hope in adultery as well. It embodies the wish to be free, free of convention, free of duty, free of the past, free to make fantasies real. We human beings have a talent for stepping off into thin air with a smile on our faces. More often than not, the freedom we long for is an illusion, and a treacherous one as well. What seemed a dizzying flight turns out to be a free-fall. But the hope is genuine, the sweet blood of that living, pulsing drive that propels each of us in the timeless search for love.

○ ○ ○

Within a month or two after I got married, I realized that I had made a mistake. Newlywed couples are just doing it ten times a day. It was really frequent and all that. Then, one night, we were in bed. I don't remember the details of it, but he didn't want to, and I said, "Don't you want to make love?"

"No," he said. I don't remember the conversation so much as the feelings of being really hurt because he didn't want me. It was from that point on that things changed for me with him. I was already unhappy with the relationship as far as everyday things, but I always thought we were real compatible with sex. That's when he probably started seeing other people.

He still had his friends and was going out with the guys and not coming home till three or four in the morning. Not telling me where he was. Probably he was with other women. But since I had no inclination what was going on, I just thought he didn't want me. I didn't know why. Looking back, it all makes a lot of sense to me now.

But I had it in my mind that you were married, and you stayed married forever, because of my religious upbringing. That's why I'm still married. But he started running around and having affairs that I never knew about.

The first one I found out about, my first son was nine months old. He had been having an affair for two years. All that time, I was planning this wonderful birth of a child. It was really weird, because when I was three or four months pregnant and was having a really horrible time with morning sickness—twenty-four-hour sickness, I call it—I woke up in the middle of the night. I can remember this dream, even though it was fourteen years ago. I dreamed that he was with another woman and I found out about it. In my dream, I was hysterical and I sat up in bed, crying and crying.

"What is wrong with you?" he said.

"I just had a dream that you were having an affair."

"You're crazy. Lay down." The next morning, he didn't even remember it, and he doesn't remember it to this day. You can say whatever you want to say, but I think it was God's way of filling me in.

After our son was nine months old, one night in church, Art went forward and talked to the preacher. He had never done that during the invitation before. We came home and went to bed. I didn't ask him about it. He didn't say anything to me. We were just laying there before we went to sleep, and I said, "You're having an affair, aren't you?"

"Yeah, I am." I tried to get him to break it off with her. But it took a while. He didn't want to do it. He didn't want to hurt her feelings. So we went through all that crap.

In the meantime, our sex life remained the same, just because we're so good together that we separate our emotional problems from the physical problems. Plus I felt that when we were together physically, it bonded us back, and I could forget everything else. So we went to counseling for several years, but we never had to have sexual counseling. He's never been inadequate, in any way. The most inadequacy has come from me in not wanting to have sex. I always live by the rule: If you want it, fine. If you don't, leave me alone. I'll do it if you want to. Looking back over the years, I can see now that you don't separate your emotions from your physical response. I thought I was doing that, but I really wasn't.

Then he had another one. And then another one. I don't know what all happened with him. Art's not real clever. He leaves big hints, so I would confront him, and he would admit over a long process of time. I never really caught him. I would get furious. By this time, we had two kids. It just ruined everything. The most recent one was four years ago.

The nursery workers at church called me one Sunday night and said,

"Your kids are still in the nursery. Art hasn't picked them up, and it's been an hour since church was over."

He works at the church as the maintenance manager. I said, "He's probably around there, or out in the parking lot."

"No, we looked out in the parking lot. Your car is gone. Nobody is here, Rebecca. He's gone."

The light bulb went on. "Okay, I'll be there to pick up the kids." I got dressed, and the phone rang. It was him. I said, "Where have you been?"

"I'll talk about it when I get home."

"You don't need to bother coming home." So we had this big old fight on the phone. He ended up coming back.

Then right after that, he started doing some maintenance work with a man whose wife all of a sudden got real involved. He started having an affair with her. She eventually joined our church, moved to our community, and did everything she could to be with him. She did not break up with her husband. They started being our best friends. One night when we were in their car, they started talking about how it's good for a man to have a really good woman friend, and how it's good for a woman to have a really good man friend. I could tell this was leading up to the point of switching around partners, so I immediately ended that relationship. I didn't want anything to do with the two of them. They had two little kids who were friends with my children, so this was really bad. They just wouldn't stop.

I confronted Art, and he admitted it. I had warned him. I said, "So help me, someday I'm going to blow up. I've had it with this."

The last straw was, we bowled on the church bowling team. She followed us everywhere, so we went the first night of the bowling league, and here they come waltzing in the door. They had signed up. I lost it. I approached her at the bowling balls, and I called her every name in the book. I told her to stay away from my husband. I did it right in front of my children. I had just reached an emotional breaking point. I didn't know any other way to handle it. I went berserk and screamed at her. People were coming from all over to see what was wrong. After about two minutes into this high-volume conversation, they found out real quick what was going on.

She denied it. She said if she was going to have an affair with somebody, it would be with somebody who would take care of her. I remember that statement, because it was such a true statement. Art's such an ass.

Nobody would want him really, once they got to know him. I thought to myself, "Then you must have just wanted him for the sex."

When you talk to Art about his affairs, he says there was actually no lovemaking involved, that it was basically sexual foreplay and oral sex. Which I think is a bunch of crap. You talk to any man, and he's not going to have an affair with a woman just for foreplay. He can do that with me at home. So the trust broke down, and as the trust has gone out of our relationship, the frequency of sex broke down.

I don't know if it's just Art or all men in general, but they don't seem to understand that if you don't have a good emotional relationship with somebody, you can't just hop into bed that night and expect them to give their all to you. You can go through the motions, but don't expect anything there. That's a problem with Art, because he wants more than just the sex act.

I talk to a lot of women, and they say, "If only my husband would be caring and holding and give me the emotional part, not just the sex act, not just do it and get off, then I would be so happy." I've got what they want in a husband. The problem is, I'm to the point that if he needs sex, then fine, he can have it. But he wants the emotional attachment, the loving, the holding and all that, and I can't give that to him anymore. It's gone. I don't love him anymore. So for me, it's, "Oh, God, here he comes. It's going to be another three-hour night. Gosh, why can't you just do this in ten minutes?"

He's wants sex very frequently, and I say, "Art why can't you ever just go through it, get it over with, get off, and leave me alone?"

"Because," he'll say, "I want to feel the closeness with you." I think now that's his way of expressing love through the making-love process, whereas a woman expresses love in other ways and ices the cake with sex, maybe. Maybe that's the difference between us. The farther apart we become as husband and wife, the more he clings to that part of our relationship, thinking that's going to make everything okay. We can have a horrible, knock-down, drag-out fight. Then that night, if we make love, the next morning he thinks everything is okay. It doesn't happen that way. My life still goes on.

In all the time he's had affairs, nothing between us has changed sexually. Our sex life has stayed the same, which is really odd, because they say with most men it will either decrease or increase. With him, it stays very much the same. So I can't tell in that way. But he just is kind of distant. Not distant sexually, but distant emotionally. So that's how I can always tell.

I stay not so much for religious reasons now, but because of my boys. They're very attached to him. I'm still from the old school that believes that two parents in a home are better than one, if there's not a lot of physical abuse, screaming and yelling. If you can muddle through, I think it's better. But it wrecks sex a lot.

I don't regret being a good girl. I'm very proud of myself. If I had had sex before I got married, I would look back at that now and regret it very much. So I'm real proud of myself. I'm trying to instill that in my sons. It's really difficult these days, but I want them to hang on to the fact that they should really wait until they are married. That's real idealistic in today's society, but that's the way I came up, and I'm satisfied with that in my life. I would hope that they could follow through in their lives, too. It's not so much a religious aspect to that, but more important is your own self-worth. It made my own self-worth really good. Something I could really be proud of.

Nowadays, you're not talking about a good time, you're talking about life and death. Nowadays if Art is going to screw around, I wish he would just go away, because if he brings anything home to me, he's a dead man. He'll never know what hit him. I can promise you that. You can read it in the paper: DEAD MAN. I'll admit it.

It's been three or four years since his last affair, and I'm starting to get itchy again, wondering. His interval is about three years or so. This time I'm just waiting on him. I'm going to get some real proof. The next time it happens, I want to get a detective, so that I have grounds to get him out, and my children can't hold it against me. He's smart enough to know that I'm waiting, so he has to be really, really careful.

It was my wife's boss, Kevin, and his wife Sandra. We were going over to their house. Jeannie and I sat down and had some dinner. There was always this undercurrent of something. Not a blatant kind of thing, not anything where they were showing you pictures of people screwing there to get you in the mood. But there was always this undercurrent, a lot of sexual innuendos and double entendres in conversation.

It was a time, too, when sexual promiscuity was fine. Maybe it wasn't fine, but it was a thing on people's minds. Affairs with other people, couples that switched and swung, everything. People were having a lot of sex. Sex was going on in the early '70s. Magazines were popping. Massage parlors everywhere. So we went over to have dinner with her boss and his wife and there were little things mentioned.

We met again. For the life of me, I can't remember how it was suggested. It was probably talked about a number of times, again and again, like brainwashing. It was a slice of the pie that gets presented enough, and it's on your mind anyway, so it gets attractive. Actually, it was more of a two-against-one thing, the overall feature. I found out later on that Jeannie and this guy had been having an affair already. I didn't know this. Kevin and I were tennis partners. Even later when she told me she was having an affair, I didn't know it was Kevin. I always suspected this other guy in her office, just because he kept a low profile. He's guilty by being too quiet. Never suspected Kevin. Kevin is an outgoing, sexual guy who would never do something like that. Nah.

So it came to this one really strange night where we went there with the intent of switching partners. There had probably been a night before where it didn't happen. But this night that it did happen, my wife and Kevin got up and went into one room, and Sandra and I got up and went into the other bedroom.

She and I are just laying there, basically saying, "You think they're doing anything?" We wound up screwing each other, but it really wasn't much to write home about, other than doing it. There was no passion or romance or anything. We did that, us in one room, them in the other room. But that thing, that taboo had been broken. Soon, we were all together in various combinations in the same room.

After Jeannie told me that she had an affair, I immediately went out and had one myself. It wasn't an affair. It was a revenge screw. But that set the stage for it to be permissible for both of us. I can see other people. You can see other people.

There was one night Kevin and Sandra came over. His wife was extremely horny, just really on. They were loose. They'd had a little wine. And we just went to town on Sandra. We took all her clothes off, and just made her feel real good.

The interesting thing was, I didn't want any part of my wife. I remember one time I was on top of Kevin's wife and Jeannie kept trying to get in there, and I was, "Nah, stay away, you." It was the intimacy that I really wanted, the one-on-one thing, and not any kind of group thing.

Although it was exciting. I can't say it wasn't exciting. Looking back at it now, it's like, "So what?" It truly was "So what?" I tell other people some of the things we did, and they just go wide-eyed, especially younger people. "Oh, wow, that must have felt great!" If I think about it in those terms, yeah, it did feel great. But, Jesus, a few times, I had an orgasm and then I actually went to a chair, lit up a cigarette and smoked, watching my wife and Sandra making out there. This was a fantasy of mine, to see two women making out. But it was cold, just cold. It was lots of fun for a little while, but it just didn't work out.

So there you are making out with the other guy's wife. It was weird. There was that spark to it of doing something outside acceptance, something strange and dangerous, one of those things you weren't allowed to do. It was a real adolescent thing to do. But the bottom line behind it all is that somebody always gets hurt from it. There is no way you can't take it personal.

The bizarre thing is, my wife continued to have this thing with Kevin heavily for years. I had another affair with somebody. In fact, Kevin is the guy who mentioned it. I was working in the music store, and he said, "Ah, you got to be getting into her pants. She's great." It was some gal at work. I was able to do that, too. That was a passionate affair, though. She blew me away. That was the first time I was really sexually attracted to someone. I wanted her. I wanted to be with her. I wanted her body. I was crazy about her. I liked the whole package. This wasn't a revenge fuck. This wasn't anything that I'd ever experienced before. She just felt good. She just was great, like a butterfly. She would lay on top of me, and it was great sex. It can be a pretty exceptional experience, that great sex one-on-one. Not that anything I ever did would be considered perverted or even that imaginative, but one-on-one, this was intimate, and it was just the two of us, and it was *nice*.

Once my wife found out about this girl, she wanted it to be just the two of us again. Once she found out that there was somebody actually interested in me, and not only interested in me, but willing to go on seeing me long-distance. This girl moved to another state. She was sending me letters now. Then she was a threat to my wife. Before that everything was hunky-dory, copacetic. But once it looked like there was a real claim on my emotions from someone, the whole thing changed for her. It was, "No, we shouldn't see other people anymore."

It just stopped, because it stopped. It wasn't anything that I wanted or needed anymore in my life. The sexual revolution had made it okay. If it wasn't for AIDS and herpes, there'd be a whole lot more going on today. There isn't any more cognizance of relationships and intimacy and what you can have with another person now than there was then. We live in such a short-term society. Everything is instant gratification. We'd be fucking like bunnies all over the place still, if we didn't die from it, if all that fear wasn't there. A lot of people believe we've reached some "new concept." I don't.

Jennifer and I moved to Phoenix, Arizona, when we'd been together about six years. We went to a human-sexuality workshop at the university. It was one of these touchy-feely, California-type deals. It was wild.

Like they would show a very erotic movie, but something that was acceptable to both men and women, like a movie of a woman masturbating. Then the leader would tell us that masturbation was really okay. Then we'd break up into discussion groups and talk about how really masturbation was great. Not much dissent.

Then we'd get back together and get into radical stuff. They would show a homosexual sex movie, and have a homosexual come and say, "Hey, what the hell? It's like heterosexual sex, except we happen to be homosexuals." Then we'd break up into discussion groups and say, "Yeah, homosexual sex is okay."

After this, we went back home and I said, "You know, I've always thought that since sex is so much fun, I don't see why there's this social taboo against having sex with other people. I mean, you enjoy it. I enjoy it. Why don't we go out and have some sex with someone else, just for fun?"

Much to my surprise, she said, "Yeah!" I thought she would say, "No! You're nuts. I want a divorce." No, she thought this was a great idea.

Now, I'll tell you what happens with open marriages. I've talked to a couple of people who've had open marriages, and the same thing invariably happens. She goes out and sleeps with about twenty different guys, and you can't get laid. She'd go out, meet this guy, and she'd say, "My husband and I feel that sexual experimentation is important. We have an open marriage."

"Wow," this guy would say. "You're really cool. That's great."

I would meet a girl and tell her the same thing. The woman would look at me and say, "You egg-sucking snake! Slime ball! Yick!" And she'd walk off.

The rules were that we did not have threesomes or foursomes. Looking back on this now, I don't know why we didn't. That would have been fun.

I would have liked that. Jealousy is interesting to me. I am not a jealous person. I have always heard that men are able to separate sex and love more than women. That's the way I feel about sex. I like sex. I don't see where it has any relations to the person that you are married to or in love with. It's a fun activity. It's like having a great meal or seeing a great movie. It's wonderful entertainment. The point of this thing is to have this fabulous orgasm that sends a natural drug coursing through your system and makes you feel good. The thought of another man having sex with my wife doesn't bother me at all.

I was a little jealous, I have to admit, when she was getting laid, and I couldn't seem to. It wasn't that I was jealous of her having sex, but I was envious that she was having all this fun and I wasn't. It *was* my idea after all.

Finally, I had a relationship with a mutual female friend of ours. She was a short, good-looking blonde. My wife was not a particularly attractive woman undressed. She had this funny-looking figure. This blonde was so sweet and cute. I've always liked blondes. She had small, pert breasts, which I also like. She was coming off a bad relationship, and Jennifer happened to be out of town. She knew about our open marriage and she said, "Why don't we go have dinner together?" Afterwards there happened to be something on TV. It happened that the only TV in her apartment was by her bed. She initiated the whole thing. We're sitting in bed together. I didn't have to make much of a pretense. I just put my hand on her shoulder. She said, "Are you making a pass at me?"

"Well, yeah," I said.

"Okay." We started having sex. This was the third woman I had slept with in my life now. I fell madly in love with her for maybe two weeks. I was just walking on air. I couldn't concentrate, I couldn't think straight. I was just nuts. Oh, boy.

As soon as we had sex, we called Jennifer up together, and she says, "Jennifer, guess what. I'm in bed with your husband." And we laughed, and talked to Jennifer. I talked to her. That was terrific and really fun. Jennifer was laughing, and she thought it was great. We would go out places together, the three of us, and make jokes about it, "Here's Harry with his harem." I'd just grin. We never slept together, the three of us. We could have, I'm sure, looking back on it now, if I'd had enough nerve to broach the subject. I'm sure I could have talked them into it. I kind of missed out on that deal. Too late now. Never again am I going to have a chance to have a threesome. Too bad.

Anyway, shortly after that we had our son. As soon as we had Gary, our lives completely disintegrated. We got a divorce. I'm not blaming it on Gary. I don't know what happened. I think we were getting more mature, and as that happened, we realized how little we had in common.

I was very naive when I met him. I thought he locked us in the house because he wanted to protect us. We were new in the area. We didn't know anybody or anything about the town. He installed a lock on the door that he can lock it from the outside, but you can't open it from the inside. A dead bolt with a key. I'm in, I can't go out. There's a six-foot fence from the front of the house to the back of the house. He kept us in there two weeks at a time while he went on the road. Two straight weeks. We never got outside. I took sick. The fire department had to climb a ladder over the two-story house onto the patio to get me out.

"Does he always do this?" they asked me.

"Yes," I said. "He takes the phones and puts them in the trunk of the car, and locks us up in the house." What kind of man was that?

It was because of all that he was doing out there. He wanted to make sure I didn't get to do it. Turns out the real-estate business that we had was a cover for him to sleep around. Him going to school all the time? A great place for the motherfucker to find girlfriends.

How come the girl lives behind me sees more of what he was doing than I did? Because we couldn't go to see him. She told me, "I'm going to give you a phone over your fence. Plug it in."

"What?" I said.

"Just plug it in. You going to find out a whole lot. He's got you canned. That's why he keeps you in a little ponytail and blue jeans, no makeup, and you can't do anything, can't leave the house."

I plugged that baby in. When the phone did ring, I found out he'd been engaged to a girl at college for two years. She asked me who I was, and I told her I was his wife.

"You couldn't be his wife. He don't have a wife."

"Yes, I am, and I've got two kids, girl." She told me he had been having dinner with her parents. Oh, she was devastated. I told her, "Come to my house. You'll have to climb the fence to get in, because he has a big lock on the door, and we're not allowed out, but I would love for you to climb that fence and be sitting here when he gets home. Or just sit on my steps, because I can't open the door."

She did come. Oh, did he shit bricks. I went to the hospital. He beat me up real bad, because the girl give me the telephone, and he said I had no right to plug it in. I was really naive. I said I was brainwashed, because I let him do me that way. But that was my fault. I don't blame nobody for that but me. I'm glad it happened. That woke me up to men and to real life.

It was a period of time when Kelly and I were both dissatisfied with each other. We weren't really communicating emotionally. Beyond that, we weren't really communicating very much at all, I guess. I thought it was maybe a phase that I was going through. I was kind of grouchy and grumpy. She was kind of grumpy and grouchy. My body would say, "Let's have sex." About that time, she wouldn't really be interested. The other half the time when she was interested, I could tell there was no passion there. Just no passion.

So, when the opportunity came along, I just considered myself single again in respect to sex. "If she's not going to be available for me sexually in any truly satisfying way, hey, it's an open game." I found myself browsing through books like *Open Marriage*. Just a very difficult, strenuous time between us.

While I was looking for a little sexual activity—and basically it was very physical, I didn't have prolonged affairs—I got the impression from what she told me afterwards that her approach to her affairs was more emotional. She wanted that emotional contact, and the sex developed out of the emotional contact.

Once it was out in the open, I was really confused and pissed off, because she had *emotional* relationships, and I'd just had a series of one-night stands. To me there was a difference. It really pissed me off. I mean it *really* pissed me off. I'd go into these rages over it, and absolutely not see the hypocrisy in my focus and the cognitive reality that I felt. What *I* did, well, that was okay, but what *she* did was really bad. I felt there was more of a betrayal, because there had been emotions poured out to someone else, while I had just been looking at leg.

It wasn't until I started going through counseling with her, and then individually, subsequently, that I realized what we were talking about was the emotional basis for a marriage to begin with, that the sex just happened to be a thing that grows out of it.

The rebuilding of the marriage has been a long, involved process that we are still coping with every day. It's a function of staying focused and supportive. The task for me is not turning my thoughts so tightly inward that I start to rebuild negative cognitive structure. Rather, I stay emotionally open and available, aware of what her needs are at any particular moment, and I kind of quiet myself down and give her the space to be who she is. I've been accused a lot in our relationship of tending to be outgoing, exuberant, and hyperactive in the extreme. When I go to extremes, I don't really pay attention to her emotionally. I overlook her needs. I turn on the stereo or television without asking her, or I'll turn them up too loud. She's right. I have in the past not been emotionally there.

What I have found as time goes by, and I have become more emotionally available to her, is, number one, to recognize my emotions, to know that they're okay, and that I don't necessarily have to hide them from her or anyone else. I say "anyone else," but certainly there are limits to that. I don't have to hide who I am. Things just get a hell of a lot easier. The sex becomes a very nice thing again.

The most difficult part for Kelly, I know, is letting go of the old models that she had of me, and not withholding herself emotionally during sex. When I say withholding herself, I mean her thinking she was going along for the ride versus being really active and passionate. Every time that we have sex and she's really involved, it's very encouraging to us both. It builds and builds and builds to the point that our relationship is certainly stronger than it was when we were first married, if for no other reason than we've been so damn persistent and desirous of making it work. But in terms of our ability to communicate and in terms of the passion involved in our sex, we certainly are right up there where we were before.

So all that seems to add up to a pretty nice package. It would have been a shame to see that go to waste had we said, "Enough of this shit! We'll both go our own separate directions."

That surely was a viable alternative at many, many junctures. As a matter of fact, only recently—and by that I mean within the last six months—has Kelly gotten to the point where the marriage isn't still just an experiment, like, "Is this going to work or is this not going to work?" Now there is a true sense that this isn't a trial run. This is a relationship again. This is it. The best of it's here and this is a good person to be with.

Tony has never been aware that I had an affair. No, not at all. He would leave me in a second. Although I have every right in the world to leave him—there's a real double standard. He's threatened to take the children and all that, so I wouldn't attempt it.

Emotionally, it just drained me totally. You think it's so wonderful and great, but you cannot divide yourself between two people. One relationship has to suffer. You cannot be equal. I thought I could be. If you have any kind of a conscience, that wells up in you, especially somebody from my religious background. I was living in hell, but not enough to quit. As long as I could play the game, I continued to do it, until it served no further purpose for me.

What I was wanting out of the relationship was not the sexual thing. I wanted the emotional part of a relationship with a man that I was not getting from my husband, the compassion, the caring, the concern and support. I've always said that if I were to marry again, I'd find a man who could take care of me. That's what I was missing—somebody to take care of me. I wasn't missing anything out of the sexual relationship. I could not ask for a better man sexually than my husband. I don't want him to do anything else. I'm totally satisfied. But we're lacking in so many other things, and that was what I was looking for. This man I was having an affair with, I can see now, preys on that with women. Most men like that do. They find out what women need, and they give it to them to reel them in. Then, pretty soon, the game-playing ends and their true colors start to come out.

This guy eventually fell in love with me, but he wanted me to love him on his terms. He got tired of playing the game of support and nurturing, kindness and caring, and "Listen to what my kids are doing." He didn't want to hear about that. He wanted me to come over for ten minutes, so he could get his rocks off. That's all he cared about. I was leaving my kids at home alone, so I could go over for a half hour or twenty minutes and see him. Just totally losing my mind. It was just stupid. That's not what I needed. I sure didn't need sex. I had plenty of that at home. I could have that anytime I wanted it. But him being a single man, he could not have sex anytime he wanted. That's what he needed me for.

I was having to sacrifice my emotional well-being for his physical well-being. If I stay with my husband, I'm still losing my emotional well-being for the satisfaction of my husband's physical well-being. So I was torn apart.

Here these two men wanted me sexually, but emotionally, I wasn't getting anything from either one of them. So I just quit everything, at least the emotional part of it. I just turned myself off. I figured if I wasn't going to get anything emotionally from a man anyway, then at least I only have to have sex with one of them. It's a pretty rotten thing to say, but it's true. I only have to give myself to one instead of both. There were times when I had to leave my lover's apartment, come home, and have sex with my husband. It's almost like being a prostitute.

I would love to have an affair. I have tried to talk women into sleeping with me. In fact, I've increased my efforts here in the last year or two without success. I haven't been able to figure out how to do it. I don't have any moral objections to doing it. It makes perfect sense for me to have a mistress, because it would take all this pressure off my wife. It would take a lot of pressure off me. I'd get laid, I'd feel better, I'd be happier. Everything would be great. It would be nice if I could find a woman who was married to someone who had the same problem, and she was unfulfilled in her sex life. We could get together once a month, have sex, and that's all there is to it. But I have not been able to find a woman like that.

I have lunch with a number of single women. I have put out some invitations, and the response I get is, "You're a nice guy, but you're married. I don't want to get involved with a married man. It would mess with my head. It would not be fun. I'd have to be sneaking around."

I promise them I wouldn't get involved, but it doesn't work. Most of them will say that they have moral objections to sleeping with a married man. That their husbands slept around and it just killed them. They could never do that to another woman, etc., etc.

I've asked a couple of married women whose husbands I don't know, and they've acted interested. The problem is logistics. I met this one gal one night and we got to talking. We got along real good, and were flirting with one another. She was about early thirties, petite, cute, and real interested in me. If things had been right, we could have maybe done something. But she had a husband at home watching the kids. I asked her if he ever goes out of town. She said, "No." And if he does, she's got the two kids. That's been kind of the situation I've found with married women. It would have to be a deal where their husband would go out of town at the same time my wife would go out of town. What are the chances of that happening?

One rule I have is I'm not going to make a pass at a woman who is a friend of my wife. It's too dangerous. She might tell, or otherwise let it be known accidentally or through mutual friends. Likewise with any wives of guys I know.

The situation hasn't worked out. You hear about guys playing around. There was this thing in the paper the other day that said in a new survey only two percent of the married men in the study reported being unfaithful within a year, which is much less than the numbers I had always heard. They were like fifty percent. Two percent is probably closer to reality. Fooling around outside marriage is a lot like the '60s, free-swinging sex myth. It's built all out of proportion. I don't think it happens very much.

We all cheat in our heads. Regardless of what anyone else says, I believe that all men within the first five seconds of meeting a woman primarily concentrate on whether she's sexually available. Whether or not they're planning to take advantage of that by trying to sleep with this woman, it's completely instinctual for us to check out her status quickly. We immediately go, "Could I have an affair with this person?" If you're in a relationship, you may discard that information, or maybe you keep flirting on the basis of that possibility without ever going ahead and trying to do something about it. But I still think that in any male-female relationship, that's the first and foremost foundation. From there, all other elements of the relationship build out. And women do that back.

I would hope to be as honest as I can be with everybody in my life. If it's one of the people closest to me, then I'm really breaking moral guidelines by lying to that person regardless of the privacy of it. That does not excuse being duplicitous. Mechanically, I appreciate the convenience of whether to be direct or to omit elements of ourselves, creating the illusions that are supposed to pass for who we really are. You can conveniently omit information forever and claim to be upright and honest, but you're just not. You're really not.

Things have been going good. Occasionally. Kids in the house now, you don't get as much or as often. But, yeah, it's been good and different. The intimacy is the best.

People get jealous of that, too. They see a long-term relationship, they get a little pissed off at you. Especially when they find out that you don't fuck around, and don't have affairs. They get really jealous.

One woman was coming on to me not long ago. She said she found me attractive, and if I gave her the slightest inclination, she would have me upstairs in the bedroom. I said, "That's really nice of you. I do find you attractive, but I've been married for a long time. I'm happy like this, and I want to stay happy like this. We work together on this project. We do the job together. That's it."

I feel a certain twinge of "I want to." But I don't want to. I wouldn't want that done to me. I don't want that sharing, that intimacy to be broken.

This woman wasn't angry. She understood it, and everything was fine. I just felt this resentment toward me ever since.

But that lie-telling that goes with that shit just eats away at me. If you can do it, fine, do it. I don't put the Holy Cross on anybody's forehead if they have affairs. For me, I've lived it once and it was a fucking nightmare of never being able to be yourself. I like being able to go home and yell if I want to and not experience any guilt from it, except for being a jerk. Not have hidden agendas going on. It takes a lot out of you personally to have to do that, and someone else is going to suffer for it besides the person who does it.

That is unless you go in there with a real cool attitude of "This is just the way I am." If you have that cool an attitude, then I think you fall into the asshole category. There's something really shallow about the whole thing. I buy into the fact, too, that if you're doing that to somebody else, you could probably do it to me. You could fuck me over just as easily and probably not bat an eye at it. So they are the kind of people I tend to stay away from now. "Whoops, nope. See you later."

I found out later that he was screwing around the whole time. All my friends didn't think I'd believe them, so they waited till we broke up and then told me. Thanks, everybody.

I figure you tell them if you know it. If you don't tell them, for Christ's sake, keep your mouth shut after. Don't go, "Oh, well, he was screwing around on you that first week you were together." That killed me afterwards.

During the affair, one person told me the truth. He wasn't a friend, he was a business associate of the guy I was dating. My boyfriend was smart enough to know this guy would tell me something, so he made a preemptive strike. He told me, "Oh, he just wants to get in your pants. He always goes after somebody that I'm going out with." So by the time this guy talked to me, I thought I had him pegged. Plus, he told me, and then he asked me out to dinner. I thought, "Ah-ha. Right. I'm going to believe you?"

Then after it was all over, jeez, everybody jumped on the bandwagon —"Oh, yeah, yeah. I saw him do things, and I heard about that."

"Why didn't you tell me?"

"I didn't think you'd believe me."

"Okay, I might not have believed you, but I wouldn't hate you like I do now. And why are you telling me now anyway?"

"So you don't go back to him."

I was recently faced with the same predicament with one of my girl-friends. Somebody told me about how her boyfriend of nine years had sent flowers to another girl, and some other things. It was all circumstan-tial evidence that he was having an affair. I tell you, I sat on it for a week before I said anything. If it was me I'd want to know, but I was afraid that she wouldn't. She's my closest friend and I really need her.

It was selfish of me, but I kept thinking, "Gosh, what if I tell her this and she hates me. Maybe I should check it out and see if it's nothing or not."

What was I going to do? Call him? Tail him? I thought about that. I almost did it. I found out where the other girl lived.

I took an informal poll among the people I know. They didn't know who I was talking about. I asked people, "Would you want me to tell you, if I thought your lover was running around with somebody else?" What was funny was how many people thought I was talking about them. All my girlfriends did. They were all saying, "Are you talking about my hus-band?"

"No, I'm not. If I was talking about your husband I'd be asking this hypothetical question of someone else."

Right away, the women jumped on it—"Holy shit, he's doing it, isn't he?"

None of the guys connected it with them at all. The guys were saying, "No, don't tell."

What do you do with that when somebody does tell you? Then you've got this horrible decision to make. You've got to confront him or you have to sneak around and check up on him, one or the other. That's one area where men have it easier. They're real quick to come in and say something like, "I heard you were screwing around on me." And they don't have any problems saying that, because they don't have this reputation as gossips and for being melodramatic, where we do.

For us to say it, we've got to get all the proof first, because we're terrified. We don't want to say anything until we've pieced it all together.

One night I told her. It's part of my upbringing—I blurted it out on the street. My mother always told me bad news on escalators. Where do you tell people bad news, in a car? I don't know a good place to tell them. I said, "I should have told you this earlier. I've known about this for a week and I didn't know what to do." Then she was real hurt, because I should have known what she wanted. We talked about it and then she wasn't angry with me anymore.

She and I sat down and made a list of all the suspicious things that he'd been doing. Then she went to him with the list and confronted him. It turned out it was nothing, it just looked bad. There was nothing more to it, which I firmly believe. Of course, then he knew that I told her and he was mad at me.

I'm sixty-two years old. I was a good little girl for twenty-one years of marriage. Then things just got stressed out. I was one of those mothers who spent most of her time nurturing the family. I fell apart when they were all starting to leave the nest. My mother was dying of cancer, and my sons were moving out.

At the time, I had gone back to work, so that we could pay for the college tuition for all three kids at the same time. This young man came to work for us as a summer intern. He was a great big, strapping farm boy who was very handsome and very personable. As a matter of fact, he was the exact age of my oldest son. We seemed to hit it off as just great friends. I developed the biggest crush that I ever experienced in my whole life. I couldn't believe this forty-two-year-old woman had a crush on a twenty-year-old man. I thought I must be sick.

By Christmastime, he and I went shopping for some gifts for people at the office, and then we went to call on a mutual friend who was sick. I confessed to him that I didn't know what was going on, and I didn't know what to think about it, but I had a big crush on him. He said, "Don't feel bad. The feeling is mutual." Which was quite a shock, but it was also quite a boost for my ego.

My husband was giving me a hard time about my wanting to go back from the Midwest to the West Coast to see my dying mother again. For whatever reason, he's always questioned everything that I did, just to get me to use the gray matter, but it's as though he's questioning whether you have good judgment or not. I took offense at it. Anyway, he was very nonsupportive in this situation.

By June of the next year, my mother had died, and I was very unhappy in my marriage. Of course, I felt a sexual attraction to this young man, but I was drawn to him by emotions more than anything else. He was supportive and sympathetic, was there to talk to all the time, whereas my husband had always been rather noncommunicative.

The young man quit the office in the fall and was going to go on to the university. I knew I would never see him again. I'd never had this kind of experience before. I certainly had never strayed outside my marriage. I was just a basket case. I was getting depressed. Finally, I was put on medication, because it wasn't normal behavior for me.

I went to an Episcopal priest and told him what was bothering me. He said, "All those feelings are normal and perfectly natural. It is just part of your upbringing that makes you feel you shouldn't have them. It's how you act on them that makes the difference." He said he hoped I wouldn't act on these feelings. "Actually, most affairs are not very satisfying anyway." I think he meant, like a lot of people my age being brought up in my generation, I probably wouldn't get a great deal of sexual satisfaction and would find it real disappointing. Then he said, "Do you have orgasms?"

"Yeah," I said. "Sometimes."

"In that case, you probably would enjoy it, but I still don't think it's what you ought to do."

My husband and I had what I considered good sex, by which I mean I would have orgasms. But we did nothing out of the ordinary, practically just the missionary-type thing. We didn't have oral sex at all. During that time, there was an occasion or two, when my husband would drink too much, that he had actually performed oral sex on me. So I knew a little bit about it, but he was so inexperienced, and he would not read anything about it. With his background, he was embarrassed to do it, unless he was drinking a lot. So there was nothing wrong with our sex life per se, but things were not going real well in just the relationship department. Therefore, it would naturally spill over into the sexual side, as it always does. So we wouldn't have sex. There weren't the feelings there for it.

My husband went to a funeral in another little town, so I called my young friend. I told him that my husband would be out real late, so maybe we could meet somewhere. He was living in an apartment with three other guys, so we met over on one of the country roads and we got into his car. I couldn't believe this. I'm making out in this car like I'm a teenager again, having sex out on a road, watching for the police to come and shine their flashlights on us like in high school. It was pretty bizarre. But it was *real* exciting, too.

I had to have medication to get through the time when this young man finally moved away, because I had become so emotionally involved with him that it was hard to separate. I had absolutely fallen in love, and I will always love him until I die, but he's just a dear friend anymore. I still keep in touch.

I had a psychic tell me one time, "You don't have to fall in love with everyone you sleep with." I thought I should adopt that philosophy. I didn't think women could do that. But *I* can. I have to care about them, but I have found that I do not have to be in love with them. And I have discovered that I thrive on this kind of excitement.

My husband was in an industry where we had these conventions every year. We would go to the hotel, and he always had a hospitality room where he was in charge two nights running. So I would go with other people wandering around from hospitality suite to hospitality suite.

This gave me a perfect opening to do what I wanted to do, because nobody was keeping tabs on me. Here I was drinking and just having a wonderful time. Everyone's in a party atmosphere. Just visiting with people and flirting and carrying on.

One night, the flirting led to something else. This young man—I'm sure he was probably fifteen years younger than me—said, "Would you like to come up to my room?"

"Sure!" I said. Then I got up there. "Oh, my God, what am I doing?" But it's amazing to me that once you do something how much easier it is to do it again. It was open season at the conventions from then on.

There was still an element of danger. You had to sneak up the back-hall stairs, or just get in the elevator and hope nobody you knew saw you —"Hi, Alice. What are you doing on this floor?" I've done that many times.

Then there was this other guy who I always thought was real good-looking. My husband and I have known him for years and years. Out of the blue, two or three years down the road, after I'd been out with a couple of people (I don't think the ones I went out with talked that much, but maybe they did), this guy comes up to me in one of the hospitality suites, and he says, "I'm in room 2210."

I look at him and say, "Excuse me?"

"You think you could come up for a while?"

"Oh, I guess so," I said. So for three years running it was always, "What time can you get away tonight?"

One year he was on the thirteenth floor. He wanted me to come over. I was staying at another hotel across the street. I figured I better not take the elevator, so I walked up thirteen floors. I got to his room and I said, "I'm getting far too old for this."

"You'll never be too old for *this*," he said.

"No, no. I mean climbing up thirteen floors."

By this point my husband had developed not only some emotional problems, but some physical problems, too, as far as being impotent. He was totally impotent and nothing could be done. Since he had this kind of upbringing where he would not try to accommodate me or satisfy me, unless he had really been drinking, he was not about to do anything. That made me really angry. I said, "I'm not willing to deny this part of my life, just because he's unwilling to do anything about his problems. If he's impotent, there's nothing I can do for him. I have tried. If he's not willing to do something for me, then I don't have to feel terribly guilty about doing things for myself."

His problems started out I suppose because of my running around. He's not stupid, you know. But we never discussed it. He never addressed the issue. He never said *anything* about it. During the meantime we were also transferred from the small town where we started to the home office. There was a lot of stress there. He was very, very tired. He would just come home on weekends. We would try to make love, and he really couldn't. They say the emotions even with men are much more tied up with sex than we realize. He had also had hernia surgery, so he was afraid that he would harm himself or that it would hurt, so that too made him back off somewhat, even when he was totally healed. All those things together made sex impossible.

There was a time eight or nine years ago where I got totally depressed. I decided that maybe it wasn't right for me to live this way and still live with my husband. So I told him I was leaving. I couldn't live like this. It was tearing me up, this double life. I said to him, "Now, you know I've been running around."

"I'm not stupid, you know," he said.

"I know you're not, but you have never confronted it. You've never mentioned it. You have never been willing to even acknowledge it, to my way of thinking."

"I just figured maybe you'd get over it. I knew you were running around at the conventions. I had times when I'd look at people and think, 'Is it him? Is he one of them?' But I know that was just my ego getting in the way, so I try not to think about it."

He's been that way about everything in life. He just tries not to think about it, so he doesn't. Then he doesn't have to deal with it. That's part of our conflict in life. I like to deal with everything, get it out, work it over, and deal with it, so you can get on with life. If it's not working, then do something about it. So I was going to leave. I had an apartment and everything.

My middle son told me, "Just be darn sure if you're leaving that you're going toward something that's better. Don't just leave to be leaving, because you'll be sorry. Once you walk out that door, even if you say it's just a trial separation, there are changes that take place. Everything will have to be renegotiated, no matter which way you end up."

He's been through a lot of traumatic times in his life, so I listened to him. I was supposed to move out on Monday morning. I went home that Sunday night and said to my husband, "I'm not sure I want to leave."

"I don't want you to leave," he said.

"I'm not sure I can change."

"I'll just have to hope that you'll want to change."

It was left at that and nothing has ever been discussed again. We went to counseling a time or two. Basically, he thinks it's all my fault, and he doesn't want to discuss it. The only thing he'll say is, "What do you want me to do?"

Whenever somebody says that, they don't have a clue what you're talking about. Nobody wants somebody else to *do* anything. What you want is for them to communicate their feelings to you and to listen to your feelings without just saying, "Why don't you just do this and this?" Giving you instructions, trying to give you a fix for it. I don't want any advice. I'm not asking for a solution. I just wanted to talk about it, so he would know what I'm feeling and what's going on here. After forty-two years of marriage, he still hasn't a clue what I'm talking about.

The sad thing was that when I was ready to leave home and I decided to stay instead, George and I were still attempting to make love occasionally, and were able to a time or two. One night he said to me, "I feel like I'm making love to you, and you're having sex with me." That took care of that as far as I'm concerned, so I would never care if I would ever have sex with him again. I found that extremely insulting. I was trying to awaken some feelings in him. I was trying to be real free and abandoned to my feelings and really enjoying it. I thought that was what we should be doing if we care for each other, that it might work out for both of us. He took it wrong. Okay, forget it.

If I cared about the situation, if it hadn't deteriorated to such a point, if I wasn't enjoying myself outside my marriage, I might insist on him going and having a penis implant or having something done. I feel badly that he's not able to experience anything. But he doesn't seem motivated to do anything about it. We're just two people living in the same house, and I couldn't care less.

Since I have this wonderful sex life on the side, I'm okay. This friend of mine, I've never quite experienced this with anybody else in my life. I mean, I stopped counting the orgasms when I am with him. We meet at a motel, and just have a wonderful time in a few stolen hours once every two or three weeks. I say to myself, "I can survive on this. I can stretch this out over a week or so."

I don't know how people can deal with life and shut sex off totally. I know people do it. Not everyone loses the capacity to do this when they get older. These men I'm with now, one of them will be fifty in October and one of them just turned forty-eight. So they're not in their prime either.

My husband retired last year, so he's home all the time—which is going to probably be the end of our relationship even superficially if he doesn't shape up pretty soon. It puts a crimp in my style, too. Nobody can call here. I've spent a lot of quarters at corner pay phones calling my friend at work, or in the case of another friend I can call his house sometimes during the day, because he works nights.

I have moments of panic. My affairs are usually a good thing for me. Then I'll have days where I just feel awful, because it is an affair and because you can't talk to them when you want to talk to them, or you can't reach them when you need them.

I called his house on Tuesday morning. He just said, "Hello!"

"What's going on?" I said.

"*Hello?*" And he hung up. That just made me feel terrible. I was depressed all day long, but I thought, "She must have been home. She wasn't supposed to be, but she must have been." He won't call me, because it will show up on his bill. I called back yesterday morning, and he said, "I hung up on you yesterday."

"Yeah, I know."

"She was standing right next to me."

"I figured that's what it was."

"I hoped you'd figure out what was wrong."

But that still makes you feel less than a person. It's got to diminish you in some way to be treated like that, to not be open and have a good, open relationship with somebody, to live in stolen moments. It may have its excitements, but there's a real downside, too.

On those days when I get depressed, I have a talk with myself and say, "Wait a minute, this goes with the territory. Let's get this into perspective. Straighten out our priorities. What is it that you really want? You want some fun and games. So you got to take some of the downside, too. My husband doesn't care enough to address his problem, so I've got to address my problem. And my problem is just getting some sex every now and then." That's the kind of lifestyle I'm living. I can't get hung up on it. Of course, I'm disappointed. I feel angry and upset for a few hours, and then I go, "I have no strings on this person and that's just the way it's going to be if I want to live this way."

I would love to have someone that I could spend the rest of my life with, someone more compatible. We would actually communicate and could have some sort of relationship. I feel like there's nothing left for me here at home other than our mutual commitment to the family. Since one of my sons and his wife are getting a divorce, my husband and I are the only stability for our grandchildren right now, so I don't really want to leave, or else I would have said, "Just forget it. This is ridiculous." My husband and I are decent to each other. With the kids there I don't really want to rock the boat. But if I met someone who really clicked, and we thought we could be kind to one another the rest of our lives, I probably would seriously consider it. At this point, if I can have some fun and a little sex along the way, that will do for now.

After our second child was three, my wife went back to work and started having an affair with this guy at the office. It became a series of affairs. I'd wind up finding out about them somehow. She really didn't want to keep them secret, is what it comes down to. It was very painful for me to face up to that, because in my first marriage I had really seen that I had screwed up the marriage through extramarital affairs. So, karmically, my second wife has an affair. This is it. I understood because of my own infidelity, and that actually helped me deal with it better. I knew what it was about. There was still the machismo thing, all the stuff that pulls on my male ego, but I knew that I could be hurt and it was my ego that was in pain. That helped in a certain fashion.

The thing that made me feel really cheated was that I had really behaved myself extremely well through the pregnancy and early babydom, when the guy just doesn't get as much sex as he could handle. I was on the road a lot and there were women available, but I said, "I'm not going to do that this time."

What came out of it was my wife came to me and said, "Look, you wanted to get married, but I never wanted a monogamous relationship." This has to do with her own issues around sex. At first I said, no, but later I went back to her and said, "Okay, let's do that. This doesn't work for me the way it is." I was getting tired of being horny and tired of having the lack of sex be a major pressure on my life. So I thought, "I'll just go out and have other relationships, and that's it." I called up an old girlfriend of mine. She and I started getting it on again, and that was nice.

Almost ten months went by. I became emotionally involved with this other woman. My wife got really mad. "Look, that's not in the agreement, that's not part of the deal as far as I'm concerned." I just didn't get it. It's not in my makeup not to get to know somebody. Plus at that particular time I was really hungry to be close to somebody, to be excited about being with somebody. And to be quite honest, I thought the marriage was all but over. My wife and I split up. This other woman and I had what was probably one of the best love affairs of my life. And as that relationship was breaking up, I finally started to understand more about my own sexuality.

I was addicted to sex and had been my whole adult life. It wasn't like the sex addiction you see referred to these days in magazines—"Oh, God, I've got to go have sex now." It never felt like a drug dependency. It was more like a part of my identity, part of what I walked around with in life—the guy who's good in bed and has lots of sex. Sex wasn't something that I just wanted, it was something I had to have. For example, I know the difference between wanting a drink and having to have a drink. I've crossed over those lines in the use of alcohol. I've also crossed over those lines not just in the use of sex, but in the use of relationships—having to have somebody there for me.

It was not just sex I was addicted to. I really was addicted to love in the form of sexual expression. A very important source of love was from a woman who loved you and expressed it through sexuality, physically, emotionally, the whole package.

Realizing that was a liberating factor above everything else in my whole life. I was literally dependent upon an outside source of love for a sense of well-being. Without any specific person being there for me, I didn't feel loved. My life was empty without that. That's the way it was an addiction.

I began to break free of this. I really had a spiritual conversion. I know it sounds weird to say that, because I didn't convert to any specific religious faith. But I really started to have a sense that there had to be another source of love that was independent of me, not internal, but in a way emanating through me. It sounds tedious and trivial to put it into words: God is love, Spirit is love, God's love for Creation, this and that. But my newfound sense of that and knowing my pattern of dependency has really helped me not to have to depend on another person to feel loved and lovable. I can access it just by taking a deep breath and being open to the feeling of love.

So now I'm back with my wife, and I don't need her for that. In fact, I don't need her. If she comes home today and says, "I don't want to do this anymore, I'm packing my stuff. I'm splitting," I will have experiences of sadness, but I would not have the need to try to make her stay.

There was another shift in my life that came out of this. I ceased to be the most important person in my life. Not just intellectually, but viscerally, I knew that taking care of my kid was more important than the other stuff. That became the reason my wife and I got back together again. Providing this child with the best, balanced environment and secure upbringing that I could provide her with rose to become more important than my problems. My sexual problems in the marriage are down to number six or seven on the list, instead of up there at number one or two.

It gives me a level of patience and objectivity that I didn't have before, even to the knowledge that maybe my wife and I will never rekindle our sexual yearning for each other. If that's the case, maybe at some point I will make some other choices about who I'm with. Yet, I don't have the need to resolve that now out of pain, or even the fear that I'm getting older, I'm going to lose it. Of course, I do occasionally have little bouts of extramarital sexual interest that happen.

It is a version of "staying together for the sake of the children." The differences are my willingness to face those issues rather than sweep them under the rug. The willingness to be honest at least with myself. Do I like that it's this way? No. I don't like that, okay? Yet it really is a priority to me, a literal priority to provide for this child. So if I'm going to provide for this child, then it's also really important to me to have a good relationship with my wife.

The irony is that we really like each other and care about each other. So none of that is really phony, we don't have to fake it. Even to the place where this morning before this interview, she said, "Oh, jeez, you're going to tell him all this stuff."

"Nah, nah," I said. "I'll talk about before our relationship."

"Oh, you'll talk about that woman and how great the sex was with her."

"You know the best sex I ever had was with you. You know that's true."

"Yeah, eight years ago."

But she could say that, and we could both laugh about it now without bad feelings, which we couldn't have done a couple of years ago.

I also have real confidence that the possibility exists for us to have a good sexual relationship free of all the neurosis that we brought to it originally. Maybe that won't happen, but it certainly has a chance to happen. If we had cut each other off, that would have eliminated the chance for us to grow together entirely.

Intimate relationships set the stage for the real issues that go on with individuals more than any other human situations. When the issues start to rise and come forward, if you leave the relationship, then that's just your way of avoiding the issues. That's what I used to do. Part of what she and I are doing is dealing with those issues. Rather than deal with them in a pressure cooker—where nothing really gets dealt with—we're letting it slow-cook, even if we haven't said that specifically to each other. It's the Crockpot version.

It happened to me a very long time ago. It was only three months with somebody that I worked with. I hadn't even been married that long. It was during those first couple of years when I thought, "Oh, God, I haven't done the right thing."

I met somebody who was totally different from my husband. Someone who was intellectual and very artistic. It was such an immediate thing for me that it scared me. I thought, "You haven't been married very long, why is this happening to you?"

We saw each other pretty intensely for those three months. Then he just said, "I can't do this anymore," and he cut it off. I really wasn't ready for that to happen. He just decided that he didn't want anything to do with me. I was hurting him too much, because I wouldn't leave my husband. So that ended, but it didn't end, because it took a long time to get over it emotionally. My husband, to this day, does not know. It's nothing that I feel like I could ever talk to him about.

I don't know how people do it, stay married for twenty-five years and that's the only person they're with their whole life. I don't believe that one person can be everything to you. It just isn't possible. But you get caught up in the state of marriage. We have our family and our kids. Everything is in this nice little package right now. So you kind of go along, and everything can be fine. You just don't like to throw a wrench into it.

My husband would be absolutely shocked to find out. Even in his wildest dreams, he could not imagine that having an affair is something that I would do. I have this image to the outside world that I'm a very good, *nice* person who really doesn't do anything wrong. Inside myself, I'm thinking, "Let's see, yes, I've done quite a lot actually. I've snuck around quite a few times in my life, although I find it something hard to deal with."

I just feel like shocking people sometimes. I'm not Pollyanna here. There's one guy at work who says, "You're just like everybody's little sister. There's some girls that you meet that you just want to fuck, and there are other girls that you want to marry. You're the one that everybody wants to marry."

"Oh, yeah," I want to say, "I could tell you a story or two." It's not so much what they think of me, but just the fact that it is such a limiting notion—that I'm not capable of sexuality, it's not in me, or that someone else wouldn't be interested in me sexually, that someone else wouldn't find me attractive enough to want me. I don't know if my husband sees that there are other men who find me attractive. Even if he sees I might be attracted to other men, he doesn't think that I would do anything about it.

Maybe I'm just at a weird stage in my life right now. I feel antsy. Maybe it's the approaching-forty thing. It's an uneasiness with the way things are. Part of me worries, "What am I looking for? What is it that's better?" Part of me is just involved with the fact that there is something very exciting about new love and new sex. That can't be duplicated, no matter how long you've been married. I had the best sex of my life with my husband when we were dating. It was just the best. But we've been having sex for fifteen years now, and it evolves into a different thing. You can really love someone deeply, and not be able to recreate the physical excitement of being with someone new.

I wonder, do people who are married fifteen years make out anymore? I don't. Does that still happen with people? The whole kissing thing can be so exciting, so very sexual. I miss that. I just want to *kiss* somebody. I want that anticipation of something exciting still to come.